THE BIBLE AND EM   D0858940

At a time of renewed interest in empire, this stimulating volume
explores the complex relationship between the Bible and the colonial
enterprise and examines some overlooked aspects of this relationship.
These include unconventional retellings of the gospel story of Jesus
by Thomas Jefferson and Raja Rammohun Roy; the fate of biblical
texts when marshalled by Victorian preachers to strengthen British
imperial intentions after the Indian uprising of 1857; the cultural-
political use of the Christian Old Testament, first by the invaders to
attack temple practices and rituals, then by the invaded to endorse
the temple heritage scorned by missionaries; the dissident hermeneutics of James Long and William Colenso confronting and com-
promising with colonial ambitions; and finally the subtly seditious
deployment of biblical citations in two colonial novels.

This innovative book offers both practical and theoretical insights
and provides compelling evidence of the continuing importance of
postcolonial discourse for biblical studies.

R. S. SUGIRTHARAJAH is Professor of Biblical Hermeneutics at
the University of Birmingham. His recent publications include
Postcolonial Reconfigurations (2003), *Postcolonial Criticism and Biblical Interpretation* (2002) and *The Bible and the Third World* (2001).

THE BIBLE AND EMPIRE

Postcolonial Explorations

R. S. SUGIRTHARAJAH

CAMBRIDGE
UNIVERSITY PRESS

CAMBRIDGE UNIVERSITY PRESS
Cambridge, New York, Melbourne, Madrid, Cape Town, Singapore, São Paulo

Cambridge University Press
The Edinburgh Building, Cambridge CB2 2RU, UK

Published in the United States of America by Cambridge University Press, New York

www.cambridge.org

Information on this title: www.cambridge.org/9780521824934

First published 2005

Printed in the United Kingdom at the University Press, Cambridge

A catalogue record for this book is available from the British Library

ISBN-13 978-0-521-82493-4 - hardback
ISBN-10 0-521-82493-1   - hardback
ISBN-13 978-0-521-53191-7 - paperback
ISBN-10 0-521-53191-8   - paperback

Contents

v

Acknowledgements

I owe a considerable debt to a number of people.

Firstly, I am indebted to Dan O'Connor for his wisdom, time and generosity. We have spent countless hours discussing details on the phone, to the delight of the telephone-company shareholders. It was his reading of the chapters and his astute comments which sharpened the argument of this volume, and without his wit the whole project would have been dull.

My thanks go to Kevin Taylor of Cambridge University Press, who saw potential in the volume and commissioned it, and to Kate Brett, who took over from him and provided continued enthusiasm for the project.

I am grateful to Vincent Kumaradoss, Daniel Thiagaraj, Kwok Pui-Lan, Clara Joseph, Marcella Althaus-Reid, Daniel Smith-Christopher, Susai Raj, John Perumbalath, Ngurliana and Hephzibah Israel for generously getting for me some rare and inaccessible texts.

I appreciate also the prompt and cheerful assistance of Dorothy Wuong of the Orchard Learning Centre and her excellent and ever helpful staff.

My sincere thanks also to Ralph Broadbent for, as ever, sorting out my computing problems expertly and efficiently.

I am fortunate to have had Jan Chapman as copy-editor. This is our second collaborative venture, and I am very grateful for the scrupulous and perceptive way in which she has gone through the text.

Finally, to my wife, Sharada, whose support and encouragement are beyond what I can express here. The sacrifices she has made, especially in giving up her own research time to enable me to finish the project, are more than I can ever compensate for.

Introduction

One of the celebrated colonial clichés is that the Bible and the gun go together and that they are almost inextricably linked. One story goes even further, in which the Bible and the gun are literally conjoined. William Colenso (1826–99), who worked as a printer in New Zealand and was a cousin of John Colenso, of whom we will hear later in this volume, picked up a cartridge fashioned out of pages from a Bible. The rolled-up paper came from 2 Samuel and bore the words 'How long have I to live?' (19.34).[1] The cartridge of rolled-up biblical verses gives a slightly different meaning to the phrase 'militant reading', an idea later to be popularized in liberation hermeneutics.

This volume is about what happens to colonial artefacts such as the Bible, beer, a gun and a printing press, and especially, in our case, the Bible, when it is imposed forcefully on the 'natives', or offered to them for their benefit. It is about the Bible and its readers and their troubled journey through colonialism. It assembles essays which demonstrate how the Bible has been used in a variety of ways by both the colonizer and the colonized. It brings to the fore personalities and issues which are seldom dealt with within the parameters of mainstream biblical scholarship. It is an attempt to retrieve hermeneutical and cultural memories in both western and nationalist discourses.

Briefly, I offer some explanation of the three themes which hold this volume together – empire, the Bible and postcolonialism. The empire itself has come in different forms, and the word has gathered many meanings. Before it became a term of abuse and acquired its current meaning of one nation-state coercively ruling another, it meant simply 'state', 'domain' or 'realm'. There were many ancient and modern

---

1 I owe this citation to D. F. McKenzie. See his *Bibliography and the Sociology of Texts* (Cambridge, Cambridge University Press, 1999), p. 108. Other books which were used for this militant purpose included works of Voltaire and Milner's *Church History*.

I

empires in the former sense, their aim to conquer other people and bring them under their control. Persians, Macedonians, Romans, Mongols and Mughals had extensive empires. When the term empire is used today, or at least in this volume, it does not refer to these empires. It is used in the modern sense, as a specific term for a system that grew out of European colonial expansion between the fifteenth and twentieth centuries. These European empires – Spanish, Portuguese, Dutch, French, Belgian and British – were an outgrowth of industrial capitalism and were marked by distinct cultural domination and penetration which have created the myth of the West as the superior 'other', a myth which is continually evoked in international disputes, and in political, cultural and theological dis-courses. The empire that this volume deals with mostly is the British empire; the Portuguese and the Spanish empires make only a brief appearance.

The Bible referred to here is largely the King James Version, which came to the colonies as the Englishman's book – a landmark text in the history of the English people. Before the First World War, this translation reigned supreme. This provincial and vernacular text of the English people became a cultural and colonial icon and eventually emerged as a key text of the empire, playing a prominent role in colonial expansion. It was more than a religious text, for its influence extended to the social, political and economic spheres. The King James Version became not only the arbiter of other peoples' texts and cultures but also set the pattern for vernacular translations and even acted as a role model for the printing and dissemination of other sacred texts. It functioned sometimes as a rigid instrument and sometimes as a flexible one but was always evolving as a medium for cultural and political expression. The focus here is not on the extraordinary story of the making and marketing of the King James Version but on some of the hermeneutical debates surrounding it, espe-cially in the colonial world. It is about how different communities of interpreters, among both the colonized and the colonizers, appropriated, reappropriated and at times emasculated their favourite texts and how, in the process, they themselves were shaped and moulded and their identity redefined. The colonial usage is a testimony to the notion that every era produces the Bible in its own image and responds to it differently on the basis of shifting political and cultural needs and expectations.

Finally, postcolonialism: it is not easy to define postcolonialism, and those in the business of doing so are well aware that the task is fraught with enormous difficulties. These difficulties are largely caused by the theory's association with many institutions. A theory which started its career in commonwealth literature has now crossed disciplines as disparate as medieval studies and sports, and each discipline has fixed the theory's meaning to suit its own needs. Even such an elementary question as 'what is postcolonialism?' elicits a plural answer. My intention here is not to provide an elaborate introduction to the work of the most eminent postcolonial critics and theorists. There are two reasons for this reluctance: firstly, as I have just said, each subject area has worked out its own theoretical clarifications, and not all of these are useful or transferable to biblical studies; secondly, I have already mapped out in other volumes the merits of postcolonialism for biblical studies and given my own critique of it.[2] Postcolonialism is used here as an interventionist instrument which refuses to take the dominant reading as an uncomplicated representation of the past and introduces an alternative reading. Postcolonialism allows silenced and often marginalized people to find their own voices when they are at loggerheads with the dominant readings. My method is to work with specific hermeneutical examples and to introduce to them critical practices which are assembled around the label 'postcolonialism', rather than apply an already worked-out complex theory which imposes artificial structures and obscures and obfuscates the material at hand. The way in which I have employed postcolonialism in this volume resonates with Robert Young's approach: 'Much of postcolonial theory is not so much about static ideas or practices, as about the relations between ideas and practices: relations of harmony, relations of conflict, generative relations between different peoples and their cultures. Postcolonialism is about a changing world, a world that has been changed by struggle and which its practitioners intend to change further'.[3]

ABOUT THIS VOLUME

The volume has five chapters, and the two poles around which they revolve are the Bible and the British empire. The first chapter, 'Textually conjoined twins: Rammohun Roy and Thomas Jefferson and their Bibles', is the first-ever contrapuntal and critical study of the gospel compilations undertaken in the nineteenth century by an American and

2 R. S. Sugirtharajah, *The Bible and the Third World: Precolonial, Colonial and Postcolonial Encounters* (Cambridge, Cambridge University Press, 2001), pp. 244–75; and R. S. Sugirtharajah, *Postcolonial Criticism and Biblical Interpretation* (Oxford, Oxford University Press, 2002) pp. 11–123.

3 Robert J. C. Young, *Postcolonialism: A Very Short Introduction* (Oxford, Oxford University Press, 2003), p. 7.

an Indian, and the hermeneutical and Christological questions they posed. During the colonial era, independently of each other and responding to different hermeneutical needs, a high-caste wealthy Indian, Rammohun Roy, and an American, Thomas Jefferson, the third President of the United States of America, produced their own versions of and selections from the gospel narratives. What Roy did in his *Precepts of Jesus* and Jefferson in his *The Philosophy of Jesus* and *The Life and Morals of Jesus* was to expunge the gospel records of their historical incidents, miracle stories and doctrinal references, herd together the moral teachings of Jesus and portray him as a great ethical teacher. This chapter investigates their textual productions and scrutinizes their narrative content, their hermeneutical presuppositions and the colonial background to their choice of extracts. It also situates their work and measures their construals of Jesus against the nineteenth-century European 'lives' of Jesus. The chapter also investigates how far Roy's and Jefferson's hermeneutical endeavours fitted into the colonial project of modernity, and it explores whether these two lay readers of the Bible set the tone for the later demythologization project which held great sway in twentieth-century biblical scholarship.

At a time when presidents and prime minsters adorn their speeches with biblical allusions to bolster the new imperium, the second chapter looks at an earlier example of how biblical texts were conscripted in the nineteenth century against a group of Indian soldiers who threatened western power and interest. This chapter, entitled 'Salvos from the Victorian pulpit: conscription of texts by Victorian preachers during the Indian rebellion of 1857', explores the reactions to this event by the clergy in England. The chapter makes use of more than a hundred sermons reported in the *Times* that were preached in London the day after the nation observed a day of humiliation and prayer. Besides these sermons, the chapter also draws on two other homiletical sources – sermons by F. D. Maurice, an important theologian of the time, and two sermons preached by the Bishop of Calcutta. The latter helps to ascertain the mood in India and how this event was viewed by the British in India. The chapter investigates, among other things, how the Bible was commandeered for colonial service, the massive over-presence of Old Testament texts, the hermeneutical practices of these preachers, the theological content, (mis)construals of India, and how these Victorian homilies became a site for articulating British national identity in terms of God's people waging war against God's adversaries. The sermons were supreme examples of how, in the formation of meanings, texts and contexts, readers obtain their identity in interaction with each of these. The chapter is a study of the extraordinary collaboration of biblical texts with pulpit-eering, Christian piety and messianic vocation, whilst at the same time revealing racial prejudices, and the skewed scholarship of Victorian Christianity. It also discusses what kinds of meaning are embedded in the texts and how readers situated within a particular historical place and time produce meanings from particular kinds of text. The Victorian clergy's appropriation of biblical narratives is also a warning to Christians that they ought to be aware of the terrors and the terrifying potential of biblical narratives, especially in emotionally charged situations.

In popular perception postcolonialism is erroneously seen as anti-western and missionary-bashing. The third chapter, 'Thorns in the crown: the subversive and complicit hermeneutics of John Colenso of Natal and James Long of Bengal', rectifies this popular negative image that all missionaries are 'evil'. It looks at the hermeneutical endeavours of two colonial missionaries who broke ranks with their fellow missionaries and used the Bible simultaneously to confront their own colonial and missionary administration, and to empower the invaded. John Colenso and James Long were two unusual missionaries of the empire days. John Colenso was supported by the Society of the Propagation of the Gospel and worked in Natal, South Africa, whereas James Long was a Church Missionary Society missionary who worked in Bengal, India. There are certain parallels between these two missionary savants. Both were moral critics of imperialism but nonetheless supported and lauded its civilizing project. What made them different was that both dissociated themselves from their own colleagues and were deeply involved in the political struggles of the day. In the case of Colenso, it was the Zulu cause, and in Long's case, it was the cause of Bengali indigo workers. This chapter focuses on their appropriation of the Bible in their struggle against the missionary homiletics and colonial presuppositions of the time. One perceived the Bible as an icon of western culture, and the other as an oriental book. Whereas Colenso rigorously pursued the then emerging historical-critical method as a way of seeing parallels between the Jews of old and the Zulus of the present, Long demonstrated the earlier marks of narrative criticism in his engagement with Indians. This chapter scrutin-izes Colenso's under-investigated and puzzlingly neglected *Natal Sermons* (four volumes), and Long's unheard-of and almost invariably overlooked *Scripture Truth in Oriental Dress*. In doing so, it brings out how, in their exegetical practices, Colenso and Long challenged the racialism, prejudice and bigotry of the time and offered an alternative form of Christian faith that was courteous, considerate and cordial, as a way of appealing to the natives. The chapter also examines the controversy caused by their hermeneutical endeavours, and the contemporary relevance of these colonial skirmishes.

Though there is a vigorous debate among Christian and Jewish scholars vis-à-vis the Old Testament, little attention has been paid to the function of the Christian Old Testament in Asia, Africa and other parts of the world. Many from these regions have been perplexed about the place they ought to give to this larger part of the Bible. The fourth chapter, 'Texts and testament: the Hebrew scriptures in colonial context', investigates the complex role of the Old Testament during the colonial period and how it was profitably mined by orientalists, missionaries and indigenous Christians and Hindus. While orientalists used it as an exact indicator of the chronology of the peoples of the world in order to prove the veracity of Genesis and to date the origins of the Hebrews, the missionaries used it as a bulwark against any cultural assimilation. The major part of the chapter, however, is devoted to the story of how the Hebrew scriptures were used as a serviceable weapon against the missionaries by the colonized in order to challenge their cultural and religious defamation, to strengthen indigenous religious customs and traditions and to redefine their identity. The two leading figures were Arumuka Navalar and Arumainayagam Suttampillai, one a high-caste Jaffna Saivite Tamil and the other a low-caste Nadar Christian. Both failed to live up to the preferred role of supine and submissive natives and went beyond their allotted and confined space. In doing so, they gained great hermeneutical purchase out of the Old Testament and found it an amiable ally. While Navalar continued to be a Saivite and read the Old Testament contrapuntally with his Saiva texts, demonstrating that the religion and rites of Israel were essentially the same as Saivism, Suttampillai remained a Christian but became more Jewish by adapting the liturgical and ritual practices of the Jews and by situating Moses and Jesus in their Jewish milieu. Both Navalar's and Suttampillai's elevation of the Old Testament did not mean that they did not value, or discounted, the New. In their particular struggles against missionary arrogance, the Hebrew scriptures provided them with powerful ammunition. Theirs is an early example of how that other gift of colonialism – the printing press – was employed in order to strengthen indigenous cultures, disseminate indigenous voices and, more tellingly, to dispute with the missionaries. The study of Navalar and Suttampillai also offers a corrective to colonial discourse analysis which is over-obsessed with the Bengali response to the western impact and forgets how other Indian communities such as the Tamils, Marathas,

Kanadigas and Malayalees responded. What was unique about Navalar was that while Bengali reformers like Rammohun Roy were defensive about the popular forms of Hinduism, he was unapologetic, even proud of them. The chapter ends with what the Bible and especially the Hebrew scriptures have to say about empires – offering their own warning to those who are tempted to establish new empires.

The profound influence of the Bible on western art, literature and music has been well documented and celebrated. The fifth chapter, 'Imperial fictions and biblical narratives: entertainment and exegesis in colonial novels', explores how biblical images and stories have been employed creatively, and at times subversively, in two novels – Sydney Owenson's *The Missionary* and Akiki K. Nyabongo's *Africa Answers Back*. True, these novels came out of different cultural and political contexts. Both, however, were written from the receiving end of imperialism, one trying to unsettle its smugness and arrogance, the other seeking to renegotiate the effects on local customs, practices and history that imperialism and the Bible have imposed. In *The Missionary* Luxima, one of the leading protagonists of the novel, time and again rejects the pre-eminence of the Bible and its teachings and tries to maintain the superior status of her own Vedas, whereas in *Africa Talks Back* one of its main characters, Mujungu, wrests it from his missionary opponent and reads it in a much broader spirit than that encouraged by the missionary. This second novel also celebrates the merits of reading aloud as opposed to silent and private reading, a habit encouraged by modernity and Protestantism. It was the vocalization of the text which enabled the 'illiterate' father of Mujungu and his wives to get biblical ratification for a controversial cultural practice – polygamy – a practice which the missionary claimed was proscribed by the Bible. Thus, the Bible as a printed text became a serviceable tool for those raised in an oral culture. The chapter also explores the serious attention paid by these two narratives to the troubled question of the religions of the empire and the umpiring role of Christianity. The novels also negotiate an uneasy tension that lies between conversion as an individual spiritual illumination and the individual's allegiance to a community. The chapter also analyses how these two novels try to map out new forms of self, family and community.

A brief word about citations from colonial writings: when quotations from colonial writings are used, the original grammar, spelling, syntax style and capitalization have been left unchanged so as to retain their integrity. For the names of people and cities, the Raj spelling is retained as an example of colonial mutilation of names. In registering what they thought they heard, colonial administrators and clerks failed to record the aural beauty of the names of peoples and cities, and instead made them look crude, even grotesque, and ridiculous. The racist and religious bigotry disclosed in their use of language is also left untouched. The easiest thing would have been to launder out these blemishes, which rightly offend us now. Such an act would have cleansed the record of the degrading and embarrassing history of prejudice and discrimination. I have left them as they are as a reminder of how things used to be, and of how, even quite recently, racist language was still widespread and deemed acceptable. Biblical citations come from a number of versions determined mainly by whose references I use. Replacing them with one version would look neat but would lose the flavour of the context in which these various versions were used.

This volume does not claim to be comprehensive. As mentioned earlier, there are other former European empires which deserve attention and other hermeneutical issues which merit careful consideration. My study deals only with the British empire and even here is limited to a specific century and circumscribed by a few selected hermeneutical issues. In the face of revisionist histories and cleaning up of the past, all that I aim to do is to offer a hermeneutical sanctuary to these marginalized and maligned discourses and to prevent their total banishment from the interpretative radar. One of the last writings of Edward Said aptly sums up the tenor, scope and execution of this volume and my hopes for it: 'The intellectual's role is to present alternative narratives and other perspectives on history than those provided by combatants on behalf of official memory and national identity and mission'.[4]

4 Edward W. Said, *Humanism and Democratic Criticism* (New York, Columbia University Press, 2004), p. 141.

CHAPTER I

Textually conjoined twins: Rammohun Roy and Thomas Jefferson and their Bibles

> [T]he chief thing is not to interpret the Gospels, but to understand them as they are written.
>
> Leo Tolstoy

Before the Victorian search for the life of Jesus started in earnest in the late nineteenth century, there were two 'lives' of Jesus compiled from the four gospels; they preceded these scholarly endeavours and have gone unnoticed by historians of biblical studies. One was *The Precepts of Jesus*[1] by an Indian, Raja Rammohun Roy (1774–1833), and the other was *The Life and Morals of Jesus* by the second President of the United States of America, Thomas Jefferson (1734–1826). Significantly, both publications came out in the same year, 1820. Motivated by practical needs, and scarcely interested in defending the authenticity of the scriptures, the Indian and the American attempted to retell the story of Jesus in a way that would reconfigure him as simply an expounder of moral precepts – a retelling that would trouble the received notions of Jesus and prove to be unpalatable to the religious establishment of the time.

Rammohun Roy and Thomas Jefferson were men of exceptional calibre. One was part of a new 'native' elite emerging as a result of colonialism, and the other was a member of the founding generation of a newly independent colony. Significantly, both paid attention to religion. They were in varying degrees tantalized, inflamed, tormented and stimulated by it. The religious landscape in Jefferson's case was largely mono-religious, and it was Christianity with all its complexities and variety that formed the background to his enterprise. In Rammohun's case, his religious ideas were shaped by the Indian religious cauldron of Islam, Buddhism, Jainism and, obviously, Hinduism, the dominant religious tradition in the subcontinent. Roy's Islamic learning in Patna and his encounter with

---

1 To give its full title, *The Precepts of Jesus. The Guide to Peace and Happiness; Extracted from the Books of the New Testament, Ascribed to the Four Evangelists* (Calcutta, The Baptist Press, 1820).

Buddhism in Tibet are fairly documented. What is often overlooked is his contact with the Jains. He lived in Rangpur from 1809 to 1814, as an assistant to the revenue officer, John Digby. Rangpur at the time was a thriving mercantile centre frequented by Muslims and Jains for commercial reasons. Roy came into contact with Jains and made an extensive study of their many texts, including the *Kalpasutra*.[2] In a way, he typified and set the tone for the new spirit which was to emerge as a result of the colonial mixing of faiths and civilizations.

The reception history of the text produced by the Raja was totally different from that of the President's text. One went unnoticed and the other made an instant impact and created a storm. Jefferson had an ambivalent attitude towards making his religious views known to a wider public. Initially he was very reluctant to make his *Life and Morals* available to the public. It was produced to satisfy his own spiritual thirst. It was only later that he decided to reveal his views on Christian religion to a small circle of relatives and friends. He wrote to Benjamin Rush, a physician and social reformer, that he was 'averse to the communication of my religious tenets to the public'.[3] As he put it, he did not want to 'trouble the world' with his views: 'It is then a matter of principle with me to avoid disturbing the tranquillity of others by the expression of any opinion on the innocent questions on which we schismatise'.[4] He wanted his beliefs known only by his close friends, whom he urged to be discreet. When there was the possibility of publishing his 'Syllabus' and 'Philosophy', the little tracts which preceded his *Life and Morals of Jesus*, his request was that his name should not be 'even intimated with the publication'.[5] At least at that time, for Jefferson, religion was a private matter; he shared his feelings with only a few close friends, and, as he put it, it is a 'matter between every man and his maker in which no other, and far less the public had the right to intermeddle'.[6] Later, however, after the bitter election, in which some of the clergy called into question his status as a Christian, Jefferson wanted to clear his name and prove that he was a better Christian than his opponents, by showing them that it was he who

---

2 Saumyendranath Tagore, *Raja Rammohun Roy* (New Delhi, Sahitya Akademi, 1966), p. 13.

3 Letter dated 21 April 1803 in Dickinson W. Adams, (ed.), *Jefferson's Extracts from the Gospels: 'The Philosophy of Jesus' and 'The Life and Morals of Jesus'* (Princeton, Princeton University Press, 1983), p. 331. Unless otherwise stated, all citations of Jefferson's letters are from Adams's *Jefferson's Extracts from the Gospels*.

4 Letter to James Fishback, 27 September 1809, p. 343.

5 Letter to Francis Adrian Van der Kemp, 25 April 1816, p. 369.

6 Thomas Jefferson, *The Jefferson Bible: The Life and Morals of Jesus of Nazareth* (Boston, Beacon Press, 1989), p. 22.

was adhering to the primitive religion of Jesus. Jefferson did not edit the gospel narratives originally with a view to publicizing his ideas. His exercise was to help him with his own devotion, to assure himself of his position as a Christian, to provide himself with a nightcap for a peaceful sleep at night. His purpose was not to provoke, scandalize or offend, nor to convert anyone.

Roy, on the other hand, did not hesitate to make his religious views public.[7] He thrived on open debate. It was the public arena which gave him the platform to popularize his own views on religion and to enter into debate with both Baptist missionaries in Calcutta and his own Bengali pundit community. Rammohun Roy produced his *Precepts of Jesus* with a view to simplifying the teachings of Jesus and popularizing them. His *Precepts* was an intentional counter-narrative to the gospel tracts the missionaries were circulating in Calcutta. He proudly justified his selection as in line with the missionary practice of the time:

for we see very often extracts from the Bible, published by the learned men of every sect of Christians, with the view to the maintenance of particular doctrines. Christian churches have selected passages from the Bible, which they conceive particularly excellent, and well adapted for the constant perusal and study of the people of their respective churches; and besides, it is a continual practice of every Christian teacher to choose from the whole Scriptures such texts as he deems most important, for the purposes of illustrating them, and impressing them on the minds of his hearers.[8]

The Precepts was a public tract aimed at proselytizing Christians, especially the Baptist missionaries.

This chapter is about the texts that Roy and Jefferson produced. In looking at these taut tracts, I hope to demonstrate how the Indian and the Virginian behaved like conjoined twins with regard to the appropriation of scriptures, explication of Jesus' teaching, debunking of dogmas, resistance against priestly control and dealing with colonialism. I will narrate the reasons behind these compositions and the nature of their textual

---

7 Roy's *Precepts* generated a heated debate between him and the Baptist missionary Joshua Marshman. Marshman made a vigorous defence of conventional Christianity through a series of articles; see his, *A Defence of the Deity and Atonement of Jesus Christ, in Reply to Ram-Mohun Roy of Calcutta* (London, Kingsbury, Parbury, and Allen, 1822). Roy defended his opposition to the narrow sense of Christianity professed by the missionaries by making three public appeals. For a hermeneutical appraisal of their debate, see R. S. Sugirtharajah, *Asian Biblical Hermeneutics and Postcolonialism: Contesting the Interpretations* (Sheffield, Sheffield Academic Press, 1999), pp. 29–53.

8 Rammohun Roy, *The English Works of Raja Rammohun Roy*, vols. I–IV, ed. Jogendra Chunder Ghose (New Delhi, Cosmo Publications, 1906), p. 559.

selection. I will also analyse the compilations and look for textual similarities and variations, and the image of Jesus they confected, and I will end with some hermeneutical reflections.

The Precepts is a collection of the sayings of Jesus arranged in the order in which they appear in the gospels. Roy provides nothing on the historical background in which these sayings emerged. The narratives relate to the birth, death and resurrection of Jesus. The miracle stories are all left out. Roy defended his deselection thus: 'These precepts separated from the mysterious dogmas and historical records . . . contain not only the essence of all that is necessary to instruct mankind in their civil duties, but also the best and the only means of obtaining the forgiveness of our sins, the favour of God, and strength to overcome our passions, and keep his commandments'.[9] For Roy, these precepts were 'entirely founded on and supported by the express authority of Jesus of Nazareth – a denial of which would not only imply a total disavowal of Christianity'[10] but also be tantamount to undermining the authority of the divine teacher himself. Roy 'selected those Precepts of Jesus, the obedience to which he believed to be most peculiarly required of a Christian'.[11]

The publication of *The Precepts* was probably the last of Roy's many attempts at dabbling in various religions. It is important to remember that Rammohun Roy had for a long time been opposing some Hindu popular practices before he turned his attention to Christianity. He saw the idolatrous worship and polytheistic practices prevalent among Hindus as the causes of moral degradation in India. It was his disgust with the popular Hinduism of his time which prompted him and provided the background for his approach to Christianity. Roy's main thesis was that the religion propagated by the missionaries, with its trinitarian doctrine and belief in supernatural deeds, was as polytheistic and superstitious as popular Hinduism. In Roy's view, the presentation of Christianity by the Baptist missionaries in Bengal as a religion of divine incarnation, sacrificial atonement, miracles and wonders resulted in the genuine message of Jesus being drowned out by the welter of these mythological claims. Such a Christianity, Roy warned, was 'calculated to excite ridicule instead of respect, towards the religion they wished to promulgate'.[12] Roy persistently reminded Christians that these doctrines professed by them would

9 Ibid., p. 552.   10 Ibid., p. 550.   11 Ibid., p. 559.   12 Ibid., p. 920.

be ridiculed by Muslims and scoffed at by Hindus: 'The doctrines which the missionaries maintain and preach are less comfortable with reason than those professed by Moosulmans, and in several points are equally absurd with the popular Hindoo creed. Hence there is no rational inducement for either of these tribes to lay aside their respective doctrines, and adopt those held by the generality of Christians'.[13]

The Precepts was Roy's way of 'purifying the religion of Christ from those absurd idolatrous doctrines and practices'.[14] Admitting that a similar attempt to rid his own Hindu tradition of polytheistic notions was only a 'very partial' success and was sufficient to discourage any similar undertaking, he went on to produce *The Precepts* because of his 'reverence for Christianity, and for the author of this religion, that has induced me to endeavour to vindicate it from the charge of polytheism as far as my limited capacity and knowledge extend'.[15] Besides rectifying the erroneous presentation of Christian faith, Roy had another reason for separating the moral teachings from the abstruse doctrines and miraculous elements. The former, he claimed 'are liable to the doubts and disputes of Free-thinkers and Anti-Christians, and the latter are capable at best of carrying little weight with the natives of this part of the globe, the fabricated tales handed down to them being of a more wonderful nature'.[16]

Jefferson's *Life and Morals of Jesus* had a long and complex 'marination' before it reached its present form. It evolved from two previous incarnations, 'Syllabus of an Estimate of the Merits of the Doctrines of Jesus compared with those of others', and 'Philosophy of Jesus of Nazareth extracted from the accounts of his life and doctrines as given by Matthew, Mark, Luke and John', which Jefferson called 'a wee-little book'. These two texts were Jefferson's vision of Christianity as he wished it to be practised. One could hazard at least two particular reasons behind the production of 'Syllabus' and 'Philosophy'. Firstly, unlike Roy's, these texts were not the result of a purely theological quest but were personal and political. As has been pointed out earlier, they were produced to refute the charges levelled against Jefferson by his clerical adversaries that he was not a Christian:

It is a paradigma of his doctrines, made by cutting the texts out of the book, and arranging them on the pages of a blank book, in certain order of time or subject. A more beautiful or precious morsel of ethics I have never seen; It is a document in proof that *I* am a *real* Christian, that is to say, a disciple of the doctrines of

13 Ibid., p. 881.   14 Ibid., pp. 875–6.
15 Ibid., p. 665.   16 Ibid., p. 567.

Jesus, very different from the Platonists, who call *me* infidel and *themselves* Christians and preachers of the gospel while they draw all their characteristic dogmas from what it's Author never said nor saw.[17]

Secondly, Jefferson wished to introduce a moral vision based on Christianity as a panacea at a time when the new republic was being torn among factionalists and social harmony was being disrupted. Just as Roy saw the social utility of Christianity in the colonial context in India, Jefferson felt that the ethical principles of Christianity would inform the moral sense of the newly freed country. Jefferson was not satisfied with his 'Philosophy' and planned for an expanded version; the result was the *Life and Morals of Jesus*. Unfortunately no text of the 'Philosophy of Jesus' survived. What we have now is the probable reconstruction worked out by Dickinson W. Adams.

How these various compilations metamorphosed into *The Life and Morals of Jesus* is a matter of conjecture and detective work.[18] The basis could have been the promise made to the Dutch scholar and Unitarian minster, Francis Adrian van der Kemp. Admitting that his earlier attempts were 'hastily done', being 'the work of one or two evenings only', while he lived in Washington, 'overwhelmed with other business', Jefferson promised him that he would undertake to go through these again at his leisure.[19] In the same letter, he said that he would like to add an account of the events in Jesus' life so that the 'world will see after the fogs shall be dispelled, in which for 14 centuries he has been inveloped by Jugglers to make money of him, when the genuine character shall be exhibited, which they have dressed up in the rags of an Imposter, the world, I say, will at length see the immortal merit of this first of human Sages'.[20]

Jefferson made clear the purpose of his compilation: 'I have performed this operation for my own use, cutting verse by verse out of the printed book, and arranging the matter which is evidently his, and which is as easily distinguishable as diamonds in a dunghill'.[21] His aim was to restrict

17 Letter to Charles Thompson, 9 January 1816, pp. 364–5 (emphasis in the original; henceforward italics in quotations are by the original author unless stated otherwise).
18 For an excellent detailed account of how *The Life and Morals of Jesus* evolved from the earlier *Syllabus* and *Philosophy of Jesus*, see Dickinson W. Adams (ed.), 'Introduction', *Jefferson's Extracts from the Gospels*, pp. 13–38 and also Eugene R. Sheridan, *Jefferson and Religion* (Thomas Jefferson Memorial Foundation, 1998), pp. 24–64. There was a tradition of presenting copies of Jefferson's Bible to the new US Senators and Representatives at the swearing-in ceremony. It was started in 1905, discontinued in the early 1950s and revived again in 1997.
19 Letter to Francis Adrian Van der Kemp, 25 April 1816, p. 369.
20 Ibid.
21 Letter to John Adams, 12 October 1813, p. 352.

his volume to 'the simple evangelists, select, even from them, the very words only of Jesus'.[22] The scissors-and-paste technique which he applied to his 'Philosophy' was pursued with greater vigour this time. *The Life and Morals* was not an attempt at harmonizing various bits of the gospels but a careful selection to suit Jefferson's heremeneutical palate. More detailed and ruthless than his earlier 'Philosophy', Jefferson did not hesitate to cut off a biblical verse in the middle of a sentence if it proved to be awkward to his religious sensibilities. What he retained was a completely demystified Jesus. It was a kind of non-miraculous biography of Jesus gleaned from Luke and Matthew. All references to miracles, Holy Spirit, and any instances which highlighted Jesus exercising authority were excluded. He ended his construal of Jesus with Jesus' death and left out narratives related to resurrection. For the teaching of Jesus, he focussed mainly on the milder admonitions, especially in the Sermon on the Mount and his most memorable parables. The result was a reasonably coherent and oddly truncated biography.

THE RAJA AND THE PRESIDENT AS TEXTUAL TERMINATORS

Firstly, I offer some fairly simple observations about the texts the Raja and the President produced. Roy's was a proper published version, printed, ironically, at the Baptist Press owned by the Baptists, whose very theology Roy's tract subverted. Jefferson's was, as Edgar J. Goodspeed called it, a 'scrap book',[23] – a cut-and-paste job, a method which was later turned into a fine-art form by the feminist biblical scholar Elizabeth Cady Stanton. Roy's *Precepts* was intended for a wider audience and was distributed free of charge by Roy. Jefferson's compilation remained hidden within his family until it was discovered by Cyrus Alder. If Roy's was a public search for religious truth, Jefferson's was a private quest, intended for his personal reading and enjoyment. One was unilingual, the other was multilingual. Roy's plan to publish *The Precepts* in Sanskrit and Bengali did not materialize. Jefferson's text had biblical verses in Greek, Latin and French.[24]

The Precepts and *Life and Morals* draw roughly the same number of verses (about 1200) from the four gospels, the vast majority from Matthew and Luke and about a hundred each from Mark. However, Roy restricts

---

22 Ibid.
23 Edgar J. Goodspeed, 'Thomas Jefferson and the Bible', *Harvard Theological Review* 40:1 (1947), 71
24 For which Greek, Latin and French versions Jefferson used, see ibid., pp. 71–8.

his selection from John to only fifty-one verses, whereas Jefferson has three times that number. For both, the King James Version was their ur-text, the regnant Protestant version at that time. The King James Version became the text for the empire not because of the excellence of its translation, as its admirers would like us to believe, but rather because of the machinations of the publishers who promoted its cause. Jefferson's text is literally a cut-and-paste job, whereas Roy's is generally a stringing together of large blocks of the sayings of Jesus, occasionally dropping a few verses here and there.[25]

In the deployment of gospel narratives, Jefferson is the more daring of the two. He casually moves texts around, paying little respect to the narrative sequence or to the canonical order in which the gospels are arranged. He hops and flits between gospels and disrupts their chronological arrangement. He freely moves passages from their settings and yokes them with others. He even moves around verses within a chapter. A notable case in point is Matthew 27. In this chapter Matthew features the suicide of Judas and his returning of thirty pieces of silver to the chief priest and the elders at the beginning of the trial; he places these episodes early in this part of the narrative. Jefferson, in his version, relocates them at the end after Pilate has handed Jesus over for crucifixion. Such a rearrangement will horrify purists raised on the canonical sequence. Roy does not engage in such zigzagging. He is fairly faithful to the canonical order, starting with Matthew, then moving to Mark, then Luke, and ending with John.

Both provide the sources of the narratives they have chosen. Just as the King James Version has columns, Jefferson pastes his texts in parallel columns. He supplies details of the chapter and the verse of each passage he has extracted. Roy simply indicates at the beginning of each segment of his selection which gospel it has been chosen from. His text runs through without any verse divisions, thus emphasizing the narrative potentiality of the gospels, a practice that later came to be advocated by those who promoted the idea of the Bible as literature.[26] Another possible reason for doing away with the numbering of verses could be that Rammohun

---

25 For example, on the Sermon on the Mount, Roy does not include the entire chapter Matt. 5. He omits vv. 33–42. The other instances are: chapter 13, vv. 38–45 are left out, and in chapter 20, Jesus' moving to Jerusalem and the announcement of his imminent death are missing (vv. 17–19).

26 The leading figures were Matthew Arnold, H. G. Moulton, Ernest Sutherland Bates and James George Frazer.

was producing *The Precepts of Jesus* for Hindus, and Hindu Shastras at that time did not have such chapter and verse identification.[27]

Slicing up the Sermon

Both Roy and Jefferson draw largely on the Sermon on the Mount in order to support their case for Jesus as a moral teacher. Roy's *Precepts* starts with Matthew's account of Jesus preaching on the Mount: 'And seeing the multitudes, he went up to a mountain'. A reader who plunges into Roy's version without reading the introduction does not not find out until the fourth page that these are the words of Jesus. Roy retains the Sermon on the Mount almost as it is in chapters 5–7 of Matthew except for some minor deletions. In his view, the Sermon 'contained in the 5th, 6th and 7th chapters of Matthew' are 'the blessed and benign moral doctrines', and they include 'every duty of man, and all that is necessary to salvation'. More importantly, for Roy, the Sermon expressly excludes 'any of the mysterious or historical' accounts.[28] Since the Sermon on the Mount contains the necessary ingredients to fit Roy's expectation of religion, he did not see any need to interfere with the text. The fact that the Sermon does not contain any article of faith about Jesus would have been an added bonus to him.

Jefferson, on the other hand, does not reproduce the entire Sermon but in effect rewrites it. He cleverly conflates Matthean and Lucan accounts and also brings in materials from other parts of the gospels which are normally not seen as part of the Sermon on the Mount. In a sense, it is Jefferson's sermon. He starts with the Matthean version of the Beatitudes but adds two segments from Luke. Jefferson's Beatitudes stop at Matthew 5.12 and attach the Lucan four 'woes', depicted in contrastive terms – poor/rich, hungry/full, weeping/laughing and rejected/accepted (6.24–6). He returns to Matthew's account and follows it until verse 47, and then he slices off Matthew's last sentence: 'You therefore must be perfect, as your heavenly Father is perfect'. As far as Jefferson's theological outlook is concerned, such a claim is redundant. It is not perfection that Jefferson is looking for but moral obligation and mutual love. Such an idea is found in Luke. So he interpolates the closing verses of chapter 6 of Luke, which

27 Rammohun Roy's own translation of the Upanishads did not carry any verse divisions. Charles Wilkins's translation of the Bhagavadgita (1785) did not carry any verse numbers, which displeased William Jones, who was to embark upon a massive project of translating Hindu sacred texts.

28 *The English Works of Raja Rammohun Roy*, p. 555.

reinforce Jefferson's theme of moral obligation: 'Be ye therefore merciful, as your Father also is merciful' (6.36). Jefferson does not tamper with Luke's chapter 6 but, like Roy, leaves it alone. By the seventh chapter, Jefferson's scissors are unusually busy again. He is contented with the first twenty verses, which have moral instructions that are compatible with the ethical vision he is advocating. They start with Jesus' saying about not judging or condemning people, which would be to usurp God's role, but forgiving them. Then suddenly Jefferson throws in Matthew's justice of measure for measure with the Lucan saying which speaks of God's boundless beneficence. From then on, he reverts to Matthew's running order, which includes the attempt to remove the mote in the brother's eye while neglecting the beam in one's own, not casting pearls before swine, and not being so cruel as to give a stone to a son who has asked for bread, or a serpent for a fish. He ends the Matthean segment with the most important of all his moral teachings – the 'golden rule' which expresses the universal wish for all people to be treated with love and justice: 'Therefore all things whatsoever you would that man should do to you, do even so to them'. As a classicist, Jefferson would have known that this was not a unique Christian saying, having its roots in the Graeco-Roman world. But what was important for him was that it resonated with the Jeffersonian notion of a universal ethic. Jefferson must have been so excited with the saying's universal applicability, that he uncharacteristically failed to note the second part of the sentence: 'for this is the law and the prophets', a Matthean addition indicating the fulfilment of the Torah. The long nights that he laboured to produce his version must have taken their toll. Jefferson, who was relentless in deleting any reference, however remote, to prophetic fulfilment, leaves this uncharacteristically uncut. He regains his severe tendency to slash any material which does not fit in with his hermeneutical presuppositions when Matthew begins to wander into a discussion about who is eligible to enter the Kingdom of God. Jefferson ruthlessly severs these three verses and brings in a passage from a later chapter of Matthew which speaks about the inner character and external action of good and evil men and Jesus' saying about how the 'idle word' is decisive for judgement (12.35–7). Jefferson might have had in mind his clerical opponents who said unpalatable things about him. He then turns to Matthew's final injunctions, that the believers must not only hear the words of Jesus but also practise his precepts. Those who enact the teaching are seen as prudent and those who do not are seen as foolish. Jefferson rounds off with the formula that Matthew uses to bring Jesus' long speeches to a conclusion. This highlights and reiterates three of

Jefferson's hermeneutical claims, namely that 'these words' were uttered by Jesus and that he was a teacher and had a distinctive style: 'For he taught them as one having authority, and not as the scribes' (Matt. 7.29).

Roy and Jefferson treated the Sermon on the Mount not only as central to Jesus' teaching but also as a rallying point for all Christians. In a letter to George Thatcher, Jefferson made his aspiration clear: 'If all Christian sects would rally to the Sermon on the Mount, make that the central point of the Union in religion, and the stamp of genuine Christianity (since it gives us all the precepts of our duties to one another) why should we further ask, with the text of our sermon, "What think *ye* of Christ?" '[29]

History with morals

What makes the Jefferson version different from that of Roy is the inclusion of historical passages related to Jesus' life. The historical narratives which find their way into Jefferson's Bible are: the birth of Jesus, his circumcision and baptism, visit to the temple, entry into Jerusalem, and the last days of his arrest, trial and death. He also includes details about Herod's rule, and the ministry and death of John the Baptist. None of these feature in Roy's *Precepts of Jesus.* Interestingly, they are found in the Virginian's version not because these narratives have historical value but because they embody two of Jefferson's cherished theological ideas: Jesus as an ordinary human person and Jesus as an expounder of moral precepts.

The events related to the temple in the life of Jesus get a fair share of attention in Jefferson's version. It is here that the twelve-year-old Jesus spends three days hearing from and posing questions to the temple authorities. The first act and the first utterance of the adult Jesus also take place in the temple. In Jefferson's Bible, the disruption of the temple occurs twice: once at the beginning of Jesus' ministry and again just before his last days in Jerusalem. In both cases, Jefferson's intention is clear – to expose the temple's mercantile aspect and its use for exploitation. Unlike Mark's version, where Jesus after his baptism inaugurates his ministry with the words 'The time is fulfilled, and the kingdom of God is at hand: repent ye, and believe the gospel' (1.15), Jefferson follows John's order of events and puts the driving out of the money changers and vendors at the beginning of his version. Soon after his baptism Jesus goes straight to the temple, the very heart of the nation's religious and political power, and confronts the authorities. Jesus' opening sentence in *Life and Morals* is: 'Take these things hence; make not my father's house an house of merchandise'. It looks as if Jefferson's choice of John was intentional and had a deliberate hermeneutical motive. In John's version, Jesus' action does not have any reference to the Hebrew scriptures. The placing of the disruption of the temple at the beginning of Jesus' ministry fits in not only with John's theological purpose but also with Jefferson's. Like Jesus' life, Jefferson's too has been marked by endless embroilments with his own clergy. Jefferson had lambasted those priests and clergy who erected artificial structures out of 'the genuine system of Jesus', made his teachings into 'an instrument of wealth',[30] and derived from it 'pence and power'.[31] The inclusion of the prediction of the downfall of the temple (Matt. 24.1–2) may be Jefferson's strategical device to wrest the power from priests who exercised political and economic influence. Surprisingly, Roy, who had similar conflicts with his own religious pundits and with Christian missionaries, completely ignores Jesus' involvement with the temple and its authorities.

Consider how Jefferson handles Jesus' entry into Jerusalem. While the gospel writers were busy finding parallels between Jesus' entry and prophetic sayings which fitted with the image of the long-awaited Messiah, Jefferson removes all passages relating to any prophetic fulfilment. When the city people are moved by the procession and pose the question 'who is this?', Jefferson cuts out Matthew's answer: 'This the the Prophet Jesus from Nazareth in Galilee'. He shows no interest in Matthew's account of the entry and inserts the Johannine version, in which the Greeks' simple request to Philip is: 'Sir, we would Jesus'.

Jefferson's treatment of the events related to Jesus' last days reveals that he had little interest in historical details. As is his practice, Jefferson does not stick with one gospel but draws on all four. For Jesus' arrest, Jefferson shows an initial preference for the Johannine version because it fits in with the Jeffersonian notion of Jesus as an ordinary human being. It is only in John that Jesus openly courts arrest twice by identifying himself as Jesus of Nazareth, whereas in the Synoptic gospels it is Judas who identifies Jesus with a kiss. Once the identification of Jesus is established, Jefferson forgets the rest of the Johannine narrative, which has a long discourse on the father–son relationship, a theme for which Jefferson has little enthusiasm. From there he goes to Matthew, who narrates the

---

30 Letter to Charles Clay, 15 January 1815, p. 363.
31 Letter to Margaret Bayard Smith, 6 August 1816, p. 376.

incident of the cutting-off of the ear of the high priest's servant. In the hands of the gospel writers this incident provides an opportunity for Jesus to perform a miracle. But Jefferson does not see it that way. The healing which follows is marginal to Jefferson's purposes. What is central is that Jesus seizes the opportunity to reject violence and its inevitable consequences – 'for all that take the sword shall perish with the sword'. Jefferson promptly removes the next three verses, which refer to Jesus' ability to summon divine help, as well as references to the scripture being fulfilled – anathema to Jefferson – and concludes with a saying of Jesus which emphasizes that he is a teacher who is simply going about his business of teaching: 'I sat daily with you teaching in the temple, and ye laid no hold on me' (Matt. 26.56). True to form, Jefferson slices away any saying that might indicate that these events had taken place because they were foretold in the scriptures. Unfortunately, the person who felt the pain of Jefferson's blade most was the servant of the high priest, Malchus. His ear remained unhealed because of Jefferson's predetermined theological agenda.

For Peter's denial, Jefferson reverts to John's version for the simple reason that it encapsulates Jefferson's cherished idea of Jesus' being regarded as a teacher. In the other gospels, the accuser identifies Peter as one of those hanging around with a Galilean or a Nazarene, whereas only in John is Peter twice accused of being the disciple of Jesus, thus reinforcing Jesus' role as a teacher: 'Art not thou also one of this man's disciples?' While the Synoptic gospels treat Jesus' status as marginal to the elite of Jerusalem by calling him 'Galilean' (Matt. 26.69; Mk 14.70) and employ a title of scorn such as 'Nazarene' (Mk 14.67), it is John who emphasizes the Jeffersonian idea of the teacher–disciple association.

The trial scene as it is reported in the gospels is a complicated discourse, each gospel writer having a different chronological order and narrative sequence and competing layers of interpretation. Jefferson goes again for John's version because it suits his theological purposes. Whereas in the other gospels the high priest seeks false witnesses to frame Jesus or tries to find out whether Jesus thinks of himself as the Messiah, in John's version the high priest's line of questioning is focussed on Jesus and his disciples, and on his 'doctrine' (as the King James Version has it), the issues Jefferson was concerned with. In Jefferson's thinking, doctrine was concocted by the clergy to mystify ordinary people. The answer of John's Jesus that he was not only teaching openly but also that he had never hidden anything from people was closer to Jefferson's agenda: 'I spake openly to the world. I ever taught in the synagogue and in the temple, whither the Jews always resort; and in secret have I said nothing' (Jn 18.20).

The crucifixion in the Jefferson version is a pathetic story of an innocent man being put to death. True to his style, Jefferson conflates accounts from Matthew, Luke and John. Probably reminded of his own taunting by his clergy, Jefferson retains the mocking of Jesus by the soldiers. For Jesus' final moment on the cross, Jefferson prefers Matthew. In Jefferson's reconstruction, Jesus does not die as the saviour of the world but as a person abandoned by God, like the figure in Shusako Endo's novel *Silence*. Jefferson promptly removes all the supernatural events described by Matthew, such as the quaking of the earth, opening of graves, raising up of saints and, more importantly, the saying of the centurion which identifies Jesus as truly the Son of God. *The Life and Morals* ends with a rather abrupt finale: 'And rolled a great stone to the door of the sepulchre, and departed' (Matt. 27.60). There was no room for the resurrection because Jefferson believed that it was a great perversion of Christianity. In Jefferson's narration, there is no appearance of a risen Lord, nor his ascension into heaven. Jesus is depicted as an illustrious teacher, noblest of them all, who dies for his ethical teaching.

Jefferson's employment of historical material in the gospels was determined by four factors. Firstly, any historical event which did not reinforce Jefferson's understanding of Jesus as a great moral teacher was excised. A conspicuous case in point is the narratives surrounding the temptation of Jesus. This event, which figures prominently in the gospels, does not feature in Jefferson's version. Secondly, Jefferson was very careful to remove any saying that would portray Jesus as a Messiah. He was troubled by the notion of Messiah and relating that to Jesus. The Caesarea Philippi incident in which Peter openly identifies Jesus as the Messiah was left out. The subject of the Messiah was one of the themes that Jefferson wanted to explore at a later date. To Francis Adrian Van der Kemp, Jefferson wrote: 'if my days are prolonged, I may yet, and it is my intention, institute an Inquiry – "what there is in the Jewish writings about a Messiah, what opinions the contemporaries of Jezus [*sic*] friends and foes had of him, and what he instilled in his disciples, what they learned of him in Public" '.[32] Incidentally, the Caesarea Philippi incident is one of the rare historical events which crept into Roy's text. The Messiah whom Roy had in mind, however, is not the Messiah who is couched in Semitic and Hellenistic idiom, but one rooted in Asiatic sensibility and more accessible to Indians. Thirdly, any event which had even a hint of a suggestion that it might have happened as a result of a

---

32 Letter to Francis Adrian Van der Kemp, 4 June 1816, p. 371.

fulfilment of prophecy came under Jefferson's customary axe. Jesus' entry into Jerusalem on a colt gained a nod from Jefferson but he was extra careful about removing Matthew's fulfilment citation, which combines Isaiah 62.11 and Zechariah 9.9: 'Tell ye the daughter of Sion, Behold, thy King cometh unto thee, meek, and sitting upon an ass, and a colt the foal of an ass' (Matt. 21.5). Jefferson includes the dividing of Jesus' clothes by the soldiers after his death, but leaves out any reference to the Old Testament prediction: 'They parted my garments among them, and for my clothing they cast lots'. Fourthly, events which had supernatural occurrences entrenched in them are cleansed of any such contamination. The angels are the hapless victims of Jefferson's cuts. Although he relies on Luke's account for the birth, he skips all the conversations and announcements of the angels, and especially Gabriel's explanation to Mary of the miraculous conception. The shepherds watching over the flocks by night do not have a visitation from the angels nor do they hear the heavenly host singing 'Glory to God in the highest'. Jefferson includes the baptism of Jesus but leaves out the supernatural events connected with it such as the heavens opening, the spirit of God descending like a dove and alighting on him, and the voice from heaven saying, 'Thou art my beloved Son; in thee I am well pleased'. Roy completely ignores this aspect of Jesus' life. In Jefferson's version, historical narratives are mobilized but subverted and restricted to a minimalist form. 'Incidents of his life require little research', he wrote to Francis Adrian Van der Kemp.[33] For Jefferson, the supernatural events were an appendage to his theological goals rather than a depiction of historical reality.

Women: dehumanized and glorified

The strong female characters, such as the Syrophoenician woman who irritates Jesus by voicing her views, are missing from the versions of Roy and Jefferson. Roy includes a part of the narrative relating to the Samaritan woman but she remains invisible. She and her question hardly figure in *The Precepts*, but Roy includes Jesus' answer to her question, which speaks about the new worship in spirit and truth replacing the old ritualistic one, an idea which Roy himself was passionate about, as his quarrels with Hindu pundits prove. When women are mentioned they are chosen for their vulnerability, piety or generosity. John's account of the woman caught in adultery features in both Jefferson's and Roy's

---

33 Letter dated 25 April 1816, p. 369.

compilations but her presence is seen as an opportunity for Jesus to wax eloquent about morality and she serves as a benchmark for future good behaviour. Jefferson incorporates the Lucan version of the anointing scene, which fits in with his motives. The woman's action in the other three gospels is seen as a perfect preparation for Jesus' death – an event in which Jefferson had little interest. Luke has his version in the early part of Jesus' ministry and portrays the performance of the woman as the warm-hearted gesture of an intrusive woman. The signal purpose of including her is to underscore her act, which should inspire men. *The Precepts* has the Widow's Mite twice, one in Mark's version and the other in Luke's. The intention seems to be to idealize her as a selfless giver. The giving by the widow acts simultaneously as an ideal picture of conduct and also as an exemplification of how men should act and live. These biblical women are enclosed, confined, and merged into the hermeneutical framework set by Jefferson and Roy, and thus do not have their own voice nor identity.

On using (or not using) John

Roy includes only six passages from the fourth gospel (3.1–21; 4.23; 6.27; 8.3–11; 9.39; 15.1–17) and he places them all at the end of *The Precepts*. A closer look at these texts will reveal that that they were all chosen because they endorse Roy's hermeneutical agenda: unity of God, purity of worship, and showing love and charity to fellow human beings. He expresses at least two interconnected reasons for the comparatively few passages from John. One is that the fourth gospel is a depository of incomprehensible doctrines: 'It is from this source (i.e. John) that the most difficult to be comprehended of the dogmas of the Christian religion has been principally drawn'. In his view, it was John's gospel which provided the foundation for the 'mysterious doctrine of three Gods in one Godhead',[34] which he saw as an unnecessary hindrance to the dissemination of an ethical Christianity in India. The second reason is related to the first. John's gospel contains a peculiar message which is not easy to communicate without 'preparatory instruction'. Unless one is properly tutored it is not easy to fathom the message of John. For instance, Roy reckons that the opening verse, 'In the beginning was the Word and the Word was with God, and the Word was God', will without any 'recourse for an explanation'[35] cause problems. In one of his appeals, Roy puts it to

---

34 *The English Works of Raja Rammohun Roy*, p. 558.
35 Ibid., p. 560.

Marshman thus: 'Would they (i.e. the Indians) not find themselves at a loss to reconcile this dogma to their unprepared understandings?'[36]

Roy begins his Johannine selection with the narrative referring to Nicodemus at 3.1–21. Roy's selection of Nicodemus could have been influenced by two factors. One is Nicodemus' identifying Jesus as 'a teacher from God' (3.2), and the other is Jesus' endorsement of the true religion based on being born 'from above'/again rather than on temple-based rituals. The Nicodemus incident is followed by the classic Johannine saying about the redundancy of the old ritual worship that went on at Mount Gerizim and at Jerusalem: 'But the hour cometh, and now is, when the true worshippers shall worship the Father in spirit and truth: for the Father seeketh such to worship him. God is Spirit: and they that worship him must worship *him* in spirit and in truth' (4.23). This saying stands in *The Precepts* minus its original context and, more revealingly, as I indicated earlier, without the chief interlocutor of the pericope – the nameless Samaritan woman. The attraction of the saying for Roy lay in its complementarity. It parallelled and matched the Vedic teaching that the Supreme Being may be worshipped anywhere with no special place of worship (Brahmasutras 4.1, 11), and that the Vedic rituals are no substitute for worship of a monotheistic god. In his disputes with his own brahminical community, Roy had drawn their attention to their own scriptures about the nature of true worship: 'Those observers of religious rites that perform only the worship of the sacred fire, and oblations to sages, to ancestors, to men, and the other creatures, without regarding the worship of celestial gods, shall enter into the dark regions' (*Isa Upanishad* 9).[37] In the 'Religious Instructions', a question and answer pamphlet which Roy produced, based on sacred authorities, he states: 'A suitable place is certainly preferable, but it is not absolutely necessary; that is to say, in whatever place, towards whatever quarter, or at whatever time the mind is at best at rest, – that place, that quarter, and that time is the most proper for the performance of this worship'.[38]

Roy's next selection from John comes from 6.27, where Jesus questions the motive of the people who followed him. His admonition presupposes that eating and being filled were not sufficient reasons for seeking him: 'Labour not for the meat which perisheth, but for the meat which endureth unto everlasting life, which the Son of Man shall give unto you: for him hath God the Father sealed'. Roy always opposed and suspected the motives of converts from the lower castes, who changed

---

36 Ibid.   37 Ibid., p. 76.   38 Ibid., p. 138.

their religion purely for monetary benefits and because of other inducements dangled before them by missionaries. He complained about the gift
of five hundred rupees and a country-born Christian woman as a wife,
which these converts received as compensation for the loss of caste.[39] He
even quoted Abbé Dubois, a contemporary Roman Catholic missionary,
to support his scepticism about and disapproval of the proselytizing that
went on in colonial India. Dubois spoke about native Christians who had
the 'habit of being six months Catholic and six months Protestant' and
who changed their allegiance 'in times of famine, or from other interested
motives'.[40] The Johannine saying about eating and not being filled is
followed immediately by the aforementioned account of Jesus' meeting
with the woman caught in adultery. Then Roy includes one of John's
ironical remarks: 'For judgement I am come into this world, that they
which see not might see; and that they which see might be made blind'
(9.39). Obviously the reference here is not to physical but symbolic
blindness. Roy's placing of this utterance soon after his questioning of
the motive of conversion may be intentional. The saying indicates the
inevitable outcome of the preaching of the gospel when some are
hardened by selfish motives and their eyes blinded. What Roy seems to
register here is that only a 'seeing', a conversion which is uncorrupted by
attractive inducements, grasps the ultimate meaning of the gospel message. *The Precepts* ends with John 15.1–17. This narrative has two sections.
In the first, the metaphor of the vine and the branches is used in order
to highlight the importance of unity among the disciples of Jesus. But
what is attractive to Roy about the passage is that it reinforces the pre-
eminence of the Father and the bearing of fruit. With all his reluctance to
use John, Roy finds in the fourth gospel an appropriate ending which
encapsulates his theological stance: 'These things I command you, that ye
love one another' (Jn 15.17). What is crucial to Roy is the Johannine
understanding of doing the truth, the sustaining of conscious, continuous
and responsible relationship.

Roy and Jefferson are ruthless in editing out two of John's distinctive
Christological affirmations: the triumphalistic assertion that Jesus is the
way, the truth and the life, which makes him a unique gatekeeper of
salvation; and the divine status attributed to Jesus ('the Father is in me,
and I am in him'). A striking example of this omission is Jefferson's
handling of John's narrative about the last supper (13.21–6). The incidents
described in the story, such as Judas' leaving the scene, and the saying

---

39 Ibid., p. 879.   40 Ibid., p. 878.

about the glorification of Christ and God, are peripheral to his hermeneutical cause and swiftly expurgated. For Jefferson the most appealing aspect of the narrative is the moral message embedded in it: 'A new commandment I give unto you. That ye love one another; as I have loved you, that ye also love one another'. The supreme example of this love is humility demonstrated by Jesus in washing the feet of the apostles, an example the disciples themselves were expected to emulate.

Commissioning of the disciples

Interestingly both Jefferson and Roy retain the commissioning of the disciples. They draw on Matthew's sending out, which discourages the disciples from going into Gentile territories and focusses on the inner renewal of Israel, which, needless to say, resonates with both Jefferson and Roy. Both of them had qualms about aggressive evangelization. To Margaret Bayard Smith, a Washington social leader and a novelist, Jefferson expressed his feelings thus: 'I never attempted to make a convert, nor wished to change another's creed'.[41] Although they retain the commissioning, they handle the narrative differently. Jefferson, in keeping with his practice, mixes Marcan and Matthean accounts, whereas Roy largely sticks to Matthew's version. Jefferson begins with Mark 6.7: 'And he called unto him the twelve and began to send them forth by two and two', and he deletes those lines which speak about Jesus giving the disciples authority over unclean spirits. Then he inserts Matthew's commission and retains 10.5 and 6, which clearly forbid mission to the Gentiles and to the Samaritans but urge the disciples to go to the lost sheep of the house of Israel. Jefferson makes certain that all the materials relating to authority over unclean spirits and the power to heal and forgive are edited out. He also cuts the most important aspect of the sending out, namely to preach 'The Kingdom of God is at hand'. An uninitiated reader who is unaware of Jefferson's idiosyncrasies will be wondering what the point of the mission is. What is the content of the message which the disciples are supposed to preach? From this point, Jefferson follows Matthew 10.9–23, which has instructions about what the disciples should take on their journey, how they should behave in houses and towns, and the inevitable persecution they will face, but deletes the verses about the master of the house being likened to Beelzebub (vv. 24, 25). From there Jefferson continues with Matthew's narrative until it reaches the stage

41 6 August 1816, p. 376.

where Jesus says: 'I have come not to bring peace but a sword'. This was too harsh a statement from Jesus and unpalatable to Jefferson's theological taste. Moreover, it did not fit in with the Jeffersonian notion of social harmony which Jesus' message was supposed to bring. His blade gets busy and he slices this verse out. Then he reverts to Mark 6.12, which reports the successful preaching activities of the disciples. As these activities of the disciples, such as casting out of demons and miraculous healing of the sick with oil, are redundant to his interpretative aims, Jefferson does not hesitate to remove them. What is important for him is the teaching aspect of the mission, especially what the disciples taught (Mk 6.30). Jefferson includes Luke's mission of the seventy. Here, too, he is careful to expunge anything to do with the power to exorcise, heal and forgive but retains the material related to the preaching activities of the disciples and the kind of behaviour expected of them.

Roy depends entirely upon Matthew's pericope about the commissioning and, unlike Jefferson, he does not juggle passages from different gospels. He erases Jesus' opening utterances about the sending aspect of the mission but makes use of the passages which describe the pains and suffering of those who engage in God's work. Roy would have immediately identified with the agony and antagonism of the disciples. He himself was faced with disapproval and hostility from his own people. 'I was at last deserted by every person',[42] he recorded in his Autobiographical Sketch. Unlike Jefferson, Roy has no misgivings about using the stern statements of Jesus on causing division and mayhem among parents and children. The saying of Jesus 'For I have come to set a man at variance against his father' must have spoken particularly to his own situation when he had a difference of opinion with both his father and his Brahmin pundits about his interpretative activities which questioned idolatry and interfered with traditional customs, activities which did not please either. As a result of his intervention in religious matters, his father was 'obliged to withdraw his countenance openly'.[43] There are two aspects of the commissioning account which must have attracted the attention of Roy. The first is the intimate and transcendent knowledge of God in such sayings as that the sparrows cannot fall to the ground without the knowledge of the father, and 'even the hairs of your head are all counted'. Such statements would have been seen as reinforcing Roy's notion of a universal principle which rules over people's destiny: 'One Being as the

---

42 *The English Works of Raja Rammohun Roy,* p. 224.
43 Ibid., p. 224.

animating and regulating principle of the whole collective body of the universe'.[44] The other aspect is the practical one of any religious teaching: 'And whosoever shall give to drink unto one of these little ones a cup of cold *water* only in the name of a disciple, verily I say unto you, he shall in no wise lose his reward'. It is not the religious ritual but the everyday praxis which serves the betterment of humankind: 'The divine homage which we offer consists solely in the peace of *Daya* or benevolence towards each other, not in a fanciful faith or in certain motions of the feet, legs, arms, head, tongue or other bodily organs in a pulpit or before a temple'.[45]

Roy was not against the proclamation of Christian faith or the presence of the missionaries. In spite of his duel with Marshman, he was helpful to missionaries and even provided his own land for building Christian schools. He did not oppose Christianity as such but he wanted a Christianity shaped according to his hermeneutical vision – moral and rational. Thus he did not want the prospective converts to embrace a faith in which they changed 'the deities worshipped by their fathers, for foreign gods, and in substituting the blood of God for the water of the Ganges as a purifying substance'.[46] He resented and remonstrated against the missionary way of proselytizing the natives by reviling Hindu tenets or offering material inducements. He made it clear to those missionaries who were active in Bengal that 'to introduce a religion (Christianity) by means of abuse and insult, or by affording the hope of worldly gain, is inconsistent with reason and justice'.[47] Roy pressed missionaries hard to convince Indians by the force of their argument, by presenting Christianity as an ethical and enlightened religion. He pointed out to them that the doctrines of Hinduism 'are much more rational than the religion which the Missionaries profess'.[48] His plea to the missionaries was to put their house in order and promote and collaborate with any religion which preaches worship of one true God, and relies on ethical principles as a means of bringing peace and happiness. Jefferson, too, was not keen on making converts of others.

Magical unrealism

In spite of the rationalistic streak of Roy and Jefferson, some of the miracles of Jesus enter the compilations. The purpose of their inclusion is not to highlight the miraculous aspect of the incidents as such but to

---

44 Ibid., p. 198.   45 Ibid.
46 The letter of Rammohun Roy to the editor of the *Christian Register*, 7 May 1824.
47 *The English Works of Raja Rammohun Roy*, p. 146.   48 Ibid., p. 147.

amplify the moral teaching embedded within the stories. Inevitably, the miracle is pushed into the background, and the teaching which surrounds the incident is brought to the fore. Both compilations include Matthew's version of the man with the withered hand (12.9–10). In this narrative the Pharisees question Jesus about the lawfulness of healing on the Sabbath. In Jefferson's Bible, Jesus takes over the question as though it is his own. Far more important to Jefferson is the moral signal that the incident sent out: showing that kindness to people who are in distress is decent human behaviour. This compassionate ethical response is much closer to Jefferson's theological thinking than the more immediate task of healing, or portraying Jesus as another faith healer. Thus Jefferson loses interest in the man's withered arm and cuts out the verse about restoring the hand. Ironically, he adds a verse from Mark which reiterates the notion that alleviating human misery is more important than observing institutional regulations: 'He said unto them, the Sabbath was made for man, and not man for the Sabbath' (2.27). The retention of the incident in *The Precepts* with a fully healed arm is difficult to fathom. Roy's explanation would have been that his readers who had been raised in 'miracles infinitely more wonderful' and 'superior'[49] to those recorded in the Bible would not be impressed by such a healing, the inclusion of which would have carried 'little weight with them'.[50]

Another healing miracle which is included in Jefferson's version is of the man blind from birth (Jn 9.1–3). Jefferson would have chosen this narrative over that of the Synoptics for the simple reason that the miracle in John is not occasioned by a request for healing (cf. Mk 8.22). The incident itself is described by the fourth evangelist with economy of style. The Virginian's Bible makes it even more taut. The disciples raise an important theological issue: what caused the man's blindness? – his sins? or those of his parents? There is an enigmatic reply from Jesus: 'Neither has this man sinned, nor his parents: but that the works of God should be made manifest in him'. The occasion of the miracle does not engage Jefferson's interest but he is attracted by the plight of the blind man as a convenient opportunity to do God's work. Jesus is seen as a person who does the work of God while he has time on earth. Once the purpose of the pericope is made clear, Jefferson neglects the man, leaves him unattended, forgets the disciples' question and haphazardly moves on to John 10, which contains a cluster of sayings about the shepherd and the sheep.

49 Ibid., p. 555.   50 Ibid., p. 615.

Here Jesus is portrayed as an ethical exemplar who, as a good shepherd, knows and loves his sheep and takes care of them by dying for them. In the Johannine miracle story which Jefferson cuts short, Jesus heals the blind man by making clay with his spittle, thus giving him an opportunity to initiate one of John's characteristic 'I am' discourses – 'I am the light of the world'. The unfortunate man whose ear was severed still remains unhealed.

Roy did not rate the miracles recorded in the New Testament as on an equal 'footing with the extravagant tales of his countryman'. He doubted that Hindus would be impressed with them, because they had been brought up with infinitely more amazing supernatural feats which were supported by authorities superior to the apostles: the biblical miracles carried 'little weight with those whose imaginations had been accustomed to dwell on narrations much more wonderful and supported by testimony which they have been taught to regard with a reverence that they cannot be expected all at once to bestow on the Apostles'.[51] There were two reasons for Roy's omission of miracles. Firstly, it was not because he doubted their authenticity or intended to slight them but because he was first drawn to 'the sublimity of the Precepts of Jesus'.[52] Secondly, the miracles were performed to impress and to accommodate those who were spiritually less gifted: 'Jesus referred to his miracles those persons only who either *scrupled to believe*, or doubted him as the promised Messiah, or required of him some sign to confirm their faith'.[53] Jefferson, too, was wary of miracles and he did not subscribe to the idea that Jesus ever performed them. The miracles attributed to Jesus and the miraculous events surrounding Jesus' life, in Jefferson's view, were corruptions of primitive Christianity. The author who preached a simple and mild philosophy was invested with 'mysteries' and 'miraculous powers'.

SKETCHING JESUS

In their portrayals of Jesus there are some remarkable parallels between Jefferson and Roy. Both saw Jesus as merely a man with an extraordinary sense of divine consciousness. The most Roy was willing to concede was that Christ was a 'Redeemer, Mediator, and Intercessor with God in behalf of his followers'. He made it clear that even such an admission on his part was no 'proof of the deity' of Jesus.[54] The titles claimed by or

51 Ibid., pp. 614–15.　　52 Ibid., p. 614.
53 Ibid., p. 613.　　54 Ibid., p. 608.

conferred on Jesus, such as Messiah, Christ or the anointed Son of God, were summarily dismissed by Roy as 'unscriptural invention'.[55] As far as he was concerned, Jesus did not assume the character of deity nor even claim equality with God; he was conscious of his inferior status to the father, declared himself subordinate to the almighty God and subjected himself to God's authority. Roy rejected outright the two-nature theory which defined Jesus simultaneously as both divine and human. Such an affirmation, he claimed, was not limited only to Jesus; it also applied to other biblical figures like Moses and even to the leaders of Israel. Roy was uneasy with claims which would make Moses, Jesus and other biblical figures gods, and the religion of Jews and Christians polytheistic and heathenish. He was willing to grant that Jesus was not a mere prophet but 'was superior even to the angels in heaven, living from the beginning of the world to eternity, and that the Father created all things by him and for him'.[56] Roy conceded that the gospels do register instances of reverence paid to Jesus by his apostles, a blind man, a leper and mariners. But their 'reverence for him as a superior' is seen within the framework of his humanity – 'as a created being'.[57] To drive home his argument, Roy cited Colossians 1.15, as affirming his human condition: 'the image of the invisible God, *the first born of every creature*'.[58] For Roy, Jesus was like the prophets of old, who were 'from time to time sent by the Almighty to afford mental rest to mankind, by imparting to them the comforts of divine revelation; and by so doing they only fulfilled the commission given them by God: but no one ever supposed that in doing so they established claims to be considered incarnations of the divine essence'.[59] At the most, what Jesus did was to 'frequently compare himself to David or some of the other prophets'.[60] For Roy, Jesus was only a medium through which God's message was revealed.

Jefferson did not lag behind in affirming Jesus' humanity. For him, Jesus was 'a first wise and good Being'[61] but 'was not a divine being'. He was 'only a man, of illegitimate birth, of a benevolent heart, enthusiastic mind, who set out without pretensions to divinity, ended in believing them, was punished capitally for sedition by being gibbeted according to the Roman law'.[62] Jefferson's contention was that Jesus did not entertain any notion of his own divine status and if he had any it was ingrained in

55 Ibid., p. 575.   56 Ibid., p. 583.   57 Ibid., p. 595.
58 Ibid., p. 584.   59 Ibid., p. 589.   60 Ibid., p. 642.
61 Letter to Francis Adrian Van der Kemp, 4 June 1816, p. 370.
62 Letter to Peter Carr, 10 August 1787, in Julian P. Boyd (ed.), *The Papers of Thomas Jefferson*, vol. XII: *7 August 1787 to 31 March 1788* (Princeton, Princeton University Press, 1955), p. 16.

him by the environment in which he grew up. Jefferson wrote to William Short: 'Jesus did not mean to impose himself on mankind as the son of god physically speaking' but it was 'inculcated on him from his infancy' by the 'fumes of the most disordered imaginations recorded in their religious code'.[63] In Jefferson's estimation, Jesus was the 'most innocent, the most benevolent, the most eloquent and sublime character that ever has been exhibited to man'.[64]

For both Roy and Jefferson, Jesus was essentially a teacher who taught uncomplicated moral truths which were made difficult and troublesome by later interpreters. Jefferson's claim had always been that Jesus preached 'simple precepts', that it was 'the speculations of crazy theologians which have made a Babel of a religion the most moral and sublime ever preached to man, and calculated to heal, and not to create differences'.[65] Roy expressed similar sentiments: Jesus preached a 'simple code of religion and morality' but was made obscure by mysterious dogmas and historical details;[66] this simple code was sufficient and well-suited to regulate the conduct of the human race. Both reduced the moral teaching to a neat formula. For Jefferson, Jesus' teachings could be summed up thus: 'That there is one God, and he all-perfect: that there is a future state of rewards and punishments; that to love God with all thy heart, and thy neighbour as thyself, is the sum of religion'.[67] Roy, too, was quite clear about the essence of Jesus' teaching, which was encapsulated in the words 'Thou shalt love the Lord thy God with all thy heart, and with all thy soul, and with all thy mind, and with all thy strength. This is the first and great commandment. And the second is like, namely this: Thou shalt love thy neighbour as thyself. There is no other commandment greater than these'.[68] Roy went on to say that if there were other teachings required for the human race to achieve peace and happiness, Jesus would not have said to the lawyer 'This do and THOU SHALT LIVE'.[69] What really mattered to Roy and Jefferson was the quality and improvement of the lives of individuals and society that the ethical teaching of Jesus could bring about, rather than affirming the nature of the person of Jesus or the efficacy of the doctrines manufactured by later theologians. Roy was annoyed, amused and surprised at the obsession of the followers of Jesus

63 Letter to William Short, 4 August 1820, p. 397.
64 Letter to Joseph Priestly, 9 April 1803, p. 328.
65 Letter to Ezra Stiles Ely, 25 June 1819, p. 387.
66 *The English Works of Raja Rammohun Roy*, p. 547.
67 Letter to Benjamin Waterhouse, 26 June 1822, p. 405.
68 *The English Works of Raja Rammohun Roy*, p. 550.
69 Ibid., p. 551.

with the nature of his person – divine or human – rather 'than to the observance of his commandments'.[70] The parable in Matthew 25 is an indication that people will not be judged on the basis of belief in Jesus' divinity but on the basis of obedience to his ethical teaching. Similarly, Jefferson remarked that we should observe 'those moral precepts only in which all religions agree' rather than 'intermeddle with the particular dogmas'.[71]

Both Roy and Jefferson viewed Jesus as a reformer of the Mosaic religion. For Roy, Jesus completed the circle which started with Moses, a long line of faithful messengers through whom God had revealed his law: 'It is true that Moses began to erect the everlasting edifice of true religion, consisting of a knowledge of the unity of God, and obedience to his will and commandments; but Jesus of Nazareth has completed the structure, and rendered his law perfect'.[72] For Roy, the proof that Jesus was the new Moses was clear from the the Sermon on the Mount, where Jesus repeatedly asserts his new role with the words 'You have heard . . . but I say unto you'. For Jefferson, Jesus was essentially a Jewish reformer, who enunciated an extraordinary ethical vision which was universally applicable. Unlike the ancient philosophers such as Epictetus, Epicurus and Socrates, and biblical figures such as Moses, whose moral teaching was concerned with and confined to 'action', Jesus 'pressed his scrutinies into the region of our thoughts and called for purity at the fountain head'.[73] Jefferson was very clear in his mind where Jesus stood in relation to Moses as a reformer of Jewish religion. In Jefferson's view, Jesus differed from Moses on three counts. Firstly, Moses did not believe in life after death whereas Jesus 'inculcated that doctrine with emphasis and precision'. Secondly, Moses made it mandatory for Jews to indulge in many idle ceremonies and observations which had 'no effect towards producing the social utilities', and which Jesus exposed as futile and insignificant. Thirdly, Moses implanted in the minds of his people the most bellicose attitude towards other nations. Jesus, on the other hand, preached 'philanthropy and universal charity and benevolence'.[74]

Roy and Jefferson showed total disregard for traditional Christological claims on the grounds that they were largely perversions of Jesus' teaching and in the main were concerned with metaphysical issues which were

---

70 Ibid., p. 919.
71 Letter to James Fishback, 27 September 1809, p. 343.
72 *The English Works of Raja Rammohun Roy*, p. 606.
73 Letter to Edward Dowse, 19 April 1803, p. 330.
74 Letter to William Short, 4 August 1820, p. 396.

beyond human understanding. Both showed scepticism about the Church's teaching on the incarnation, resurrection and ascension. These were, in Jefferson's reckoning, concocted deceits by different Christian denominations: 'The immaculate conception of Jesus, his deification, the creation of the world by him, his miraculous powers, his resurrection and visible ascension, his corporeal presence in the Eucharist, the Trinity, original sin, atonement, regeneration, election, orders of Hierarchy &c.' were impostures and have 'resulted from artificial systems, invented by Ultra-Christian sects, unauthorized by a single word ever uttered' by Jesus.[75] In his appeals, Roy, too, consistently questioned Christological doctrines such as the incarnation, the virgin birth, atonement and resurrection, which were seen as central to the form of Christianity propagated by the Baptist missionaries. He not only undermined the uniqueness claimed for the incarnation of Christ but complicated it further by locating it within the Hindu tradition. Roy's riposte to the grand claim of the missionaries was that he did not see any difference between the incarnations of Jesus and Ram:

You cannot surely be ignorant that the Divine Ram was the respected son of Dushuruth, of the offspring of Bhuggeertuth, and of the tribe of Rughoo, as Jesus was the reputed son of Joseph, of the House of David, and the Tribe of Judah. Ram was the King of the Rughoos and of Foreigners, while in like manner Jesus was the King of the Jews and Gentiles. Both are stated in the respective sacred books handed down to us, to have performed very wonderful miracles and both ascended up to Heaven. Both were tempted by the Devil while on the earth, and both have been worshipped by millions up to the present day. Since God can be born of the Tribe of Judah, how, I ask, is it impossible that he should be born of the Tribe of the Rughoo, or of any other nation or race of men?[76]

The link between Ram and Jesus might have made Jesus recognizable to Hindus. But Jesus' incarnational status did not accord him a position of esteem. On another occasion, Roy reminded a Christian opponent that 'If the manifestation of God in the flesh is possible, such possibility cannot reasonably be confined to Judea or Ayodhya, for God has undoubtedly the power of manifesting himself in either country and of assuming any colour or name he pleases'.[77] As pointed out earlier, for Roy, Jesus was only an intercessor and 'such intercession' does not 'prove the deity of or the atonement of Jesus'.[78] The fact that Roy kept the

75 Letter to William Short, 31 October 1819, p. 391n.
76 *The English Works of Raja Rammohun Roy*, pp. 892–3.
77 Ibid., p. 908.   78 Ibid., p. 608.

conventional Christological aspects out of *The Precepts* is an indication of how he stood in relation to them.

Roy and Jefferson were anxious to demonstrate that Jesus never anticipated or insisted that his followers should accord him divine status and that, rather, he debunked such a claim. Roy cites the words of Jesus: 'Why do you call me good?' (Mk 10.18). In Roy's view, all that Jesus was interested in was that his followers should fulfil their duty towards God by obeying his commandments. Roy reminded his missionary opponents of many sayings and parables (e.g. the parable in Matt. 25) which clearly indicated that the judgement would not be on the basis of belief in his divinity but on the basis of humanity's response to God's commandments.[79]

Similarly, both found it difficult to subscribe to the atoning power of Jesus' death as an indispensable marker for salvation. Jefferson's extracts end clinically with the Matthean and Johannine versions of the burial of Jesus: 'Now, in the place where he was crucified, there was a garden, and in the garden a new sepulchre, wherein was never a man yet laid. There laid they Jesus. And rolled a great stone to the door of the sepulchre, and departed' (Jn 19.42; Matt. 27.60). Jefferson left out the resurrection because he regarded it as a breach of the original content of the gospel. Roy was equally dissatisfied with the doctrine of atonement. He pointed out that there was not 'even a single passage pronounced by Jesus, enjoining a refuge in such a doctrine of the cross, as all-sufficient or indispensable for salvation'.[80] He taunted his missionary opponents about the form in which Jesus atoned for sin – in his divine nature or in his human capacity? Whatever the case, in Roy's view, the former was inconsistent with the nature of God because God in divine form cannot be subjected to death and pain, and the latter was inconsistent with the justice ascribed to God: 'it would be a piece of gross iniquity to afflict one innocent being, who had all the human feelings, and who had never transgressed the will of God, with the death of [*sic*] the cross, for the crimes committed by others'.[81] Roy not only was dismissive of the way the missionaries interpreted the atonement of Jesus but he reframed it. He found the idea of atoning 'unscriptural' and offered an alternative: 'prayers and obedience are preferred' as a 'means of pardon'.[82] Like Jefferson's *Life and Morals*, Roy's *Precepts* did not have any scenes which depicted the last days of Jesus in Jerusalem. The concluding words of

79 Ibid., p. 553.   80 Ibid., p. 571.
81 Ibid., p. 604.   82 Ibid., p. 704.

The Precepts sum up Roy's theological intention and motive: 'that ye love one another' (Jn 15).

Although Roy and Jefferson portray Jesus as a human being, they do not dwell on his human frailties. The harsh and demanding sayings of Jesus are conveniently left out. For instance, the cursing of the fig-tree for not yielding fruit out of season: Jefferson has Jesus staying at Bethany but skips the cursing of the fig-tree. The closest Jefferson comes to the cursing is in the Parable of the Barren Tree (Lk. 13.6–9), but Jefferson reads it as the fate that befell those who failed to produce good works. We do not see Jesus being livid at an unrepentant generation or urging his disciples to take revenge for petty reasons, such as refusal to entertain them, or rebuffing the towns which oppose their activities. This is a noble, sanitized, emotionally subdued and one-dimensional Jesus, who does not demand any risk or implore his followers to pluck out an offending eye or cut off a foot. This is not the Jesus who anticipated that his preaching would bring strife, tension and deep division.

Roy and Jefferson have reconfigured a Jesus who is not the person familiar to those raised up on biblical images of prophet, miracle worker, healer, and saviour. The only biblical figure with whom their Jesus could be identified is a wisdom teacher, though not one of the Cynic variety, which is popular in some recent constructions of Jesus. Roy's and Jefferson's attitudes to Jesus were not static; they evolved over the years. Jefferson began with a negative feeling and moved to a full embrace of Jesus, whereas, Roy's early enthusiasm – 'no other religion can produce anything that may stand in competition with the precepts of Jesus'[83] – gave way to placing Jesus within a Vedantic framework. Their Jesus is a concocted figure, imagined, filtered and transmitted for private and public purposes. In Roy's case it was a matter of appropriating the special hero of another religion as a way of clarifying one's own piety. Christians who look up to Jesus as the Son of God and the saviour of the world will find Roy's portrayals of Jesus troublesome. Neither Roy nor Jefferson acknowledged that Jesus was the long-awaited Messiah. They did not grant Jesus any authority except the power of his message. Their Jesus was a great individual but not sufficiently humanized for ordinary people to identify with him. Those who are engaged in advocacy hermeneutics will find this Jesus disappointing. He was not a rebellious figure who was likely to turn the world upside-down but a robot programmed to utter moral platitudes. Jefferson left out one of the radical messages of Jesus

---

83 Ibid., p. 615.

which came to be known as the Nazareth Manifesto (Lk. 4.17–18). Jesus has been removed from the masses and does not speak for them. To their credit, Roy and Jefferson constructed a Jesus who was not a racial Aryan Christ, a fixation that dominated the Germanic, French and Anglo-Saxon quests for Jesus.[84] Roy, unlike his fellow Bengalis, P. C. Moozmudar or K. M. Banerjea, did not Aryanize Christ nor, like the succeeding Indian Christian converts, did he use Vedic images like *prajapati* (Lord and Saviour of Creation) to explicate Jesus.

To sum up this section: the Jesus they constructed was dull and uninspiring, and embraced by both liberals and conservatives. The moral certitude that Jesus demonstrated does not translate into a more specific political and economic blueprint which sets out the distribution of wealth and equal access for the disadvantaged. The Jesus they sought to unearth was not the Jesus of history unravelled by serious historical investigation, or the Christ of faith systematized by the dogmatic subtleties or liturgical practices of the church. It was the Jesus of subjective experience. It was a Jesus, on the one hand emptied of conventional Christological traits, but on the other invested with extraordinary ethical eloquence. He was an object of reverence and admiration, full of dullness and moral platitudes.

CROUCHING DOGMAS, HIDDEN DANGERS

What really mattered to both Jefferson and Roy was the quality of life rather than the dogmas of various religious traditions. Both despised the theological tenets, ecclesiastical teachings and metaphysical doctrines professed and advocated by traditional Christianity. For them the force and influence of any religion was predicated upon the type of moral standards it prescribes for its adherents rather than the substance and the subtleties of the theological doctrines it imparts. Besides their conviction that doctrines were corruptions of the teachings of Jesus, their aversion to dogmas rested on three views: they were beyond human understanding, historically they had provoked bitter strifes, and they were totally unconnected to morality. One of the Christian doctrines which came under their hermeneutical sniping was the doctrine of the Trinity.

---

84 For examples of a racially motivated Jesus in western theology, see Alan Davies, *Infected Christianity: A Study of Modern Racism* (Kingston, McGill-Queen's University Press, 1988); Shawn Kelley, *Racializing Jesus: Race, Ideology and the Formation of Modern Biblical Scholarship* (London, Routledge, 2002); Halvor Moxnes, 'The Construction of Galilee as a Place for the Historical Jesus – Part I', *Biblical Theology Bulletin* 31:1 (2001), 26–37 and 'The Construction of Galilee as a Place for the Historical Jesus – Part II', *Biblical Theology Bulletin* 31:2 (2001), 64–77.

Both saw the notion of three persons in one God as polytheistic and thus violating the monotheistic principle. Roy scoffed at its 'unscripturality and unreasonableness'.[85] He further added that no self-respecting Hindu would be attracted by it. In his Second Appeal, he made clear his apprehension:

If Christianity inculcated a doctrine which represents God as consisting of three persons, and appearing sometimes in the human form, and at other times in a bodily shape like a dove, no Hindoo, in my humble opinion, who searches after truth, can conscientiously profess it in preference to Hindooism; for that which renders the modern Hindoo system of religion absurd and detestable, is that it presents the divine nature, though one, as consisting of many persons, capable of assuming different forms for the discharge of different offices.[86]

Jefferson squarely blamed Athanasius for forcefully ousting the pure and simple unity of God with 'the hocus-pocus phantasm of a god like another Cerberus with one body and three heads'.[87]

Both Jefferson and Roy were of one accord in saying that dogmas are 'not essential to religion'[88] and are 'totally unconnected with morality, and unimportant to the legitimate objects of society'.[89] For them religion consisted of two aspects: moral precepts and dogmas. In moral aspects all religions more or less agree. Jefferson wrote: 'every religion consists of moral precepts and of dogmas. In the first they all agree. All forbid us to murder, steal, plunder, bear false witness &ca. and these are articles necessary for the preservation of order, justice, and happiness in society'. Where the various religions differed was in their particular doctrinal stipulations, where 'all differ; no two professing the same'.[90] Roy too held the view that dogmas were subject to 'doubts and disputes'.[91] Besides, they were liable to cause doubts among 'Freethinkers and Anti-Christians'; they had even caused bitter disputes among different Christian denominations which were more dreadful than those that went on between Christians and infidels.[92] Roy knew the history of Christianity and he was able to draw on the sordid doctrinal controversies between Arians and Trinitarians 'who were excited by their mistaken religious zeal to slay each other',[93] and the violence and outrage experienced by Roman

85 *The English Works of Raja Rammohun Roy*, p. 687.
86 Ibid., p. 675.
87 Letter to John Smith, 8 December 1922, p. 409.
88 *The English Works of Raja Rammohun Roy*, p. 612.
89 Letter to James Fishback, 27 September 1809, p. 344n.
90 Ibid., p. 344n.
91 *The English Works of Raja Rammohun Roy*, p. 567.
92 Ibid., p. 556.   93 Ibid., p. 609.

Catholics and Protestants over 'the different sentiments they have held with respect to the doctrine of an exclusive power of granting absolution, and leading to eternal life, being vested in St Peter and his successors'.[94]

Jefferson recalled the bitter schisms of the past and present. In the early days it was Nazarenes, Socinians, Arians, Athanasians, and now it was the turn of Trinitarians, Unitarians, Catholics, Lutherans, Calvinists, Methodists, Baptists and Quakers. These causes varied from metaphysical speculations to denominational rites and liturgical vestments, which were totally unrelated to morality, and unimportant to the welfare of society. Jefferson recalled how the church has disputed whether Christians should be baptized 'by immersion, or without water; whether his priests must be robed in white, in black, or not robed at all'. One can see a tone of exasperation in Jefferson's letter to James Fishback: 'what blood, and how many human lives have the words "this do in remembrance of me" cost the Christian world!'[95] Jefferson wrote to Benjamin Waterhouse, a physics professor at Harvard, asking what the effect of Jesus' teaching would have been without Christianity's cumbersome dogmas: 'Had the doctrines of Jesus been preached always as purely as they came from his lips, the whole civilized world would now have been Christian'.[96]

As an example of how doctrinal differences in other religions wrecked peace among their adherents, interestingly, both Jefferson and Roy cited Islam, whose disciples of the prophets quarrelled among themselves:

Among the Mohometans we are told thousands fell victims to the dispute whether the first or second toe of Mahomet was longest.[97]

Mussalmans, on the other hand, can produce records written and testified by contemporaries of Muhammad, both friends and enemies, who are represented as eye witnesses of the miracles ascribed to him; such as his dividing the moon into two parts, and working in sun-shine without casting a shadow. They can assert, too, that several of those witnesses suffered the greatest calamities, and some even death, in defence of that religion.[98]

The solution proposed by Jefferson and Roy to doctrinal difference is to preserve the essence of all religions – unity of one God and the practice of morality – and to ignore 'extraneous' dogmas which harm communal harmony. Jefferson remarked: 'Reading, reflection and time

---

94 Ibid., p. 611.
95 Letter to James Fishback, 27 September 1809, p. 344n.
96 Letter dated 26 June 1821, 405.
97 Letter to James Fishback, 27 September 1809, p. 344n.
98 *The English Works of Raja Rammohun Roy*, p. 615.

have convinced me that the interests of society require the observation of those moral precepts only in which all religions agree (for all forbid us to murder, steal, plunder, or bear false witness) and that we should not intermeddle with the particular dogmas in which all religions differ, and which are totally unconnected with morality'.[99]

However, the anti-dogma stance of Roy and Jefferson was not complete. Both held onto belief in the after-life. Surprisingly, in view of their rational approach, the Raja and the President, who insisted on an intense and more human living here on earth, were not troubled by the belief in eternal life, and eschatology became part of their theological agenda. In *Tuhfat-ul* Roy wrote that 'every religion claims that the true Creator has created mankind for discharging the duties connected with the welfare of the present and future life by observing the tenets of that particular religion'.[100] Jefferson made clear to William Short where he stood on this question. The prospect of future life might have been a minority interest to Jews but for Jesus and Christians immortality was pivotal to their spiritual well-being: 'Moses had either not believed in a future state of existence, or had not thought it essential to be explicitly taught to his people. Jesus inculcated that doctrine with emphasis and precision'.[101] Unlike the dominant theological view of the time which predicted punishment and torments for the unrepentant, Roy and Jefferson did not provide any overdramatized details but hoped that in time all would be redeemed and reconciled to God. Neither speculated about the nature of the next world or about the soul after death. According to Roy, these are 'hidden' and mysterious.[102]

The question by the Sadducees concerning the resurrection, a concept which Roy found incompatible with rational thinking, found a place in *The Precepts*. For Roy, the crucial aspect of the narrative was not the resurrection itself but the ability of Jesus to answer the questions of the Sadducees properly: 'Master thou hast well said' (Lk. 20). After such a response from Jesus, as the gospel put it, nobody dared to ask him any questions.

Roy and Jefferson were not conjoined on all matters. They differed with regard to the removal of sins. Roy's position was that one can get right with God through 'sincere repentance', and that this required no compensation from the wrongdoer or expiatory sacrifice on the part of

99 Letter to James Fishback, 27 September 1809, p. 343.
100 *The English Works of Raja Rammohun Roy*, p. 948.
101 Letter to William Short, 4 August 1820, p. 396.
102 *The English Works of Raja Rammohun Roy*, p. 947.

God. He wrote: 'Numerous passages of the Old and the New Testament to the same effect, which might fill a volume, distinctly promise us that the forgiveness of God and the favour of his divine majesty may be obtained by sincere repentance, as required of sinners by the Redeemer'.[103] The parable of the Prodigal Son is the supreme example, where no prior conditions are required before the son is reconciled to the father. Marshalling an array of texts and biblical examples, Roy was able to prove that the Bible disclosed that God has 'shewn mercy to mankind for righteous men's sakes'.[104] For Jefferson, mere repentance was not enough; it had to be accompanied by a change of course in one's life. Jefferson did not like the idea of 'efficacy of repentance' alone as sufficient means for reconciliation. Repentance is concomitant with a moral conversion which manifests itself with 'a counterpoise of good works'.[105] Or, as Bonhoeffer was to put it later, there is no such thing as cheap grace.

Pundits, priests and their malevolent practices

The religious interventions of Roy and Jefferson naturally led to brushes with their own religious leaders – Christian clergy in the case of Jefferson, and Hindu pundits and Christian missionaries in the case of Roy, the latter having the misfortune of facing the wrath of two formidable religious authorities. Roy and Jefferson believed that priests had ruined simple religions like Hinduism and Christianity, which demanded mere obedience to God and duty towards fellow human beings, by adding unfathomable doctrines and meaningless rituals, thereby making the believers depend on the priests themselves. Jefferson's denominational background was Anglicanism and at least as a young man he did not show any resentment towards Christianity. His attitude took a different turn when he was introduced to the writings of Lord Bolingbroke, a Tory and a deist moral philosopher. It was under Bolingbroke's influence that Jefferson's Anglican beliefs gradually gave way to deistic thinking, which led him to question and dispense with the Christian scriptures as the authentic vehicle for revelation and replace them with reason and nature.

Jefferson firmly believed that the doctrines of Christianity had been deliberately fabricated by the clergy in order to make the lay people rely on them, and thereby increase their wealth and power. In a letter to William Baldwin, Jefferson stated:

103 Ibid., p. 552.   104 Ibid., p. 608.
105 Letter to William Short, 13 April 1820, p. 392.

but a short time elapsed after the death of the greater reformer of the Jewish religion before his principles were departed from by those who professed to be his special servants, and perverted into an engine for enslaving mankind, and aggrandizing their oppressors in church and state: that the purest system of morals ever before preached to man has been adulterated and sophisticated, by artificial constructions, into a mere contrivance to filch wealth and power to themselves.[106]

He was particularly severe on Calvin for introducing additional absurdities on top of those that Jesus had already purged from the old Jewish religion. Jefferson saw his present task as in line with the spirit of the reformers but this time fulfilling the promise they had failed to keep:

Our saviour did not come into the world to save metaphysicians only. His doctrines are levelled at the simplest understandings and it is only by banishing Hierophantic mysteries and Scholastic subtleties, which they have nick-named Christianity, and getting back to the plain and unsophisticated precepts of Christ, that we become *real* Christians. The half reformation of Luther and Calvin did something towards a restoration of his genuine doctrines; the present contest will, I hope, complete what they begun, and place us where the evangelists left us.[107]

It was not until he became a presidential candidate that the clergy turned their attention towards him. His interference in the state–church issue, especially his attempt to disestablish the church in Virginia, and his accommodation of Nonconformists and Jews did not endear him to the Anglican clergy. Their opposition became evident during the 1800 election year, when they attacked him and called him an infidel, an atheist and a womanizer. Jefferson, in turn, blamed them for making a mild and simple philosophy into a theological muddle. He accused them of abusing the 'pure and holy doctrines of their master'.[108] To him, their theology was mere 'Abracadabra of the mountebanks calling themselves the priest of Jesus. Their security is in their faculty of shedding darkness'.[109]

Roy was a Brahmin and he was embroiled in a series of disputes with his own brahminical community as well as with Christian missionary preachers. The evidence of his early iconoclastic tendencies was seen when, aged sixteen, he produced a tract in Persian with an Arabic introduction – *Tuhfat-ul Muwahhiddin* (*A Present to the Believers in One God*) (*c.* 1804). It was a trenchant criticism of the superstitious

---

106 Letter dated 19 January 1810, p. 345.
107 Letter to Salma Hale, 22 July 1818, p. 385.
108 Letter to Charles Clay, 29 January 1815, p. 363.
109 Letter to Francis Adrian Van der Kemp, 30 July 1816, p. 375.

practices and priestcraft which were prevalent in all religions. Roy attacked religious interpreters for replacing simple natural faith in the Supreme Being: 'Hundreds of useless hardships and privations regarding eating and drinking, purity and impurity, auspiciousness and inauspiciousness, &c., have been added, and thus they have become causes of injury and detrimental to social life and sources of trouble and bewilderment to people'.[110] In this tract, which was full of allusions to the Koran, Roy blamed the Mujtahids (religious expounders) for inventing 'passages in the form of reasonable arguments in support of these articles of faith, which are evidently nonsensical and absurd'.[111] He dismissed 'belief in a just God possessing human attributes such as anger, mercy, hatred and love'[112] and ruled out any rituals, priestcraft and intermediaries as a way of accessing God: 'There is no necessity of an intermediate agency, for guidance to salvation, and there does not seem any necessity of the instrumentality of prophets or revelation . . . Prophets and others should not be particularly connected (or mixed up) with the teaching of a faith'.[113] Later, when he was involved in the abolition of sati and attacked the practice of idolatry, he clashed with the orthodox pundits over the interpretation of scriptures. He recalled that some of them became 'ill-disposed towards me, because I have forsaken idolatry for the worship of true and eternal God!'[114] He found that to his irritation, 'in defiance of their sacred books', the Bengali brahminical pundit community was obsessed with three things: (a) denying access to sacred books by concealing them within the 'dark curtain of the Sanskrit language' and 'permitting themselves alone to interpret, or even to touch any book of the kind';[115] (b) sacrificing scriptural authorities for the preservation of their own 'self interest' and 'temporal advantage';[116] and (c) 'deriving pecuniary and other advantages from the numerous rites and festivals of idol-worship . . . to the utmost of their power'.[117] In the preface to his translation of *Ishopanishad*, Roy wrote:

Many learned Brahmans are perfectly aware of the absurdity of idolatry, and are well informed of the nature of the purer modes of divine worship. But as in the rites, ceremonies, and festivals of idolatry, they find the source of their comforts and fortune, they not only never fail to protect idol worship from all attacks, but even advance and encourage it to the utmost of their power, by keeping the knowledge of their scriptures concealed from the rest of the people.[118]

---

110 *The English Works of Raja Rammohun Roy*, p. 947.
111 Ibid., p. 946.   112 Ibid., p. 948.   113 Ibid., pp. 953–4.
114 Ibid., p. 3.   115 Ibid.   116 Ibid., p. 5.
117 Ibid., p. 91.   118 Ibid., p. 66.

Roy found in Christianity the same sorry state of affairs – clergy manipulating congregations and holding on to power and position, and later interpreters adding doctrines contrary to the earlier teaching. He blamed those 'Greek, Roman, and Barbarian converts' who besmirched the religion of Christ by mingling it from time to time with 'absurd, idolatrous doctrines and practices'.[119] Roy would have concurred with Jefferson that a dogma-free ethical Christianity had a lot to offer to humanity: 'I presume to think that Christianity, if properly inculcated, has a greater tendency to improve the moral, and political state of mankind, than any other known religious system'.[120]

HERMENEUTICAL ODYSSEY

Roy began by admiring biblical teachings for their social utility in particular but progressively isolated them from the Christian context and made them congruent with the Hindu ideal of happiness: 'You ought to know that our religious faith and yours are founded on the same sacred basis, viz. the manifestation of God in the flesh, without any restriction to a dark or fair complexion, large or small stature, long or short hair'.[121] At a time when the characteristic missionary view perceived Christianity as a unique vehicle for God's revelation and Hinduism as a corrupted alternative, Roy returned to his own Hindu tradition, which he conceived as an inclusive and open religion. In his *Brahminical Magazine*, Roy asserted the relaxed attitude of Hinduism: 'It is well-known to the whole world, that no other people on earth are more tolerant than the Hindoos, who believe all men to be equally within the reach of Divine beneficence, which embraces the good of every religious sect and denomination'.[122] As Herbert Stead said: 'He was a genuine outgrowth of the old Hindu stock; in a soil watered by new influences, and in an atmosphere charged with unwonted forcing power, but still a true scion of the old stock'.[123] Roy believed that every sacred text had to be reread and reinterpreted to meet the contextual needs of the time. Therefore, he did not feel the need to exchange his textual tradition for another. He claimed that the Vedanta was 'common with the Jewish and Christian scriptures'.[124] He was willing

---

119 Ibid., p. 876. 120 Ibid., p. 875.
121 Ibid., p. 892. 122 Ibid., p. 148.
123 Sophia Dobson Collet, *The Life and Letters of Raja Rammohun Roy*, ed. Dilip Kumar Biswas and Prabhat Chandra Ganguli (Calcutta, Sadharan Brahmo Samaj, 1900), p. 380.
124 *The English Works of Raja Rammohun Roy*, p. 563.

to embrace and celebrate moral tenets of every religion, but despised their dogmatic constraints and institutional proscriptions.

The strong rationalist streak which was evident in the earlier works of Roy underwent changes over the years as he became involved in various cultural, political and religious activities. The relentless rational spirit he exhibited during the *Tuhfat-ul* days mellowed. He gave up deistic belief and began to accept that the Vedas were a divine revelation. His later writings are replete with expressions which claim that the Vedas are 'an inspired work',[125] a 'means of imparting divine knowledge',[126] 'the divine guidance',[127] 'revered from generation to generation',[128] and the law of God revealed and introduced for our rule and guidance. The texts which were once theologically awkward are now not dismissed as incongruent, or as later accretions to the Vedic teaching, but explained and given theological justification. For instance, the plurality of gods and goddesses who crowd the Vedas, together with the worship of sun and fire, are now explained as included for the sake of those who have limited understanding and who are 'incapable of comprehending and adoring the invisible Supreme Being'.[129] In the end, for Roy, the Vedas became the route to salvation:

If the spiritual part of the Vedas can enable men to acquire salvation by teaching them the true eternal existence of God, and the false and perishable being of the universe, and inducing them to hear and constantly reflect on those doctrines, it is consistent with reason to admit that the Smriti, and Agam, and other works, inculcating the same doctrines, afford means of attaining final beatitude.[130]

For Roy, the Vedas prove that 'faith in the Supreme Being, when united with moral works, leads men to eternal happiness'.[131]

Jefferson, on the other hand, began by distrusting the Bible. In the early stages of his life, the Bible did not dominate his thinking. The ethical vision of the moralists of antiquity, or 'heathen moralists' as Jefferson put it, held sway over his thinking. Jefferson in his youth accepted the jaundiced view of Bolingbroke, the Tory philosopher: 'It is not true that Christ revealed an entire body of ethics . . . If mankind wanted such a code . . . the gospel is not such a code'. The New Testament for Jefferson was a 'very short, as well as unconnected system of ethics', like 'short sentences of ancient sages'.[132] These writings contained 'allusions, parables, comparisons and promises', and had only

125 Ibid., p. 36.   126 Ibid., p. 131.   127 Ibid., p. 181.
128 Ibid., p. 179.   129 Ibid., p. 36.   130 Ibid., p. 131.   131 Ibid., p. 106.
132 Gilbert Chinard (ed.), *The Literary Bible of Thomas Jefferson: His Commonplace Book of Philosophers and Poets* (Baltimore, The Johns Hopkins Press, 1928), p. 50.

occasional significance.[133] He believed that Jesus did not reveal 'an entire body of ethics, proved to be the law of nature from principles of reason and reaching all duties of life'. On the other hand, he found profundity in the writings of the ancient philosophers: 'A system thus collected from the writings of ancient heathen moralists, of Tully, of Seneca, of Epictetus, and others, would be more full, more entire, more coherent, and more clearly deduced from unquestionable principles of knowledge'.[134] At that stage in his life the teachings of the ancient moralists supplied him with a strong moral vision. It was only later in his life that he found in the teachings of Jesus a set of moral teachings surpassing the standards of antiquity.

Jefferson's *Life and Morals* was a signal that he had moved away from the dogmatic clutches of Bolingbroke. To declare openly that he considered 'the precepts of Jesus, as delivered by himself, to be the most pure, benevolent, and sublime that has ever been preached to man'[135] was a sign of Jefferson's departure from his earlier antagonistic days. *The Life and Morals* was the product of a doctrinally mellowed and sober Jefferson. Now he was able to claim that the moral precepts of Jesus were 'far superior' and 'more pure, correct and sublime than those of the ancient philosophers', and that he found their philosophy 'short and deficient' and restricted to individuals and to immediate family, whereas Jesus' teaching 'embraced with charity and philanthropy our neighbors, our countrymen and the whole family of mankind'.[136] He might not have embraced every Christian tenet but he had no doubt about the superiority of the morality of Jesus over the heathen moralists he had favoured earlier.

COLONIAL INNOCENCE

Roy's life and work were located at the very beginning of British colonialism, which was yet to take a more malign form. Roy was one of the beneficiaries of the benign mercantile form of colonialism. It was the period of the East India Company, whose administrators had a more healthy attitude towards India and her people and culture than the liberal rulers who followed them. The innocence inherent in Roy's thinking was influenced and shaped by the modernizing projects initiated by the British in India. Not only Roy, but other leading Indian nationalists also, both

133 Ibid.   134 Ibid.
135 Letter to Jared Sparks, 4 November 1820, p. 401.
136 Letter to Edward Dowse, 19 April 1803, p. 330.

the Brahmins and Dalits such as Vidyasagar and Jytoi Rao Phule, were blind to the pernicious role of capitalism. Marvelling at the way the British were successful in modernizing themselves, Roy and these leaders were persuaded that India had a great deal to learn from the British experience, and they were convinced that India's future material and cultural improvements were dependent on the British occupation of India. Roy was even able to offer a personal testimony: 'From the personal experience, I am impressed with the conviction that the greater our intercourse with European gentlemen, the greater will be our improvement in literary, social, and political affairs'.[137] The other example of Roy's innocence was that he saw the British as liberators of India from the long rule of the Muslims. He even offered 'thanks to the Supreme Disposer of the universe' for the presence of the British. He concluded his Third Appeal with these words:

I now conclude my essay by offering up thanks to the Supreme Disposer of the events of this universe, for having unexpectedly delivered this country from the long-continued tyranny of its former Rulers, and placed it under the government of the English, – a nation who are not only blessed with the enjoyment of civil and political liberty, but also interest themselves in promoting liberty and social happiness, as well as free inquiry into literary and religious subjects, among those nations to which their influence extends.[138]

Ironically, while welcoming British rule in India, Roy was supporting and sympathizing with the struggles of other nations to establish political freedom. He was enthused by the French and American revolutions. He celebrated with a dinner when he heard that Spanish imperialism was overthrown in South America. He was thrilled about the political freedom of western nations, but he did not envisage such a state for India. Taking so much interest in religious, social and educational reforms, he was uncharacteristically silent on the issue of the rapid deindustrialization that was going in Bengal at the time as a result of the East India Company policies. A local paper lamented that Roy, who had spent much time on 'theology and literature, paid little attention to what was passing around him in the political world and to the changes which the ever varying regulations of the local government had undergone within that period'.[139] Roy's view was that India was not ripe for self-rule. For him, practical

---

137 *The English Works of Raja Rammohun Roy*, p. 917.
138 Ibid., p. 874.
139 *Bengal Hurkaru*, 25 June 1832, in Jatindra Kumar Majumdar (ed.). *Raja Rammohun Roy and Progressive Movements in India: A Selection from Records (1775–1845)* (Calcutta: Art Press, 1941), p. 488.

considerations, financial benefits and cultural gains, outweighed political aspirations. In a letter, Roy wrote that 'application of European skill and enterprize' would render India 'powerful, prosperous, and happy' and the 'change would be so great, both in the condition of the people, and the appearance of the country, as to bear no more resemblance to what it does at present, than it does now to the wildest parts of Africa'.[140] It was these pragmatic reasons which led him to suggest that Indians should be reconciled to the present state of things and pray for British rule to 'continue in its beneficent operation for centuries to come'.[141] He supported European settlement in India and in his testament said that such a settlement would 'continue the connection between Great Britain and India on a solid and permanent footing' provided India was 'governed in a liberal manner, by means of Parliamentary superintendence, and other legislative checks'.[142] Jefferson, on the other hand, was questioning the audacity and effrontery of the British parliament to enact laws for its American colonies and supervise trading rights. Colonialism at that time was seen mainly as a mercantile enterprise, and Roy and Jefferson colluded with it by supporting free trade. One of the tracts Jefferson produced, *A Summary View of the Rights of British America*,[143] questioned the authority of the British government to deny the right to free trade for its American colonies. Roy supported the free traders against the monopolists regarding the import of salt.

Roy did not side with the subalternist perspective (that of the marginalized), unlike James Long, whom we will meet in the chapter 3. Roy paid little attention to and was not aroused by the plight of the agricultural workers. He was unmoved by the hardship inflicted by indigo planters on farmers from his own province. Instead of castigating the exploiters, Roy commended them:

I found the natives residing in the neighbourhood of indigo plantations evidently better clothed and better conditioned than those who lived at a distance from such stations. There may be some partial injury done by some indigo planters: but, on the whole, they have performed more good to the generality of the natives of this country than any other class of Europeans, whether in or out of service.[144]

---

140 Letter of January 1832, in Majumdar (ed.), *Raja Rammohun Roy and Progressive Movements in India*, p. 454.
141 *The English Works of Raja Rammohun Roy*, p. 198.
142 Ibid., p. 316.
143 For the full text, see Thomas Jefferson, *Writings*, ed. Merril D. Peterson (New York, Library classics of the United States, 1984), pp. 105–22.
144 *The English Works of Raja Rammohun Roy*, p. 917.

Jefferson's track record is not an unblemished one either. He thought that
Native Americans and Blacks were incapable of civilized life. He found
the Indians physically weaker than the European labourers,[145] and their
'reason much inferior'.[146] He confessed that he was yet to meet a Black
who could utter a 'thought above plain narration'. He even dismissed
some Blacks who achieved literary fame at the time, such as Phyllis
Wheatley and Ignatius Sancho. The former's work, he said, was beneath
the 'dignity of criticism',[147] and the latter, compared to the 'epistolary
class' in which he had taken to place himself, he was 'compelled to enroll
at the bottom of the column'.[148]

CONCLUDING REFLECTIONS

The re-editing/rewriting of the gospels by Roy and Jefferson falls within
the Bhabhian theoretical notion of blasphemy. Blasphemy, in Bhabha's
word, is a 'transgressive act of cultural translation'. He defines blasphemy
as that which 'goes beyond the severance of tradition and replaces its
claim to purity of origins with a poetics of relocation and reinscription'. It
is not 'merely a misrepresentation of the sacred by the secular; it is a
moment when the subject-matter or the content of a cultural tradition is
being overwhelmed, or alienated, in the act of translation'.[149] This is
precisely what Roy and Jefferson were engaged in. They challenged the
gospels as the immaculate oracles of God and re-imagined them for their
own context. True, they did not challenge the content of the gospels.
Their achievement was to bring out and highlight the other 'enunciatory
positions and possibilities' embedded within the biblical narratives. In the
process, the Raja and the President seemed to desecrate the perfection of
the gospel narrators' story.

The hermeneutical enterprise of Jefferson and Roy encapsulated the
colonial mood of the time: peoples, cultures, lands and artefacts must be
investigated, codified and classified. To these investigations, the Raja and
the President added one more – that of the sacred texts. For Jefferson,
those 'facts in the bible which contradict the laws of nature, must be
examined with more care, and under a variety of faces'.[150] The fact that

145 Jefferson, *Writings*, ed. Peterson, p. 801.
146 Thomas Jefferson, *Notes on the State of Virginia*, edited with an introduction and notes by
    William Peden (Chapel Hill, The University of North Carolina Press, 1955), p. 139.
147 Ibid., p. 140.
148 Ibid., p. 141.
149 Homi K. Bhabha, *The Location of Culture* (London, Routledge, 1994, p. 225.
150 Letter to Peter Carr, 10 August 1787, in Boyd (ed.), *Papers of Thomas Jefferson*, vol. XII, p. 16.

the Bible was inspired should not deter one from examining its veracity. For instance, he wanted his nephew to scrutinize the evidence of inspiration in accounts such as the one described in the Book of Joshua, namely the sun standing still for several hours. The Bible, for Jefferson, was a kind of frontier which should be tamed and anything which was wild and out of control had to be annihilated. For him, the Bible was an instrument in his ambitious quest for success, and a means to achieve the American dream. For Roy, it was not a question of dispensing with the unwanted and awkward elements in the Bible. As a Brahmin, he knew that Vedic texts are never eliminated. The unappealing texts simply drop out of circulation and recede into the background, yielding their place to narratives more appropriate for the time. Roy treated biblical texts just like the Puranas. He re-grounded those elements which were relevant to his time – the moral teachings of Jesus – and he showed no interest in the other bits of the New Testament. For Roy, unlike for Jefferson, Jesus' ethical teaching was not a vehicle for individual advancement but for the social comfort of the whole community. The very Bible which was seen as such a powerful tool in the hands of the clergy of North America and the missionaries in colonial India, became the most serviceable tool in the hands of the Raja and the President in their task of fashioning an alternative vision.

But the alternative vision, at least in the case of Roy, remained an elitist one. Roy, unlike previous reformers such as Tukaram or Kabir, did not have his origins in humble surroundings. He was an upper-crust Brahmin through and through. His class and caste separated him from the masses. His influence did not reach the ordinary people nor did his work excite their imagination as Gandhi's did later. Gandhi himself had an ambivalent attitude towards Rammohun Roy and his contribution to modern India. Roy did not interact with the popular movements of the time. While the vernacular Bengali movements of the nineteenth century were making use of Vaishnavite and Sufi traditions in order to overcome caste discrimination and exploitation of women, Rammohun Roy was turning towards the texts composed by the upper caste – the Upanishads – to accommodate the social conventions and the demands of modern India. As Sumanta Banerjee noted, neither Rammohun Roy nor the other reform groups of the time 'ever cared to seek inspiration from these contemporary reformist movements among the lower orders of Bengal'.[151]

---

151 Sumanta Banerjee, *The Parlour and the Streets: Elite and Popular Culture in Nineteenth Century Calcutta* (Calcutta: Seagull Books, 1989), p. 72.

Roy's much applauded translation of the Sanskrit Veda was not intended for the ordinary people but was aimed at an elite who were erudite enough to comprehend the notion of an abstract and an incorporeal deity. The texture and unemotional style of Roy's Bengali is a testimony to this.[152] It is true that at a time when doubts were raised about the serviceability of Bengali for a wider world of intellectual activity, Roy did create a prose which was 'a suitable medium for debates on social and theological problems'.[153]

There is a hierarchy of biblical writings in operation in Jefferson's hermeneutics. High in the order are the gospels and they are seen as the only authentic repositories of Jesus' teaching. Besides containing the moral teaching of Jesus, they record the fundamentals of Christianity expressed 'in the preaching of our saviour, which is related in the gospels'.[154] The New Testament epistles, for Jefferson, were occasional writings. Although these epistles contained fundamentals of the gospels they were 'promiscuously mixed with other truths'. These other truths were included to edify and explain matters related to morality and worship. Moreover, they were incidental writing undertaken to meet contextual needs. Hence, these other truths embedded in them should not be 'made fundamental'.[155] Among the New Testament writings, the Pauline letters received a severe rebuke. In Jefferson's view, 'Paul was the great Coryphaeus, and the first corrupter of the doctrines of Jesus'.[156] What was significant for him in the gospels was that they embodied the 'the principles of the first age', and the subsequent development of Christianity was seen as a 'corruption' of Jesus' teaching and 'having no foundation in what came from him'.[157]

One of the striking aspects of Roy's and Jefferson's compilations is their postmodernity – how the same text can animate two separate responses and locate itself in two culturally varied continents. How do we account for the general tenor of similarity of their ideas? In the absence of any concrete documentary evidence, one is forced to conclude that the

---

152 Pradyumna Bhattacharya, 'Rammohun Roy and Bengali Prose', in *Rammohun Roy and the Process of Modernization in India*, ed. V. C. Joshi (Delhi, Vikas Publishing House, 1975), pp. 195–228.

153 Sisir Kumar Das, 'Rammohun and Bengali Prose', in *Rammohun Roy: A Bi-Centenary Tribute*, ed. Niharranjan Ray (New Delhi, National Book Trust, 1974), p. 136.

154 Julian P. Boyd (ed.), *The Papers of Thomas Jefferson*, vol. 1: *1760–1776* (Princeton, Princeton University Press, 1950), p. 550.

155 Ibid.

156 Letter to William Short, 13 April 1820, p. 392.

157 Letter to Jared Sparks, 4 November 1820, p. 401.

hermeneutical projects of Roy and Jefferson were one of the unplanned concurrences of history. It was one of those extraordinary coincidences in which similar patterns of thinking were developed simultaneously by two different thinkers who had no direct or indirect contact. Moreover, their intellectual and philosophical lineages were so dissimilar that any chance of borrowing or mutual influence was extremely remote. Colonial historians would like to attribute Roy's achievement to the introduction of western forms of learning in India. But Roy's intellectual landscape was far more complicated and was derived from a number of philosophical, religious and literary worlds. Before he was introduced to western learning, his intellectual thinking was stimulated by a fusion of Persian-Arabic literature, Muslim rationalism, the secular historical writings of the Mughals and Vedantic philosophy. The comparative religious studies which he was to undertake later must have been influenced by Mushin Fani's seventeenth-century Persian tract, *Dubistan-i-Mazahib*, which competently analysed five religions known to the author: Magism (the ancient religion of Iran), Hinduism, Judaism, Christianity and Islam. This tract was quite well known in the eighteenth century, and William Jones, the pioneer orientalist, looked upon it favourably. The traces of rationalism, especially in his *Tuhfat-ul* (more about this later), could, according to Brajendranath Seal, be tracked down to the Muslim rationalism of the Mutazalis of the eighth century and Muwahhidin of the twelfth century. The Vedantic school of thinking which came to dominate Roy's thinking came from Hariharanda Tirthaswami, a leading exponent of the time. Only after studying English in 1807 and settling in Calcutta in 1815 did Roy come to have closer contacts with a variety of English thinkers of the time – utilitarians, rationalists and Christian missionaries. The later works of Roy show his acquaintance with contemporary western thinkers such as Locke, Hume and Bentham. It is possible, as Sumit Sarkar has pointed out, that the Hindu intelligentsia of nineteenth-century Bengal 'maybe Rammohun, too, to some extent . . . after they had mastered English, turned their backs entirely on such traces of secularism, rationalism and non-conformity in the pre-British Muslim-ruled India.[158]

Jefferson's intellectual heritage was largely restricted to western and Judaeo-Christian forms, namely individualism and rationalism, which

---

158 See Sumit Sarkar, 'Rammohun Roy and the Break with the Past', in *Rammohun Roy and the Process of Modernization in India*, ed. V. C. Joshi (Delhi, Vikas Publishing House, 1975), pp. 52–3. For the various influences on Roy's thinking, see also Shyamal K. Chatterjee, 'Rammohun Roy and the Baptists of Serampore: Moralism vs. Faith', *Religious Studies* 20:4 (1984), 669–80.

were the distinctive markers of the newly independent nation, and both of which saw dogmas and institutions as a menace to individual progress and happiness. Jefferson's interpretative practice could be traced to and placed within the humanistic and Reformation traditions. The interpretative aim of the humanists was guided by the high investment they placed on ancient sources. Their urge was to go back to the beginning, to the classical writings. This was the very aim of the Reformation too – to go back to the Bible as a way of testing the doctrinal claims of the church against the authentic teaching of Jesus. Jefferson's hermeneutics clearly falls within this category. The temptation is to attribute the normative status which Roy accorded to the scriptures to the influence of the Protestant tradition. But the strategy of employing scriptures for religious and social reform is not an exclusively Protestant trait. The practice existed in India even before it was energized by Protestant principles. Indian reformers, especially various sects within Hinduism, had used both texts and non-textual traditions for questioning idolatry, polytheism and the evils of caste. Roy's earliest tract, *Tuhfat-ul*, is suffused with allusions to Koranic verses. He employed them to critique idolatrous practices. Roy's method, according to Saumyendranath Tagore, was based on that of the Mimamsa method for arriving at the truth: 'the method being to start with a particular piece of evidence found in Sastra, to doubt its validity, and question its authenticity, then begin a re-examination of the issue and thus arrive at a conclusion'.[159]

In some respects, the compilations of Roy and Jefferson stand in the heritage of Tatian. Tatian, in about 160 CE, harmonized the gospel accounts by interweaving the four gospels into one single narrative and produced the *Diatessaron*. Tatian was principally prompted by the problems caused by the plurality of the gospels, multiple accounts of the same events, and the discrepancies enscripted in them. As we have seen so far, the need to amend the narratives in the case of Roy and Jefferson, was provoked by the need to free the teachings of Jesus from what were seen as later accretions, corruptions and doctrinal glosses. Jefferson's letter to his nephew Peter Carr underscores the reason:

I forgot to observe when speaking of the New Testament that you should read all the histories of Christ, as well of those whom a council of ecclesiastics have decided for us to be Pseudo-evangelists, as those they named Evangelists, because these Pseudo-evangelists pretended to inspiration as much as the others, and you

---

159 See Tagore, *Raja Rammohun Roy*, p. 14. For Roy's use of mimamsa see *The English Works of Raja Rammohun Roy*, p. 157.

are to judge their pretensions by your own reason, and not by the reason of those ecclesiastics.[160]

The aspiration of Roy and Jefferson to make the scriptures simple and uncomplicated did not always produce the desired results. Their versions duplicate events. For no apparent reason, Roy has both Mark's and Luke's versions of the Widow's Mite. Jefferson includes Mark's and Luke's instructions to the disciples not in his customary fashion of mixing and matching them but as two separate narratives placed at different locations. Jefferson makes Jesus drive away the moneylenders in the temple twice – at the beginning of his ministry and in his last days in Jeruasalem. Roy inserts a number of utterances of Jesus which stand in *The Precepts* as orphans without immediate narrative habitat.

In their hermeneutical enterprise, Jefferson and Roy treated the Bible differently. For Jefferson, the Bible was essentially a historical document. When his neighbour, Robert Skipwirth, asked for a list of books which would suit the taste and status of a Virginian gentleman for a private library, Jefferson listed the writings of Locke, Xenophon, Epictetus, Seneca, Cicero, Bolingbroke, Sherlock, and the sermons of Sterne under religion whereas the Bible was placed under history. The religious books that his nephew was advised to read included the works of Middleton and Voltaire. The Bible was basically a record of human history rather than a depository of divine revelation. He encouraged Peter Carr to 'Read the bible then, as you would read Livy or Tacitus'.[161] In the same letter he called the New Testament 'the history of a personage called Jesus'.[162] Jefferson turned to the Bible fairly late in his life, not until 1809, when he found in its pages a set of moral teachings that eclipsed the standards set by the classical philosophers: 'We all agree in the obligation of the moral precepts of Jesus, and no where will they be found delivered in greater purity than in his discourses'.[163] For Roy, sacred texts were largely theological documents which promoted faith in the Supreme, moral works that led men to eternal happiness, but their authenticity and reliability was judged by the type of social comfort they promoted.

The compilations of Roy and Jefferson undermined inerrancy, altered the canonicity of the Bible and supported their hermeneutical aims. The singular purpose of Roy and Jefferson was to move the interpretative base

160 Boyd (ed.), *Papers of Thomas Jefferson*, vol. XII, p. 17.
161 Ibid., p. 15.
162 Ibid., p. 16.
163 Letter to James Fishback, 27 September 1809, p. 343.

away from priestly guilds and custodians of the canon, and particularly from the power of the institutional authorities to corrupt the text and control interpretation. Their deletion of histories, dogmas and mythologies was not aimed at invalidating the Bible but at privileging their own version of it. The hermeneutical principle at work here is, to use Jefferson's phrase, to weed out the 'hay from stubbles'. In his view, the gospel narratives were clear in distinguishing what Jesus thought was central to moral life and what was peripheral to it. What Jefferson did was to carry further the tradition of the gospels by deleting any material which muddied the moral truth taught by Jesus. Similarly, Roy conceived his task as removing any element which was 'destructive of the comforts of life, or injurious to the texture of society'.[164] Their interest was not to analyse the gospels but to unearth their ethical component. The compilations of Roy and Jefferson can be taken as counter-gospels, not superseding the canonical versions but, rather supplementing them.

How do we assess the work of the President and the Raja? There is no ruling model by which to judge their enterprise. Those interpreters who were brought up with the Bultmannian proclivity for slicing up the gospels into various chunks and who engaged in the modernistic task of demythologizing would, up to a point, relish the work of Roy and Jefferson. In an era when the gospels as stories were treated as plot and characterization, Jefferson's and Roy's way of breaking the stories into little segments would not find favour. Unlike the writers of the nineteenth-century 'lives' of Jesus, Jefferson and Rammohun Roy did not find it necessary to make a long and detailed study of the linguistic evidence or of the complex questions of the sources, nor did they engage in a comparative analysis of contemporary biblical scholarship. Both undertook their enterprise before biblical criticism became the preserve of linguistic specialists.

Jefferson and Roy trusted the texts that are much more to the liking of today's liberal voices within the scholarly guild. They did not question the integrity of the redacted gospels but only of the doctrinal, historical and supernatural elements included in them. They also did not dwell on the question of why the stories surrounding Jesus had been invented or remembered. In one sense, both were literalists. They were literalists not in the traditional sense of believing everything to be true, but what they believed as authentic they took to be literally true. Jefferson did not hesitate to accept that the moral teachings which he extracted from the

---

164 *The English Works of Raja Rammohun Roy*, p. 119.

gospels had come from 'the mouth of Jesus himself'.[165] Roy, too, believed in the actual words of Jesus and their 'excellent authority'. In his Second Appeal, Roy made it clear that neither in his introduction to *The Precepts of Jesus* nor in the defence of these precepts had he 'expressed the least doubt as to the truth of any part of the gospel'.[166] Roy and Jefferson were not blind literalists who believed that every word was dictated by God. Jefferson did not feel it necessary to accept all of Jesus' teachings, because he perceived him as a mere man and the 'first of the sages'. He made it clear to William Short that 'it is not to be understood that I am with him in all his doctrines'.[167] His material outlook did not endear him to the 'spiritualism' advocated by Jesus. The other teaching which troubled Jefferson was the eternal punishment awaiting unrepentant sinners.

Roy, too, exposed the hazards of too much dependence on ancient textual authorities, and held the view that truth was to be upheld and followed whether there was textual warrant or not: 'the truth of a saying does not depend on the multiplicity of the sayers, and the non-reliability of a narration cannot arise simply out of the paucity of the number of narrators'.[168] For him, it was pointless to hold on to texts irrespective of their status if they advanced idol worship, polytheistic practices and selfish gains. This does not mean that Roy rejected the authority of the scriptures. For him, the ultimate realization was attained not through the evidence of the scriptures alone but also on the basis of commonsense, rationality, praxis and God's grace. He redefined praxis as serving the betterment of the everyday life of people rather than sacramental or ritualistic acts. For Roy, the ultimate criterion of truth was that it should be 'followed' and put into practice and should not be 'remote from reason and repugnant to experience'.[169] In his view, the practical aspect of Christianity was important, otherwise Christianity would be 'altogether regarded as existing only in theory'.[170]

Finally, as a way of bringing this chapter to a close, let me engage in a hypothetical speculation. How would Jefferson and Roy react to today's world, where there is a virulent form of fundamentalism which is trying to forge a unified and single form of religion whether Christianity, Islam or Hinduism. Both men, in their own way, thrived on dissension and advocated an inclusive and open form of faith – they would have been

165 Letter to John Adams, 12 October 1813, p. 352.
166 *The English Works of Raja Rammohun Roy*, p. 567.
167 Letter to William Short, 13 April 1820, p. 391.
168 *The English Works of Raja Rammohun Roy*, p. 957.
169 Ibid., p. 956.   170 Ibid., p. 571.

appalled to see such intolerance within religions and between religions. In his *Notes on the State of Virginia*, Jefferson wrote: 'Difference of opinion is advantageous in religion'.[171] He made it clear that in the newly freed country 'neither Pagan, nor Mahamedan nor Jew ought to be excluded from the civil rights of the Commonwealth because of his religion'.[172] He would have been particularly horrified to hear the words 'Missed you at the Bible study' being spoken in the White House nowadays. Jefferson's Bible was vastly different from that of President Bush, which is replete with angels, miracles and a Messianic attachment to American moral values and their applicability to the rest of the world.

Granted that the Hinduism that Roy propounded was too elitist, abstract and beyond the understanding of ordinary people, he would have been alarmed at the virulent form of Hinduism manifesting itself among certain sections of the Indian population. He would have sympathized with the attempts of nationalist Hindus to find an answer to the seemingly insurmountable religious differences and cultural diversities which characterize India. But he would have found it difficult to support them when they argue for an exclusive India which equates with Hinduism. While unashamedly acknowledging his Hinduness, it was Hinduism which enabled Roy to argue for an inclusive, plural and tolerant India. It was the truth he saw in Hinduism that allowed him to see truth in Christianity and Islam. This represented a positive strategy capable of containing conflict and promoting tolerance. The religious tolerance he aspired to came not necessarily from western secular values but from within Hinduism. Like Asoka and Akbar before him, who sought to base religious tolerance on the teachings of Buddhism and Islam,[173] Roy was trying to derive religious tolerance from within Hinduism and discover connections between religions. He would have been dismayed to see the current revivalists, be they Hindu or Muslim or Christian, trying to forge religions as mutually exclusive, bounded, rigid and closed traditions. While encountering different religions, Roy was enchanted by and engrossed in them, whereas the current religious revivalists are perplexed and apprehensive about them. He was for collaboration and reciprocation, whereas the present mood is to sever ties, show mutual hostility and limit understanding. The Hinduism that Roy championed was not the Hinduism for which the present Hindu nationalists are arguing. What his

---

171 Thomas Jefferson, *Notes on the State of Virginia*, p. 160.
172 Boyd (ed.), *Papers of Thomas Jefferson*, vol. 1, p. 548.
173 Ashis Nandy, *Time Warps: The Insistent Politics of Silent and Evasive Pasts* (Delhi, Permanent Black, 2001), p. 80.

hermeneutical enterprise tried to do was to show us the richness of the pluralistic qualities of Hinduism. He exhibited openness and had confidence in his own faith. When there was a murmur among Hindu students about Alexander Duff's distribution of Bibles to them, Roy intervened:

Christians like Dr Horace Hayman Wilson have studied the Hindu Shaster and you know that he has not become a Hindu. I myself have read the Koran again and again; and has that made me a Mussalman? Nay, I have studied the whole of the Bible, and you know I am not a Christian. Why then do you fear to read it? Read it and judge for yourself.[174]

This is an appropriate text with which to end the chapter, because Roy's advice should be the guiding principle for any hermeneutical undertaking.

174 Collet, *The Life and Letters of Raja Rammohun Roy*, p. 281.

CHAPTER 2

Salvos from the Victorian pulpit: conscription of texts by Victorian preachers during the Indian rebellion of 1857

We fight for independence. In the words of Lord Krishna, we will, if we are victorious, enjoy the fruit of victory, if defeated and killed on the field of battle, we shall surely earn eternal glory and salvation.

Rani Lakshmi Bai

The Englishman never goes to a place without a Bible. It precedes, or closely follows, his sword.

A. Madhaviah

'Bring me a sword.'

1 Kings 3.24

If the first casualty of war, as the cliché goes, is truth, the second casualty to sustain heavy collateral damage is text. In war, along with truth, texts of various kinds, ranging from reports of the battle to religious texts that justify it, also fall victim to the hands of both proponents and opponents. This chapter is about the misuse of biblical texts when they were conscripted by Victorian preachers and employed as potent textual weapons during the Indian insurrection of 1857.

In the middle of the nineteenth century there was a passionately fierce and violent reaction against the penetration, presence and powerful influence of the British in India. Hindus and Muslims fought side by side, their collective outrage directed at their common enemy, the British – in the form of the East India Company – who were blamed for disrupting both the religious and the political traditions of the country and intensifying the suffering of the people. This rebellion, or mutiny, was an affair mainly restricted to the northern states of India. It became embedded in the consciousness of the British and was more than the term implies, becoming briefly an all-out war, though in today's geopolitical parlance it would have been called terrorism, and the rebels terrorists. It was a momentous event and has been exploited in both India and

Pakistan to support national movements.[1] The background and the causes of the rebellion remain an embattled terrain and are more complicated than merely a response to cartridges lubricated with pig fat or cow tallow, as claimed in popular myth-making. Equally complicated are the theories of interpretation which emerged in the aftermath of the event.

BAD COMPANY, BAD CONSCIENCE

The history of the event has been competently chronicled elsewhere, as well as the analysis of it, so all we need here is a brief note on the background, the causes, and how it was perceived by the different protagonists. The rebellion was triggered off by a series of religious and political measures introduced by the East India Company, which by this time had become more than merely a mercantile outfit and had come to act as a surrogate British government in the Indian subcontinent. Indians became increasingly suspicious of some of the changes and regulations introduced by the British, and viewed these measures as threatening their way of life. In the early part of the nineteenth century the colonial administration, spurred on by some of its overtly Christian officers and some Christian missionaries, at times supported by Indian reformers, passed a series of acts which were perceived by other Indians as unnecessary and an arrogant attempt to intervene and disrupt their ancient customs. The granting of freedom to Hindu widows by abolishing sati and allowing their remarriage, the suppression of female infanticide and the dissolution of gangs known as 'Thugges'[2] are some of the examples of foreign intrusion into indigenous habits. Besides meddling with Indian practices, the general tone of the British at the time was one of cultural arrogance. This was exemplified by T. B. Macaulay, the legal member of the Council in Calcutta, who, in spite of the discovery of a glorified India by the orientalists, dismissed Indian culture as made up of 'medical doctrines which would disgrace an English farrier, Astronomy which would move laughter in girls at an English boarding school, History, abounding with kings thirty feet high and reigns thirty thousand years long, and Geography, made up of seas of treacle and seas of butter'.[3] What he said about

---

1 For how school textbooks in Pakistan and India selectively narrate the event as a national struggle for independence, see Krishna Kumar, *Prejudice and Pride: School Histories of the Freedom Struggle in India and Pakistan* (New Delhi, Penguin Books, 2002), pp. 87–101.

2 Criminals, alleged to be followers of the goddess Kali, who were held up as prime examples of moral degradation in India.

3 T. B. Macaulay, 'Minute of the 2nd of February 1835', in *Speeches by Lord Macaulay with His Minute on Indian Education*, ed. G. M. Young (London, Oxford University Press, 1935), p. 351.

Indian literature was equally damaging: 'It is, I believe, no exaggeration to
say that all the historical information which has been collected from all
the books written in the Sanscrit language is less valuable than what may
be found in the most paltry abridgements used at preparatory schools in
England', and he went on to claim that 'a single shelf of a good European
library was worth the whole of native literature' – a claim which has now
become one of the most celebrated and castigated in postcolonial discourse.[4] The fear and scepticism of Indians were further fuelled by a
circular letter to the government by a certain E. Edmund which proposed
that 'The time appears to have come when earnest consideration should
be given to the subject, whether or not all men should embrace the same
system of Religion.'[5] There was a widespread belief that the covenanted
officers were using their privileged position to impart the knowledge
of Christianity and that the government wished to convert Indians to
Christianity.

The ordinary people might not have had access to the devious designs
of Edmund or the chauvinistic writings of Macaulay; what really caused
discontent among them was the way the traditional governing arrangements which affected their daily life had been rapidly altered by the
British. Some of the political actions of the government went against
the customs and practices of India and increasingly marginalized the
people in their own land. Among their grievances were: the resumption
of revenue on free lands, which increased poverty; the forced sale of lands
for unpaid debts and revenue arrears; the abolition of *taluqdar*, who
enjoyed the status of minor rajahs; the introduction of stamp duty; the
isolation of the Muslim rulers and failure to show respect to them; the
creation of a market in property; heavy assessment of land, which ruined
both landlords and cultivators who depended on it; the abolition of the
custom of bestowing Jagirs (grants of lands or presents), which had
increased prosperity; the power accorded to bankers and moneylenders
to manipulate civil courts to evict traditional landed families from their
properties; and the ruthless and gluttonous employment of the doctrine
of lapse in order to annex a number of Indian states which had no direct
heir. Syed Ahmed Khan, a leading Muslim reformer of the time and
himself a beneficiary of Company patronage, writing soon after the tragic
events, summed up the mood thus: 'It [i.e. the rebellion] results from the

4 Ibid., p. 349.
5 Syed Ahmed Khan, *The Causes of the Indian Revolt*, Oxford in Asia. Historical Reprints
  (Karachi, Oxford University Press, [1873] 2000), p. 55.

existence of a policy obnoxious to the dispositions, aims, habits, and views, of those by whom the rebellion is brought out [*sic*]'.[6]

The interpretation of the revolt also varies from colonialist, nationalist and subalternist perspectives. All three cover the same territory. Colonial historians are more sensitive to Indian ambitions, but also defend the excesses of the British forces and portray the rebellion as an ungrateful act motivated by the selfish and personal ambitions of Indian princes and perpetuated by wicked Mussulmans and wily Brahmins. Nationalists in both India and Pakistan see the uprising, which took place before the partition of the subcontinent in 1947, as the first war of independence. They are more sympathetic to the anger and frustration of the rebels, and go to great lengths to detail the atrocities of the British. National liberation was not an issue at the time, and, more revealingly, some Indians fought on the side of the British. It was Vinayak Damodar Savarkar, progenitor of the Hindutva doctrine and who has now become the icon of the Hindu nationalists, who mooted the idea that the revolt was a national war of independence. He wrote that when he 'began to scan that instructive and magnificent spectacle, I found to my great surprise the brilliance of a War of Independence shining in the "The Mutiny of 1857"'.[7] Radical historians, with subalternist leanings, who challenge the liberal view that the whole episode was a result of disgruntled feudal landlords and princely families, reconfigure it as an uprising of ordinary people.[8]

SACKCLOTH AND ASHES

The unexpectedness of the uprising and the exaggerated reports of civilian casualties, especially the attacks on British women and children, or, as R. Cumming preaching at the Scottish National Church, Covent Garden, put it, 'helpless babes and unoffending women',[9] heightened the

---

6 Ibid., p. 2.

7 V. D. Savarkar, *The Indian War of Independence: National Rising of 1857* (London, 1907), p. i.

8 For a conventional Eurocentric view of the event, see Christopher Hibbert, *The Great Mutiny: India 1857* (London, Penguin Books, 1980), and Saul David, *The Indian Mutiny 1857* (London, Viking, 2002); for an Indian national reading of it, see Savarkar, *The Indian War of Independence*; for a subaltern reading, see Gautam Bhadra, 'Four Rebels of Eighteen-Fifty-Seven', in *Selected Subaltern Studies*, ed. Ranajit Guha and Gayatri Chakravorty Spivak (New York, Oxford University Press, 1988), pp. 129–75; and for a critique of subaltern historiography of the uprising, see Darshan Perusek, 'Subaltern Consciousness and Historiography of Indian Rebellion of 1857', *Economic and Political Weekly*, 11 September 1993, pp. 1931–6. For a vigorous defence of Muslim involvement and for the genuine mood felt at the time, see Khan, *The Causes of the Indian Revolt*.

9 *The Times*, 8 October 1857, p. 8 col. 4.

indignation in Britain. Within Christian circles the letters of Alexander Duff proved to be influential.[10] His detailed description of the atrocities, tinged with evangelical passion, caused a great deal of agony among British Christians. The revolt was read as a divine judgement on the national failure to propagate the gospel. The failure to spread Christianity, coupled with the humiliation of early defeats at the hands of Indians, prompted the churches in Britain to call for a day of national humiliation, repentance and prayer. Such an idea had been unheard of since the Cromwellian period until it was revived during the Crimean War. Olive Anderson attributes this revival to a different theological lineage – the influence, presence and strength of quasi-Calvinism in the 1850s:

> Here was an interpretation with a different theological ancestry, namely, the emphasis placed by the Reformers especially the Calvinist Reformers upon the special providence of God, upon the efficacy of prayer in bringing to pass what would not otherwise have come to pass, and upon sin as a crime visited by penalties from God or as a breach of the covenant of grace.[11]

A day of humiliation was to be observed, by proclamation of the Queen, on 25 September 1857. The statement made clear the purpose of the occasion:

> We, taking into our most serious consideration the grievous mutiny and disturbances which have broken out in India, and putting our trust in Almighty God that He will graciously bless our efforts for the restoration of lawful authority in that country, have resolved, and do, by and with the advice of our Privy Council, hereby command, that a public day of solemn fast, humiliation, and prayer be observed throughout those parts of our united kingdom called England and Ireland, on Wednesday the 7th day of October next, that so both we and our people may humble ourselves before Almighty God in order to obtain pardon of our sins, and in the most devout and solemn manner send up our prayers and supplications to our Divine Majesty for imploring His blessings and assistance on our arms for the restoration of tranquillity; And we do strictly charge and command that the said day be reverently and devoutly observed by all our loving subjects in England and Ireland, as they tender the favour of Almighty God.[12]

A similar proclamation was issued for Scotland.[13] The day of humiliation and prayer was not observed by Protestant churches alone. Roman

---

10 Alexander Duff, *The Indian Rebellion: Its Causes and Results in a Series of Letters* (London, James Nisbet, 1858).

11 Olive Anderson, 'The Reactions of Church and Dissent towards the Crimean War', *The Journal of Ecclesiastical History* 16 (1965), 214.

12 *The Times*, 28 September 1857, p. 4 col. 2.

13 There was also a day of humiliation and prayer in India. The Governor-General, Lord Canning, reluctantly agreed to one after much petitioning. To the chagrin of missionaries, all faithful

Catholics and Jews too joined in. Cardinal Wiseman, in his pastoral letter to the Roman Catholic churches directing them to observe 2 October as a national day of humiliation and prayer, commented: 'We are only natives of one country, subjects of one Crown, and we must take our portion of common sorrow, drink equally of the same bitterness, and take upon ourselves the yoke and burden of our fellow-citizens, however far away'.[14] A service was held in India in July 1857 at St Paul's Cathedral in Calcutta, where Bishop Daniel delivered the sermon.[15] An order of service was designed for the day. Before the exhortation, the following scriptural verses were read, drawing attention to the national failure:

O Lord! correct me, but with judgement; not in Thine anger, lest Thou bring me to nothing.

I will arise and go to my Father; and will say unto him, Father, I have sinned against Heaven and before Thee, and am no more worthy to be called Thy son.

God is our refuge and strength; a very present help in trouble.

The lessons set apart for the day were Daniel 9.1–19, which describes how people in desperate need call upon God to forgive their sins for the sake of God's name and his loving kindness; and Acts 12.1–17, which tells the story of the attempt to restrain God's messenger. The implications of these texts were all too clear: the nation had failed and its attempt to bring God's message, as in the case of the apostles, had been thwarted.

There was a special collect for the day which legitimized the moral imperative of the empire:

Teach the natives of British India to prize the benefits which Thy good Providence has given them through the supremacy of this Christian land; and enable us to show more and more, both by word and good example, the blessings of thy holy religion. May those who are now the slaves of a hateful and cruel superstition be brought to lay aside their vain traditions, and turn to Thee, the only true God, and Jesus Christ, whom Thou hast sent. And so, if it be Thy good pleasure, establish our empire in that distant land on a surer foundation

---

subjects of the British crown, including Muslims and Hindus, were invited to offer 'supplication to Almighty God'. Alexander Duff wrote: 'It was felt that, whatever might have been the *design* or *intention* of its framers, it could not but practically and in effect reflect insult and dishonour on the God of Heaven, and thus, instead of deprecating his wrath, provoke fresh visitations of *His* sore displeasure'; Duff, *The Indian Rebellion*, p. 146. The Hindus, along with some maharajahs in Bombay, offered to observe the day with a puja at the temple, which made Duff even more furious.

14 *The Times*, 28 September 1857, p. 4 col. 3.
15 Daniel Wilson, *Humiliation in National Troubles: A Sermon Delivered at St Paul's Cathedral on Friday, July 24th, 1857* (Calcutta, Bishop's College Press, 1857), pp. 1–31.

than heretofore, that we Thy people, and sheep of Thy pasture, may give Thee thanks for ever, and show forth Thy praise from generation to generation.[16]

The set Psalms for the day were 77 and 79, both of which speak of public calamity.

The service was seen as 'England, the prince among nations, bowing low in supplication before the great Lord of all'. *The Times* devoted nearly five pages to the matter on the day after the service and reported in detail sermons preached in the London area.[17]

In the rest of this chapter I propose to look at the sermons preached on the national Day of Humiliation and analyse the following: conscription of the Bible for colonial enterprise; textual selection; the preponderance of Old Testament texts; interpretative practices of the preachers; theological content; construal of India. I will also analyse how these homilies became a vehicle for defining British national identity in terms of God's forces fighting against God's enemy. The sermons were a classic example of how colonial relationships were forged and how the dominant self defined the other and in turn defined itself by the exclusion of the other. I will focus mainly on the sermons preached in the London area and reported by *The Times* on the day following the service of humiliation. I will also draw on two other sources: sermons preached by Bishop Daniel Wilson in Calcutta, to indicate how the event was observed and theologically assessed in India;[18] and the sermons by F. D. Maurice, who was known for his socialist leanings and who, like many others, was overwhelmed by the tragic events in India and was one of the few who tried to articulate its implications from a slightly different theological perspective.[19] In other words, this chapter is an effort to understand from the postcolonial vantage-point the remarkable collusion of biblical text, homiletics and Christian piety, while revealing racial attitudes and lopsided interpretation at work within the Christian discourse of the nineteenth century.

16 *The Times*, 1 October 1857, p. 4 col. 5. F. D. Maurice found the prayers composed for the occasion were 'cold and formal'; *The Life of Frederick Denison Maurice Chiefly Told in His Own Letters*, vol. 11, (1884), p. 314. More of Maurice later in the chapter.

17 It was a reference in Brian Stanley's *The Bible and the Flag* which brought my attention to these sermons. See his *The Bible and the Flag: Protestant Missions and British Imperialism in the Nineteenth and Twentieth Centuries* (Leicester, Apollos, 1990), p. 181.

18 Daniel Wilson, *Humiliation in National Troubles*, and *Prayer the Refuge of a Distressed Church: A Sermon Delivered at St Paul's Cathedral, Calcutta on Sunday, June 28th, 1857* (Calcutta, Bishop's College Press, 1857).

19 Frederick Denison Maurice, *The Indian Crisis* (Cambridge, Macmillan and Co., 1857).

ONWARD CHRISTIAN PREACHERS

Firstly, I offer some simple facts. *The Times* reported 193 sermons preached in London. Some churches had three services – morning, afternoon and evening – and a collection was made to support the families of the British victims in India. The preachers were predominantly from Protestant traditions, the exception being two Jewish rabbis. All were, predictably, white and male, affectionately addressed by *The Times* as reverend gentlemen. The Bible lessons came largely from the Hebrew scriptures and only twenty-one lessons refer to texts from the New Testament. It was the Hebrew scriptures which provided the textual weapons in the preachers' crusade against the rebels. It may not come as a total surprise that the largest number of biblical citations and allusions are from the Book of Psalms. The mood of the Psalmist captured the moral dilemma and the personal and national anguish faced by the British at that time. Notwithstanding the work of the sub-editor at *The Times*, these sermons exhibit a basic consensus which gives them cohesion, namely the active and direct providence of God in the affairs of the British, the British as victims, a chance once again to make Britain worthy of her call, and an opportunity to preach repentance and prayer as way of avoiding God's chastisement. The sermons were a potent mixture of nationalism, xenophobia and biblical evangelism.

Most of the sermons centred on justifying the service of humiliation by citing biblical precedents. Biblical passages which alluded to humiliation, praying and fasting were activated to endorse the service. The obvious choice, and a great biblical exemplar, was Ezra: 'Then I proclaimed a fast there, at the river of Ahava, that we might afflict ourselves before our God, to seek of him a right way for us, and for our little ones, for all our substance' (8.21). C. J. D'Oyly reminded his listeners of the significance of fasting by recalling the words of Isaiah who spoke of fasting as a way of sharing bread with the hungry (Isa. 58.7). The other example which suited the preachers was that of Jehoshaphat, who, on hearing of the impending invasion from Edom, 'set himself to seek the Lord, and proclaimed a fast throughout all Judah' (2 Chr. 20.3). The Book of Jonah, too, provided a biblical precedent for fasting: 'So the people of Nineveh believed God, and proclaimed a fast' (3.5). On rare occasions when New Testament passages were invoked, it was a text from Acts which provided legitim-ation: 'But now [God] commandeth all men everywhere to repent: because he hath appointed a day, in which he will judge the world in righteousness by that man whom he hath ordained' (Acts. 17.30, 31). For the act of humiliation, the example of King Josiah was employed. Preaching to his Calcutta congregation, Bishop Daniel Wilson reminded them of King Josiah, who humbled himself before God, tore his garments and wept before him, when he heard what God had spoken against Judah and Jerusalem. The bishop urged that all our kings, princes, rulers and governors would 'follow the example of good King Josiah'.[20]

J. S. Wilkins likened the day to the one when the Jewish people were caught up in a similar distress, surrounded by the army of Cyrus, which was engaged in cruel practices. The Jewish people were asked by the prophet to retire and take stock: 'Come, my people, enter thou into thy chambers, and shut thy doors about thee; hide thyself as it were for a little moment, until the indignation be overpast' (Isa. 26.20). Wilkins urged his worshippers to do likewise and spend the day in reflection. C. J . D'Oyly chose the passage linked to the Jewish Passover, 'What mean ye by this service?' (Exod. 12.26), in order to explain the significance of the day's worship. He assured the congregation that the exodus passage was relevant for their time because a great catastrophe had affected the most important part of the British empire and it was the duty of the British people at home to 'pray to God to bless our arms; and to support the cause of Christianity against that of the Mohammedan and the Hindoo'.[21] He further assured them that if they prayed earnestly, their prayer would prevail. Dr. Croly pointed out that the Old Testament abounded in services of this kind, which brought 'instances of beneficial effect'. He also recalled events from English history when such services were held during the time of the French war, when cholera ravaged the country, and during the Russian war. On all those occasions, he reminded worshippers that the 'affliction of which we complained was almost immediately abated'.[22] To those who derided the service, Prebendary James told his Hanover Chapel congregation that if, in the past, peace was brought to the country after the Crimean War and a dreadful disease like cholera was curbed as a result of the nation humbling itself before God, 'so shall it be now, if we turn from our wickedness, and in faith and penitence humble ourselves in the sight of God'.[23]

---

20 Wilson, *Humiliation in National Troubles: A Sermon Delivered at St Paul's Cathedral on Friday, July 24th, 1857* (Calcutta, Bishop's College Press, 1857), p. 10.
21 *The Times*, 8 October 1857, p. 6 col. 5.
22 Ibid., p. 5 col. 6.   23 Ibid., p. 7 col. 1.

BIBLICAL VERSES AS INCENDIARY DEVICES

Biblical images were dredged up to find parallels between the British who were caught up in the thick of the trouble in India and those in Britain. The plight of the British was seen from the perspective of various biblical characters. Sometimes they were seen as like Job, helpless and at the mercy of God: W. Upton Richards appealed to Job, the symbol of the eternal unjust victim: 'Have pity upon me, have pity upon me, O ye my friends; for the hand of God hath touched me' (19.21). 'This', according to Upton Richards, 'was now the cry of our country men and country women in the far East to their relations and friends at home'.[24] Sometimes the British were seen as like David: Canon Dale recalled the words of Israel's tragic hero, 'Lo, I have sinned, and I have done wickedly'.[25] F. D. Maurice, preaching at Lincoln's Inn, invoked the parabolic image of the Prodigal Son and composed his own version of the Prodigal's speech: 'We have sinned against Thee, in that we have not taught our sons, whom we have sent forth to trade or to rule in any province of our empire, that they are servants of the Son of Man, and therefore are to treat all men as His brethren and theirs'.[26] Sometimes the predicament of the British was seen as like that of Esther. George Mansfield, in his sermon, recalled the efficacy of the intercessory prayer of Esther, which helped to overthrow the plot against the Jews in Persia, and tried to convince his congregation that a similar action undertaken by the British would crush the devious scheme against them in India.[27] Most of all, the preachers saw an easy identification with several of the Psalmists who experienced a similar state of anguish and distress and who were faced with various life-threatening situations through oppression by enemies and betrayal by friends. The fact that most of the sermons were based on texts from the Psalms confirms that the Psalmists encapsulated the mood the British were in – persecuted, alienated and betrayed. The sermons based on texts such as 'Let the sighing of the prisoner come before Thee; according to the greatness of thy power, preserve Thou those that are appointed to die' (79.11) and 'God is our refuge and strength, a very present help in trouble' (46.1) spoke eloquently of the plight of the British in India.

The texts were expounded to describe the horrific things that were going on in India. One such text was 1 Samuel 11.1–11, which became part

---

24 Ibid., p. 7 col. 2.   25 Ibid., p. 5 col. 2.
26 Maurice, *The Indian Crisis*, pp. 13–14.
27 *The Times*, 8 October 1857, p. 6 col. 3.

of the textual armoury. At least two sermons referred to the incident narrated in this passage so as to ascribe biblical proportions to the events in India. The situation in Cawnpore (now Kanpur) was likened to the people of Jabesh-Gilead who were exposed to great dangers from the king of the Ammonites, Nahash (1 Sam. 11.1–11). For a congregation well-versed in biblical stories, these allusions were only too obvious. The British were facing humiliation and physical affliction like the Jews. The Ammonites had been threatening to carry out mutilations on the Jews by gouging out their eyes. Since Victorian clergy were reluctant to give the gory details to a polite Sunday congregation, W. Upton Richards hinted at the atrocities, saying that they were 'too horrible to be related', but 'the cry of wailing had reached us from Cawnpore and other places'.[28] Reports and rumours were circulated at that time of the cutting of the noses and breasts of British women.[29] Like the Israelites, the British were now under threat, humiliated and physically disfigured. Faced with such a humiliation, the course of action was clear. The threats of the rebels had to be put down. Just as a message was sent to Gibeah to inform Saul of the Jews' extremity, the heart-rending case of the British had now reached England. When Saul heard the cause of the Jews' worries, his anger was kindled greatly. The implications for the British were blatantly obvious. The only thing left now was to act as Saul did – to rise against the enemy and massacre them and disperse those who survived.

The misrule of the British was also seen as a repetition of a biblical type. E. R. Jones, choosing Hosea 14:1, observed that Britain was chargeable with a sin like that of Israel: bad management of native landholders and magistrates; immorality of some of the British, which included covetousness; encouraging heathen festivals; affirming caste; and discouraging missionaries and native converts. Daniel Wilson, the Bishop of Calcutta, saw the current rebels and traitors as God's rod of anger, as was the Assyrian monarch of old who was sent against a hypocritical nation.[30] There were other preachers who invoked parabolic images. India was seen as a talent given to the British which they had wasted by not acting properly: J. S. Wilkins, preaching at St Jude's, Gray's Inn Road, warned that, as in the parable, if the British failed to act prudently,

---

28 Ibid., p. 7 col. 2.
29 For a record of violence against women and children, see Hibbert, *The Great Mutiny*, pp. 168–97. These rumours, according to Karl Marx, were circulated by a clergyman sitting in Bangalore, hundreds of miles away from the scene of action. Marx, writing at the time on the revolt, called these reports 'circumstantial accounts'; Karl Marx, 'The Indian Revolt', in *The Portable Karl Marx*, ed. Eugene Kamenka (New York, Penguin Books, 1983), p. 353.
30 Wilson, *Humiliation in National Troubles*, p. 9.

India would be 'wrested from us and given to others'.[31] Wilkins also used another parabolic phrase to describe the action of the Indians: their protest was like the surreptitious act of the enemy who sowed tares while men slept.

THE NEW INSTRUMENTS OF GOD

Some of the sermons advocated the idea that the baton had been passed on to the British and that they were the new Israel and the new elect. That Britain was uniquely blessed with economic prosperity, political freedom and social peace and was destined to lead the world was indeed a widespread opinion in the 1850s. The British had replaced the Jews as God's chosen people with a special vocation, and the empire was given to teach the divine purpose. Some sermons reflected this new sense of election: 'Our wondrous empire in the East was God's gift; we won it not by our own sword . . . It was given to us that we might teach the nations the way of salvation'.[32] India was seen as a 'solemn deposit' placed in the hands of the British because, as a special favour, God had endowed the nation with 'great spiritual privileges' designed to spread the knowledge of the true faith. Wheler Bush claimed that the British were the 'blessed and favoured instruments of God' leading India to her salvation.

Using the text 'God shall enlarge Japheth, and he shall dwell in the tents of Shem' (Gen. 9.27), G. H. M'Gill told the congregation that European nations descended from Japheth had now succeeded the Jews, the sons of Shem, as the new favoured people of God. He reminded his listeners that, though they might not have acquired the blessing by fair means, and, like Japheth, the British might be forced to flee for a while, it would not be too long before God's purpose was finally accomplished and Japheth enlarged to dwell securely in the tents of Shem. Preaching on the same text, R. Bickerdike provided further evidence for the new role of the British. He went on to say that the fulfilment of Japheth's enlargement came to be realized when 'Europe possessed over [*sic*] other continents'. As regards dwelling in the tents of Shem, 'it was fulfilled partially by the Romans dwelling in the land of Canaan and other Asiatic countries, but more particularly by the English dwelling in Hindoostan'.[33] The images of Japheth and Shem would have struck a chord with the congregation. In the legends of Anglo-Saxon history, Japheth, the third of the three sons of

31 *The Times*, 8 October 1857, p. 7 col. 6.
32 Ibid., p. 6 col. 2.   33 Ibid., p. 8 col. 2.

Noah, rechristened Seth, was seen as the ancestor of the kings of Wessex and England.[34] In the eighteenth century, Indians were seen as descendants of Shem who had lost the monotheistic idea of God and turned to pantheistic worship.[35] The hermeneutical significance was obvious: England was fulfilling its mission as the new Israel by leading the wayward Indians back to the worship of the one God.

The priestly function, which had been the task of priestly families among the Jews, now seemed to be transferred to the British. The administration of the empire was seen as the new ecclesiastical task. M'Caul, in his sermon, told his congregation that 'We, like Israel of old, had had conferred upon us the high commission of being a kingdom of priests'. He went on to say that the new clerical assignment was 'to teach nations the way of salvation'.[36] Biblical narratives thus provided the core hermeneutical resources which enabled the preachers to boost the national image as the new Israel and place the British within the sacred history.

PAIN AND PUNISHMENT

This was an age in which the clergy were over-absorbed with the idea of human depravity and divine punishment for sin. Many sermons undoubtedly endorsed this view. The tumultuous events in India had come at a time of 'national prosperity' to remind the people of their old trespasses. It was, as the Dean of Westminster reminded them, the brothers of Joseph and the widow of Zarephath who forgot their sins in the days of prosperity and remembered them during the days of calamity. The Indian rebellion was seen as divine retribution, and the nation must repent of its sins. A wide variety of reasons was given for provoking the wrath of God. They varied from the personal to the spiritual, the corporate to the political. The divisions between them were not always clearly demarcated. Some of these were seen as committed by the British themselves at home, and some by the British in India, which most believed were the cause of the rebellion, though Indians were also blamed for the present state of affairs.

At Westminister Abbey, the Dean said that, just as Joshua searched and found out Achan, who brought shame and confusion, the British too

---

34 Peter Calvocoressi, *Who's Who in the Bible* (London, Penguin Books, 1990), p. 97.
35 P. J. Marshall, (ed.) *The British Discovery of Hinduism in the Eighteenth Century* (Cambridge, Cambridge University Press, 1970), p. 22.
36 *The Times*, 8 October 1857, p. 6 col. 2.

should search and cast out the 'accursed things' which might bring God's wrath upon them. Among the 'accursed things' he listed two. One was trafficking in opium, a 'poisonous drug, which was so destructive both to the body and soul of millions in the East', of which the East India company exported 100,000 chests to the unwilling Chinese. The other was the slave trade and slavery.[37] C. H. Spurgeon, the famous Baptist preacher of the day (versions of his sermon were heard by 23,546 persons), pointed to communal and individual sins 'which should induce us to humiliate ourselves in the dust and beg the mercy of the Almighty'. His 'glaring faults and sins of the community' included the toleration of prostitutes in the Haymarket, Regent Street and other public places: 'If there were a crime for which God would punish England, it would be for allowing infamy to stalk our streets in public, exhibiting itself decked in the robes of a harlot in such a fashion as to insult the modesty of every decent person who approached it'.[38] Among the individual sins that Spurgeon listed were pride, oppression of the poor, illiberality and carnality. He told his congregation it was for these sins that God was punishing them. For Prebendary James, the terrible happenings in India were caused not by the incompetence or the maladministration of those in high office but by gross violation of the Lord's day in the English metropolis. His other national guilt included sins of swearing, drunkenness, extravagance and exhortation. Charles Phillips, choosing the text from Jeremiah, 'O Lord, though our iniquities testify against us, do thou it for thy name's sake: for our backslidings are many; we have sinned against thee' (14.7), came out with his own list of national sins. These included God's word being despised, his sanctuary neglected, his Sabbath profaned and his mercies abused. Besides these religious misdemeanours, Phillips enumerated sins committed in public life and in daily transactions – false weights and measures, adulterated goods, trading on Sundays and bands playing in parks, and the spirit of avarice created by market speculation, which he saw as prostration before mammon: 'All religious principles, all holy considerations, were offered up on the shrine of mammon'.[39]

The various preachers came up with a number of sins committed by the British in India. There were four concrete examples. The first was the exclusion of the Bible from the government schools, where the Vedas, the 'Shasters' and the Koran were systematically taught. The second was the discouragement of conversion, and the failure to support converts.

---

37 Ibid., p. 5 col. 3.   38 Ibid., p. 8 col. 5.   39 Ibid., p. 7 col. 3.

The most celebrated case in point was that of Prabhu Din Panda, a high-caste Brahmin sepoy, who was dismissed from the army because the colonial administration felt that his change of religion might prejudice recruitment among the high castes. The Victorian clergy construed the dismissal as the government's tacit approval of the caste system. The Din Panda incident occurred in Meerut, the very place where the uprising began. This was interpreted by Richard Chaffer as an indictment of the failure of the British to honour the trust placed in them. The third was the failure to eradicate idolatry. Unlike the Israelites in Canaan, who extirpated all offending symbols, the British failed 'to destroy the altars and the idolatrous worship of the country'.[40] Bishop Wilson castigated the government for placing the holy places of the heathen under the special charge of collectors rather than leaving them to native priests. The fourth example was racial superiority: 'It was proverbial that when Englishmen went into other countries they invariably looked down upon the people as an inferior race of beings to themselves; and this arrogance rendered us objects of extreme dislike'.[41] Maurice thought the Indian disaster was caused by a 'very low' order of '*our* morality and *our* Christianity'. For him it was a clear call to reform English Christianity from within: 'I am sure the priests of the land, the educated classes of the land, fathers and mothers of families, teachers, can do much more (and are therefore more guilty than all Downing Street and Leadenhall Street[42]) to reform India by reforming England'.[43]

Another reason for provoking the wrath of God was the personal sins committed by the British in India: 'The lax and licentious lives of European residents have too often corrupted, instead of enlightened'.[44] Bishop Wilson, preaching to an audience composed largely of Europeans, listed their gross personal vices: licentiousness, open fornication, liaisons with native women, rise of prostitution among European and Indian women, visiting playhouses, horse racing, ships sailing on Sunday, and the neglect of personal and family prayers. As Edward Headland put it, 'The crowning sin of England in respect to India had been the godlessness of her soul'.[45] He also blamed the failure of the pastoral ministry which neglected the basic spiritual care for the people.

---

40 Ibid., p. 6 col. 1.
41 Robert Liddell, *The Times*, 8 October 1857, p. 5 col. 6.
42 The street where the East India Company was located.
43 Maurice (ed.), *The Life of Frederick Denison Maurice*, vol. 11, 1884, p. 313.
44 *The Times*, 8 October 1857, p. 5 col. 5.
45 Ibid., p. 7 col. 2.

Sometimes the blame is apportioned to the earlier generations of East India Company men who had been ambitious, covetous and ungodly. Robert Clive and Warren Hastings are singled out, the former for his duplicity and the latter for his involvement in the Rohilla War. Other unlawful acts committed by the administration included the annexation of Oudh and the seizure of Benares. Robert Liddell told the St Paul's Knightbridge congregation: 'We had won that country, annexed province after province, and held them mainly by the sword; and now we had been smitten with the sword'.[46] The understanding was that the present government, which had done so much to improve the life of Indian people, had been punished for the wrongdoings of an earlier generation. Canon Dale agonized with his listeners how far 'our own sins may have contributed to draw down upon the sufferers this most appalling and unsparing judgement'.[47] It was not the simple question of fathers having eaten sour grapes and the children's teeth being set on edge. Christianity's failure, some claimed, was due to the callous actions of the British in India which went against the spirit and teaching of Christianity: 'Men of whose land we took forcible possession could hardly be expected to regard our religious teachings with much respect'.[48]

Blaming the victims

Some placed the blame squarely on the Indians for provoking the wrath of God. James Jackson saw the revolt as not driven by 'any oppression on our part, or any wrong they can justly complain of '[49] but the savage and the faithless nature of the Indians themselves. British rule, he told the assembled faithful, had been 'the best and most beneficent that any country ever experienced'.[50] G. H. M'Gill attributed the cause 'to the gentleness and kindness with which the sepoys have been invariably treated', which had been misperceived by the Indians as a sign of 'weakness'.[51] For many the revolt was a betrayal of what the British had done for the Indians, especially for the sepoys. Robert Liddell expressed the feeling thus: 'We raised that army among the natives themselves, trained it according to our own military tactics, fought with it, conquered with it, and then made our boast, "what could we not do with such forces?"'[52] Now 'God has smitten us with the very means we have fostered'.

---

46 Ibid., p. 5 col. 6. 47 Ibid., p. 5 col. 2. 48 Ibid., p. 6 col. 1.
49 Ibid., p. 6 col. 2. 50 Ibid. 51 Ibid., p. 7 col. 5.
52 Ibid., p. 5 col. 6.

W. Hinson captured the mood when he said: 'We have sinned in sinking our Christianity before the prejudices of the isolators, and there can be no doubt that the present judgement was sent on account of this'.[53]

But all the sermons admit that the greatest sin of all was not 'advancing the knowledge of Christ and His gospel in India',[54] and the 'failure to bring the religion of the Bible'.[55] This was the most unforgivable sin of all – the British negligence of the command of the saviour 'Go ye and preach the gospel to every creature'. In keeping with the self-pitying mood, J. G. Packer blamed the British for not doing their duty: 'if we had done our duty by them, and Christianized them, they would not only have been good soldiers, but they would have been good subjects, good neighbours, kind, and forebearing to one another in love'.[56] The inaction and the misbehaviour of the British both at home and in India, according to the preachers, had resulted in the 'sad lowering of the Bible standards'[57] and not holding India 'according to the principles of the New Testament'.[58] Not fulfilling the mission was described variously as 'our crying sin', our 'national shame'[59] and a 'national error'.[60] Alexander Duff spoke for many when he wrote from India that 'the present calamities are righteous judgements on account of our culpable negligence in fulfilling the glorious trust committed to us'.[61] Or, as Wheler Bush put it, the creed of the British in India was 'a mixture of heathenism and infidelity' and a 'temporizing and vacillating policy',[62] which caused the wrath of God. They had disregarded the command and were experiencing the truth of the words of the prophet: 'Therefore have I also made you, saith the Lord of Hosts, base and contemptible before all the people'.[63] The preachers agreed that the rebellion was a challenge to Christianity and a judgement of God for the official compromise with the heathen religions. The underlying theological presupposition behind these sermons was that 'whom the Lord loveth he chasteneth'. The rebellion had a purpose. These present afflictions would make Britain morally more responsible for India and compel her to give up self-interest: 'Our duty to India as a nation would now take precedence of our own selfish schemes of mere profit'.[64]

53 Ibid., p. 7 col. 5.   54 Ibid., p. 5 col. 2.   55 Ibid., p. 8 col. 1.
56 Ibid., p. 7 col. 5.   57 Ibid., p. 8 col. 3.
58 A. Reed, *The Times*, 8 October 1857, p. 7 col. 6.
59 Revd. Hessey, *The Times*, 8 October 1857, p. 7 col. 1.
60 Henry Christopherson, *The Times*, 8 October 1857, p. 7 col. 1.
61 Duff, *The Indian Rebellion*, p. 224.
62 *The Times*, 8 October 1857, p. 7 col. 2.
63 B. M. Cowie, *The Times*, 8 October 1857, p. 5 col. 1.
64 *The Times*, 8 October 1857, p. 7 col. 2.

God strikes those whom he loves most, and pain was part of God's plan, which was tied up with judgement and the conversion of God's people. The sequence which Boyd Hilton has identified in the homilies of the nineteenth-century evangelicals was evident in the humiliation-day sermons: sin, suffering, contrition, despair, comfort and grace.[65]

UNEASY AMALGAM: RETRIBUTION AND VENGEANCE

The sermons made it clear that the culprits must be punished for their crime, and that this vengeance was a just recompense and a repayment for villainous acts. The preachers seemed to have conveniently ignored the words of Benjamin Disraeli. Perturbed by the prevailing bellicose mood of the time, he said: 'I protest against meeting atrocities by atrocities. I have heard things said, and seen them written of late, which would make me almost suppose that the religious opinions of the people of England had undergone some sudden change; and that instead of bowing before the name of Jesus, we are preparing to revive the worship of Moloch'.[66] *The Times* described Disraeli's speech as an 'ill-judged effusion'.[67] The hope that the clergy would take note of Disraeli's 'mercy for mutineers' and that it would induce some tolerance among them did not materialize. Retribution was conceived by the preachers not as a brutal revenge but as a moral necessity to right the scales of justice. It was seen as an act of mercy towards the rest of the empire. Moreover, 'vengeance belongeth' to God. F. Garden even suggested that if the English did not engage in the task of bringing justice on the guilty, England might be out of tune with biblical thinking: 'We must throw ourselves out of sympathy with the whole of the Old Testament, no less than the New, if we refuse to enter into this'.[68] The line between recompense and revenge is not always neat and clear. Among the preachers there were 'hawks' and 'doves'. The hawks represented a kind of theology which flourished in the nineteenth century, and which advocated a theory of atonement that bordered on fetishizing the blood of Christ, believing that sins must be paid for with blood. The implications for the colonial trouble were clear. Just as the sins against God must be paid for with blood, crime against

65 Boyd Hilton, *The Age of Atonement: The Influence of Evangelicalism on Social and Economic Thought 1785–1865* (Oxford, Clarendon Press, 1991), p. 8.
66 *The Times*, 2 October 1857, p. 4 col. 3, and also Michael Edwardes, *Red Year: The Indian Rebellion of 1857* (London, Cardinal, 1975), p. 162.
67 *The Times*, 2 October 1857, p. 4 col. 3.
68 *The Times*, 8 October 1857, p. 6 col. 5.

God's chosen instrument – the British – must be paid for by pain and punishment. This was the colonial equivalent of refusing to be soft on crime. The doves, a minority, took another line. For them reconciliation was brought about not by meeting violence with violence but by showing mercy, love and forgiveness. But it was the punitive voice which was predominant among the sermons.

There were some sermons which were preoccupied with an intemperate demand for vengeance. John Baillie's was an extreme example of that mood. Preaching at an afternoon service at All Souls' Langham Place, he advocated drastic measures: 'the avenging work must be done – the outraged law of society must be vindicated'.[69] Basing his sermon on the text 'What wickedness is this that is done among you?' (Judg. 20.12), he drew attention to the fact that the current crime committed in British India was similar to one that visited Israel and involved the rape of a helpless woman. The Judges passage that Baillie chose refers to a complicated moral tale which depicts a gruesome crime unique even by Old Testament standards. To summarize the Judges text briefly, in its narrative context: to satisfy a baying group of Benjaminite ruffians, a concubine of an itinerant Levite was offered as a sop by their host. She was raped and tortured by the mob and thrown upon the doorstep. The following morning, her husband prepared to move on as if nothing had happened. His heartless response on seeing her underscored his vile nature: 'Get up so that we can go'. He put her on his ass and travelled home, cut her body into twelve pieces (whether this started to happen while she was still alive is unclear from the text) and dispersed them throughout the territories of Israel. In the version of events he then reported to the tribes, he simply erased the triple abuse his concubine had faced at the hands of her host, the mob and also himself, saying, 'me they sought to kill', thus confirming his depraved nature. The tribes of Israel responded to the heinous crime by demanding the miscreants be returned to be dealt with. When this demand was resisted by the Benjaminites, Israel approached God by means of an oracle. God did not promise victory, and the men of Israel lost the battle. They wept before God and enquired again, and they lost a second time. They enquired a third time, and this time God promised victory: 'Go up; tomorrow I will give them into your hand'. Baillie used this narrative, conveniently overlooking its complexities, to tell his congregation that 'our own case was exactly parallel'.[70] In his view this was not the time to assess the rights

---

69 Ibid., p. 7 col. 3.   70 Ibid., p. 7 col. 3.

and wrongs of British rule in India, but 'this monstrous enormity must be visited; these burning tears of our bereaved must be wiped; . . . and the only possible method is, the avenger must go against the murderer'. He warned his audience that such an action would cause political inconveniences and that England might lose her sepoys as Israel lost her exterminated tribe, but for the sake of the vast population of the Indian people, Baillie told his listeners 'this vast gang of murderers must be put down, and their very name become an execration'. He said that there were already faint wails about 'European brutality and torture of the mild Hindoo sepoy'. 'No', he told the worshippers, 'our wail was for the Sepoys' victims, for our butchered mothers, our murdered children, our darkened homes', and 'the wail should not cease until God has smitten before us the branded criminals from the earth'.[71] The message was clear: as in the biblical story, violent rape had to be met with violence.

There is an interesting moral twist to the story which Baillie failed to take up. After the victory Israel wept again, this time not because they could not defeat the Benjaminites but precisely because they had defeated them. The Israelites were distressed now because one of their tribes, the tribe of Benjamin, faced extermination, for the Israelites had slain all the Benjaminite women, and the men who escaped found themselves without any women. The British in India did not have any such moral qualms. The retribution was swift and barbaric. The violence unleashed was unimaginable and, as Edwardes put it, 'the city of Delhi was put to the sword, looted and sacked with the ferocity of a Nazi extermination squad in occupied Poland'.[72] Duff even provided biblical warrant for such a revenge attack. When eyebrows were raised about the ruthless methods of scripture-quoting Colonel James Neill, Duff came to his rescue, saying that he was engaged in a divine mercy mission, designed to act as warning for all evil-doers. For Duff, General Neill was a perfect exemplar of Paul's notion of the beneficial effects of God's chastisement: 'He sternly grasped the sword of retributive justice; and, as "the minister of God, who ought not to bear the sword in vain – a revenger to execute wrath on them that did evil" (Rom. 13.4) – he resolved to strike terror into the souls of the evil-doers and their miscreant sympathisers'.[73]

Not all sermons demanded the blood of the Indian troublemakers. There were preachers who were an exception to the violent tone adopted

71 Ibid., p. 7 col. 3.
72 Edwardes, *Red Year*, p. 59.
73 Duff, *The Indian Rebellion*, p. 246.

by many. There were four doves among the 193 preachers: Pearsall, Owen, Sparrow and Maurice. 'Loving the enemy', the fundamental tenet of Christianity, was often overlooked in the heat of the vengeful mood. Spencer Pearsall, a Baptist minister, preached a sermon which was exceptional in that he spoke about the Christian duty of loving the enemy. He chose two texts from the New Testament – 'Father forgive them' (Lk. 23.34) and Stephen's last words, recorded in Acts, 'Lord, lay not this sin to their charge'. He reminded his listeners that loving their enemies was a profound Christian tenet which distinguished it from other religions. For him, loving the enemy was the new commandment. He cited the example of Stephen as the most cogent confirmation of the veracity and integrity of Christianity. Pearsall pointed out that Stephen's last words were not about himself but about pardoning his murderers, authenticating the spirit of Jesus living in him, and thus Stephen's act was worthy of emulation. W. Owen, a Congregational minister, took a similar line. In his sermon he told those gathered in his Pentonville church that Christ taught us 'how to feel towards our enemies, and how to act towards them', and that Jesus did not encourage 'wild justice of revenge', but advocated 'compassion even towards our enemies'.[74] Another who called for a calmer assessment of the situation was W. Sparrow. He talked about the characteristic human response under these testing circumstances being indignation and a desire to take revenge on the culprits, rather than thinking in terms of justice. A dispassionate look at the events in India would remind people of their Christian duty. Generous and impressive retaliation, he said, would be to release those Indians who had long been shackled by the chains of Satan, 'and render blessing for cursing'.[75]

Maurice, who was one of the chief architects of shifting the orthodox theology of the time from atonement to incarnation, advised against any victimization. His less punitive stance was based on the liberal notion of family as a secure and abiding force which acknowledged the fatherhood of God and brotherhood of man.[76] In a sense, his leniency had its roots in his Boyle Lectures of 1846, entitled *The Religions of the World and Their Relations to Christianity*, a pioneering theological critique of other faiths at that time, which made a great impact on a number of theologians of his generation. In these lectures Maurice advanced the idea that the people of other faiths, as 'partakers of the self-same Spirit; in their words and acts

74 *The Times*, 8 October 1857, p. 8 col. 7.
75 Ibid., p. 6 col. 2.
76 Maurice, *The Indian Crisis*, p. 9.

they manifest its presence',[77] but at the same time imposed the notion of Christian superiority under the mask of universalism. The implication of such an inclusive theology was that one needed to show respect to people. He advanced two reasons against any punitive measures. One was that the Asiatics were made in the image of God and, as such, 'share all the blessings that belong to Europeans', and the other was that the English could not teach the love of God if they did not show others 'that He is a God Who maketh inquisition for blood; Who must have the land purged which has been defiled with it; Who, of old, destroyed cities where horrid crimes had been committed, and destroys them now'. He went on to say that to demonstrate the forgiveness of God, the English should forgive 'as He forgives'.[78]

A VIEW FROM THE PULPIT: INDIAN IMAGES

The sermons contained a great deal of material describing India. One can discern early signs of orientalism in their representations of India, which is seen variously as a proud possession of Britain, and as a country culturally and morally void in contrast to Britain's civility, learning and superior spirituality.

The sermons acknowledged the pride in possessing India. 'Our Indian empire is a historical marvel, without a parallel' and the 'national heart has throbbed with pride',[79] claimed R. Wheler Bush. M'Caul told his congregation it was 'God's gift'.[80] While the land, its wealth and natural beauty were praised, its people were seen as depraved. India was portrayed as a land of 'lying and cunning where a rupee can buy any testimony from a witness, and a shawl any deliverance from a judge'.[81] The chief villains were Mussulmans and Brahmins. The normal Indian mind was described as 'barbaric, diabolical and Satanic'. This depraved state, according to Harvey Brooks, was the direct result of these heathen assimilating the very characteristics of the gods whom they worshipped. Citing David Livingstone, the pioneer missionary to Africa, Harvey Brooks informed his faithful that people who worshipped false, impure and cruel gods were themselves clones of these vile deities and creatures of evil passion. The unutterable horrors which they represented were linked directly to idol

---

77 Frederick Denison Maurice, *The Religions of the World and Their Relations to Christianity* (London, Macmillan and Co., 1886), p. 199.

78 Maurice, *The Indian Crisis*, p. 11.

79 *The Times*, 8 October 1857, p. 7 col. 2.

80 Ibid., p. 6 col. 2. 81 Ibid., p. 8 col. 5.

worship. The impression the congregations would have gleaned from these sermons was that one could not expect impeccable moral behaviour from natives who derived pleasure from self-mutilation, wallowed in human sacrifices, prostrated themselves beneath the wheels of jugger-nauts, abandoned their sick and old to decay on the banks of the Ganges (and, if they were too long in dying, suffocated them with the mud of the river), and whose festivals were marred with murders and thieving.

The sermons disclosed colonial contempt in depicting the natives as corrupt before the advent of the British. India, before British rule, was described as 'a scene of anarchy, plunder and murder'. Such negative portrayals provided a case for supplanting this decadence with British benevolence, and thus paving the way for a peace, prosperity and security which India had never experienced before. The sermons did not fail to remind the congregation of the benefits bestowed on India. Dr Hamilton, who preached at the Scottish Church in Regent Square, presented a whole list of English achievements in India, which he saw as a 'great blessing'. Among the blessings he listed were: termination of bloody feuds among Indian states, revitalization of Indian industries which had led to a com-fortable existence for cultivators and artisans, infusion of European litera-ture and science among the 'myriad minds' of the high classes, inculcation of 'British probity and truthfulness' among Indian traders and capitalists, suppression of such time-honoured institutions as widow-burning and infant-drowning, and introduction of English law and impartial English courts of justice.[82] Such an idealized picture overlooked the predatory nature of British rule: 'We have not laid waste or plundered or depopu-lated the land as our predecessors in conquest, the Mugul and Mahratta princes did; . . . we have not drawn a revenue and exacted a tribute to be expended in governing the mother country, but all the revenues have been expended in governing the country itself'.[83] Commercial adventures were often seen as innocent of imperial ambitions.

But the severest fulminations were directed against the Indian soldiers. Sermon after sermon vilified them. They were depicted in contradictory terms as beasts and children. J. J. Toogood told his congregation that the Indian soldiers had violated all the laws of humanity and divested them-selves of any characteristics of civilized men. In his view they possessed a beastly nature: 'They have excited each other to madness; they claim a ferocious kindred with our savage animals; they are as blood-thirsty and insatiable as the tigers in their jungles; and they have been guilty of

82 Ibid., p. 8 col. 5.   83 Ibid., p. 6 col. 3.

atrocities horrible beyond conception'.[84] Another preacher said the Indian soldiers were as children rebelling against their father, as Absalom rebelled against his father.[85] Their biggest crime, according to J. J. Toogood, was that they had gone against all the civilized rules of engagement by rising against their own officers and murdering them, their cruelty thus surpassing all that had been recorded in history. In the colonial lexicon, the images of beast and child were a way of speaking and having authority over the other. One warranted taming, and the other needed protection and care. The sermons provided a canvas for painting a British identity which was undergirded by muscular Christianity in contradistinction to the supposed inadequacies of the Indians. The British gained their moral superiority through creating monsters and beasts out of the Indians.

The sermons rarely registered the voices of the Indians. Their story was hardly heard. When on rare occasions they appeared, they replicated unconsciously the intentions of the oppressor: W. Cadman referred to a sepoy who was converted in Meerut, who, when dismissed from the army as a consequence of his conversion, was supposed to have said: 'You will allow me to serve your king but not your God'.[86] J. S. Wilkins recalled a statement by another Indian: 'Your government alone prevented India from becoming a Christian country'.[87] In creating a space for colonized people, the power of the colonizer was exercised through speaking for the Indians as if they were fellow citizens. At their best, Indians could only reflect the intentions of the British.

Obviously, the insurrection in most of the preachers' minds was not a war of independence. Nor was it an uprising of an oppressed people. For most of them, it was a seditious, insubordinate and barbarous act committed against a benevolent ruler. As such, this common communal insurgency had met with punishment befitting the crime. C. H. Spurgeon saw the event not as freedom-loving nationalists aspiring to liberate their land from the bondage of a cruel oppressor, but as a 'revolt of treasonous and seditious subjects fomented by ambition and the vilest lusts'.[88] He went on to say that he would not defile his lips by detailing the bestialities of the mutineers. Since the rebels were not prisoners of war in the conventional sense of the term, Spurgeon suggested that their arrest and punishment were a justifiable judicial act. The British troops were seen as instruments of this justice. Spurgeon's description of the Indian rebels as criminals who did not deserve the status of soldiers has a contemporary

---

84 Ibid., p. 6 col. 6. 85 Ibid., p. 8 col. 2. 86 Ibid.
87 Ibid., p. 7 col. 6. 88 Ibid., p. 8 col. 5.

parallel. The Taliban and al-Qa'ida prisoners at Guantanamo were seen as unlawful combatants and, as such, according to Donald Rumsfeld, the Secretary of State for the United States, were not entitled to the protection of the Geneva Convention.

It is evident from the sermons that the preachers were clear about the remedy for this rebellion – the reconquest of India. The aim was twofold: firstly to assert the supremacy of Britain, and secondly to Christianize the natives. B. M. Cowie regarded the re-taking of India as a sign of British valour, whereas for Henry Christopherson it was a case of exerting British influence within the current world order: 'We are not now fighting for a colony, we are fighting for our *prestige* therefore our security among the empires of the globe'.[89] For Anthony W. Thorold, the seizure of India was a humanitarian cause and a sign of good governance. Dr Croly was unequivocal about exercising the military muscle of the British: 'That city which had been the rallying place of rebellion, where a mock king had been installed to insult the power of Britain, must be razed to the ground in order to teach the lesson that the just might of England could not be aroused with impunity'.[90]

B. M. Cowie prescribed conversion as a cure for those in their depraved state: 'The only remedy given from Heaven against the natural depravity of man was the religion of Jesus Christ. Hearts must be subdued before such beings as those who had now risen against the English could become trustworthy and faithful, and the way to bring this result about was to exhibit Christianity in a way worthy of its Divine Author'.[91] In C. Bull's view, Christianization was the only way to make the natives 'loyal and devoted'.[92] Another preacher asserted that England's mission was to 'reclaim these kingdoms of darkness and of Satan, and bring them beneath the sway of truth, light, and knowledge'.[93] This task was to be assigned to those who were 'more specially connected with the Church of England'.[94] The other suggestion was to Christianize the leadership of the army. F. J. Stainforth, in his sermon, admitted that India could not be held without the native army but they should be officered by Englishmen and therefore it was necessary that we 'should improve the Christian character of those officers and non-commissioned officers who represented our power in foreign lands'.[95]

89 Ibid., p. 7 col. 1.   90 Ibid., p. 6 col. 1.
91 Ibid., p. 5 col. 1.   92 Ibid., p. 6 col. 5.
93 B. G. Johns, *The Times*, 8 October 1857, p. 8 col. 3.
94 *The Times*, 8 October 1857, p. 6 col. 1.
95 Ibid., p. 5 col. 4.

Some of the sermons pressed the idea of spiritual subjugation further and went on to advocate material conquest. A few had mercantile ambitions too: 'We must build our churches there as well as our factories, and send out our missionaries as well as our collectors of revenue, not only our brave soldiers, but that valiant army whose weapon is the sword of the spirit; not only our nobles and merchant princes, but our bishops, priests and deacons'.[96] R. W. Brown summed it up for all: 'Our task is to save India, and the harmless and fearful and peaceful population from the curse of a pampered and licentious soldiery – to protect, to civilize, to regenerate, to educate, to raise them in the scale of nations until they are fitted for our institutions'.[97] Maurice, too, advocated the propagation of the gospel, but he preferred a softer approach. More to the point, he did not want the Muslims and Hindus to replicate the western manifestation of Christianity and become clones of the British. He rephrased the words of Jesus: 'When He stood on the mountains of Galilee, in the sight of the fishermen who were to be His messengers to the world, He did not say, "Go, and make them Galileans like yourselves." He did not say, "Go, and convert them from their religions to another religion"'.[98] Instead of bombarding India with a gospel wrapped in western trappings, Maurice wanted to preach a gentle and universalist gospel of God's redeeming love in Jesus: 'If we believe that God is the Father of men in Christ Jesus, that He has redeemed mankind in His Son – if we hold this faith as firmly as we hold the law of gravitation – the Shasters and Koran will be as little to withstand it'.[99] Maurice thought the gentle blowing of the trumpet would bring down the walls, but the history of mission has shown that, at least in Asia, walls hardly trembled.

THE BROWN MAN'S BURDEN

The uprising was not necessarily an anti-Christian movement, but, inasmuch as it was anti-British, missionaries as well as other Europeans became the focus of attack. Indian Christians faced the brunt both from their own countrymen because of their closeness to the missionaries, and from some of the British, who viewed everyone as Hindu irrespective of their religious affiliation. There were reported cases of Indian Christians being persecuted for their religious beliefs. Those who had the misfortune

---

96 Ibid., p. 6 col. 2. 97 Ibid., p. 5 col. 5.
98 Maurice, *The Indian Crisis*, p. 12.
99 Ibid., pp. 16–17.

to fall into the hands of the rebels were forced to renounce their faith and were ill treated or killed if they refused. Among the Christians who died in the revolt were two well-known figures of the time. One was Dhokal Parshad, the headmaster of a school of the American Presbyterian Mission, who with his wife and four children was lined up on the parade ground at Fategarh along with the Europeans. The sepoys offered him and his family a chance go free if he would first renounce Christianity. He stood firm and replied in the words of St Polycarp, 'What is my life, that I should deny my Saviour? I have never done that since the day I first believed on Him, and I never will'.[100] The whole party was then fired upon with grapeshot, and the survivors were dispatched with swords. Another instance of martyrdom was that of the wealthy Muslim convert Wilayat Ali, a catechist of the Baptist Mission in Delhi. Fatima, his wife, who survived the revolt and witnessed his torture and eventual death, recounted the ordeal thus:

They were dragging him about on the ground, beating him on the head and in the face with their shoes, some saying, 'Now preach Christ to us; now where is your Christ whom you boast?' and others asking him to forsake Christianity and repeat the *kalima*. My husband said 'No, I never will; my saviour took up the cross and went to God; I take up my life as a cross, and will follow Him to Heaven'.[101]

It is impossible to say how many Indian Christians suffered but the death toll was about twenty. Of the missionaries and chaplains and members of their families the number is given as thirty-eight.[102]

In the aftermath of the uprising, the violence unleashed by the British did not make any concessions to Indian Christians. For colonialists, the 'other' was often undifferentiated. Hence Indian Christians too were

100 Julius Richter, *A History of Missions in India*, tr. Sydney H. Moore (Edinburgh, Oliphant Anderson and Ferrier, 1908), p. 205.

101 For a full narrative of her account, see Rajaiah D. Paul, *Triumphs of His Grace* (Madras, The Christian Literature Society, 1967), pp. 224–9. For the full list of the names of the Indian Christians who were killed during the revolt, see pp. 229–30.

102 The Christian community in the middle of the nineteenth century was comparatively small. Of the 300 million Indian population of the time, there were only 492,882 Protestant native Christians, 865,643 Roman Catholics, and about 300,000 Syrian Christians. The number of Indian Christians in north-western India, to which the revolt was largely confined, were two to three thousand. Mission work had not been long established in some of these areas. For instance, the whole of northern India had only 275 vernacular day schools and 25 boarding schools, whereas Madras province had 824 vernacular day schools and 32 boarding schools. Southern India, where most Indian Christians lived, was not affected at all. For figures of the Christian population, and for the numbers of Christian missionaries, lay workers and schools, see M. A. Sherring, *The History of Protestant Missions in India from Their Commencement in 1706 to 1881* (London, The Religious Tract Society, 1884), pp. 440–7.

attacked. A notable case in point was that of Professor Yesudas Ramchadra of Delhi College. He was a mathematical genius, who embraced Christianity in 1852. His book, *The Problems of Maxima and Minima Solved by Algebra* (1850), attracted the attention of Dr Augustus De Morgan of Cambridge, who not only alerted the East India Company to the potential genius of a native but also made arrangement for his book to be published in England. One night when Ramchandra was returning from the house of a European, he was badly beaten by two English officers who forced him to make *salam*. They did not care whether he was a Christian or not. Humiliated that he was attacked by persons of the same faith, Ramchandra wrote a letter to the Governor of Delhi, which revealed the reason for his unwarranted attack: 'I made many *salams* instead of one, and cried I was a Christian, Sir, and employed in the Prize Agency and after that he [i.e. the officer] proceeded towards the Dewan Khas abusing me and saying that I was black as jet'.[103]

How many of the Indian Christians sided with the rebellion is hard to tell. H. Hipsley, a Quaker, who toured India soon after the revolt, in his proposal for the introduction of the Bible in government schools drew attention to the fact that 'not one native Christian was found to be implicated in the Mutiny of 1857, though they were not the class on which the much coveted Government patronage had been freely bestowed'.[104] There were, however, cases of native Christians throwing in their lot with the British. '*The only body of natives* in India', wrote Alexander Duff, 'who, throughout the present terrible crisis, have, *on principle and from conscience* displayed without known exception, devoted loyalty towards the British Crown, is *the body of native Christians connected with every evangelical church and communion*'.[105] Duff, in one of his letters, drew attention to the trustworthiness of the native Christians though they were few in number:

In them, participation in the transcendent benefits of a common and glorious faith has overcome the antipathies generated by foreignness of race and the humiliation of conquest, and merged all in the love and fellowship of Christian brotherhood. The reality of their good-will and affection towards us, – and to their credit it ought to be specially noted, – has, in various ways, been made manifest throughout the progress of the recent awful rebellion. No sooner did

103 See also Paul, *Triumphs of His Grace*, pp. 209–11 for the full text of his letter. Also pp. 203–7 for Ramchandra's own account of how he escaped the terrible events of 1857.
104 H. Hipsley, *The Bible in the School: A Question for India* (London, Alfred W. Bennett, n.d.), p. 17.
105 Duff, *The Indian Rebellion*, p. 181.

the intelligence reach Calcutta of the massacres at Meerut and Delhi, than the educated native Christians of all denominations met in our Institution, and drew up a truly loyal and admirable address to the Governor-General. A similar address was also forwarded from the large body of native Christians in the district of Krishnaghur; offering, at the same time, any assistance in their power with carts or bullocks, &c. The native Christians at Chota Nagpore, – a hilly district, – offered their personal services as police guards, or in any other capacity. The native Christians in the district of Burrisal, East Bengal, were ready, if called on, or accepted, to form a local military corps for the defence of that quarter.[106]

RESPONSES, REFLECTIONS

The suddenness of the uprising, the ferocity with which the violence was unleashed, and the fact that women and children were among the victims, quickly created an atmosphere of distress which bordered on hysteria in England. The pulpits reflected this mood.

These were the halcyon days of preaching. C. H. Spurgeon and Joseph Parker were among the princes of pulpit. In that pre-television age, according to a survey of the time, an average sermon lasted one hour and eighteen minutes. It was common to base theological propositions firmly on passages of the Bible, or proof-text them. A traditional sermon was about expounding biblical verses, and the principal task of the preacher was to expound these verses to congregations. In the mid-Victorian era, people universally believed that the Bible contained the word of God. Therefore, in one sense, the Bible itself was the real preacher; the role of the preacher was to bring out its riches, and, more to the point, he was expected to speak with certainty and authority. Persuasive preaching was about affirmation of assurances and not about presentation of speculative theories, which was to congest the interpretative arena later. The sermons of the Day of Humiliation stand within this tradition of assured and confident preaching.

The Old Testament as a weapon of mass destruction

The Old Testament became a veritable textual battleground in which definitions of national identity, and divine election and the stereotyping of the enemy were continually determined and clarified. The preponderance of Old Testament citations in sermons could be attributed to the

---

106 Ibid., p. 192.

numerous passages which seem to encourage state-sponsored revenge. The Old Testament was used as one extended proof-text. The torrent of rich xenophobic venom which is expressed in some passages of the Old Testament was extracted and forged as a lethal weapon to advance the vengeful agenda of the preachers. In their devotion to chapter and verse of the Hebrew testament, the preachers were undaunted by cultural, historical and political differences and distances, and they easily adapted themselves to the thought-world of the Hebrew tribes. The original context and meaning of texts was unimportant. They saw their own fate and reality reflected in the Hebrew narratives.

The over-reliance on the Old Testament by these preachers resembled that of the Puritans. The Puritans massively plundered the Old Testament in order to find validation and consolation for their cause. In the 1850s, according to Olive Anderson, the educated classes in England, under Carlyle's influence, were becoming 'rapidly enthusiastic about mid-seventeenth century puritanism'.[107] The Puritans were admired for their self-discipline and fearlessness. Like the Puritans, the Victorian preachers imagined that they too were a group led by God in the struggle against idolaters and tyrants. In the Old Testament the Victorian preachers found not only slaying of enemies enshrined and endorsed, but also incitement to such action. The theme of the Humiliation Day sermons was similar to that of the Puritans: those who opposed the British opposed God, and hence their battle was the Lord's. Divine purpose and British interests were often fused. The voice of God blended with the voice of the invader.

What these sermons overlooked was the ambivalent attitude within the Hebrew tradition towards war and the importance of preserving life. The Hebrew writers were committed to and at the same time puzzled by violence and warfare as they tried to make sense of it. Though Hebrew narratives abound with belligerent passages, there are other passages which modulate such a bellicose stance. The Hebrew writers showed concern about the ethical implications and the justness of war. There is, for example, the condemnation of Jehu's excesses (Hos. 1.4), the feeling of guilt after a war (Num. 31), God's redeeming love for the powerless, as in the case of the release of the Hebrew slaves, and, of course, a natural sympathy for the weak and the oppressed.[108] A telling illustration of the

107 Olive Anderson, 'The Growth of Christian Militarism in Mid-Victorian Britain', *The English Historical Review* 86:338 (1971), 51.

108 For a detailed study of war ideologies in the Hebrew Bible, see Susan Niditch, *War in the Hebrew Bible: A Study in the Ethics of Violence* (New York, Oxford University Press, 1995), especially pp. 134–49 for passages in the Hebrew Bible which are critical of war.

anti-war mood is the barring of David from building the temple in
Jerusalem because his career was tainted with waging great wars and
shedding much blood (1 Chr. 22.8). The Victorians absorbed the vitriolic
and vengeful language of some of the Hebrew writers, but ignored the
contrary language found in Hebrew texts, the gospels and Paul. Just as the
Puritans had jettisoned the vocabulary of mercy and forgiveness and chose
the most confrontational lexicon of the Old Testament, these pulpiteers
rejected the reconciliatory and compassionate message of the Bible and
opted for an antagonistic tone. The preachers imagined, like the Puritans
before them, that they were wrestling against adverse conditions to secure
a way of life. The sound of Joshua's trumpet suited their cause and
circumstances rather than the peaceable passages of the Bible which
extolled the virtues of the meek inheriting the earth or the turning of
the other cheek to the enemy.

What the preachers almost forgot in the heat of the moment was that
the Hebrew scriptures also spoke about the treatment of those taken as
prisoners of war. When the king of Israel asked Elisha if he should slay
them, the answer he received was: 'You shall not slay them. Would you
slay those whom you have taken captive with your sword and with your
bow? Set bread and water before them, that they may eat and drink and
go to their master' (2 Kings 6.20–3). These preachers were preoccupied
with God as the warrior, celebration of warfare, and the narratives which
celebrate the daring acts of Israelites.

Licensing extermination

Seeking recourse to an imagined elect people of God may have been an
attractive theological proposition for the Victorian clergy but it was a
frightening and doom-filled one for those who did not belong to the
chosen fold. The popularity of the notion of Britain as a new Israel, a
favoured nation with a divine destiny, helped to boost the idea that the re-
taking of India was a noble cause and a high duty which God had
bestowed upon the English, and, therefore, the brutal retaliation was an
honourable and an inescapable undertaking for the British. The crushing
of the Indian rebels was a just and necessary cause.

The most troubling aspect of Britain as the latter-day Israel was that
India became, in the imagination of the preachers, the new Canaan. The
implication was that Indians, like the Canaanites, could be destroyed
and exterminated. M. Gibbs captured the new hawkish stance: 'He gave
them possession of the land of Canaan, subduing the people who had

previously inhabited it, and to him they were responsible for the righteous administration of the trust he had confided to them'.[109] Just as the Israelites were told that it was their duty to destroy the Canaanite altars and their idolatrous worship, the duty of the British was to do the same in India. A Jewish rabbi, Mark, went to the extreme of suggesting that the crimes of the sepoys were equal to those of the Canaanites, and, anticipating Joseph Conrad's Kurtz in *The Heart of Darkness*, he told his worshippers at the Margaret Street synagogue that the Indian sepoys 'should be exterminated'.[110]

The image of a new Israel licensed the British to project themselves as true believers faithful to God, and, in the current circumstances, as innocent victims. The flip-side of this was that the Indian rebels became the impure, unfaithful oppressors of God's chosen and hence they should be punished for harming God's people. The metaphor, new Israel, has multiple meanings. What the preachers latched on to was not the image of a wandering people but of a people who were at war with their enemies.

Biblical warrants and urgency

The attitude of these preachers betrayed many of the prevailing notions about the Bible. The verbal inerrancy of the Bible was largely acknowledged. There was a cherished belief in its contents as an intimate part of religious thought and life. The preachers and their congregations had a reverence for the Bible in the great Protestant tradition. There was an unquestioning acceptance of the factuality of the biblical stories as narrated in the Bible. The Victorian Christians read the Bible with an earnestness that indicated their conviction that they were reading the very words of God. This was a time when an average churchgoer believed in Joshua's halting of the Sun, Balaam's speaking donkey and Jonah's whale. It was seen as a depository of absolute theological truth, and such an understanding gave the Bible an astonishing sense of homogeneity and contemporaneity. In a sense, the Bible became a modern book in that it provided a commentary on the current situation and therefore was useful in the present context. For preachers the Bible, was not an archaic record but a progressive document which enabled them to ground themselves in the present and shape the future. The Bible was the word of God, and it spoke to his people through contemporary events in their lives and

109 *The Times*, 8 October 1857, p. 6 col. 1.
110 Ibid., p. 8 col. 6.

history. M. Gibbs observed that though his text, Judges 1.1–5, applied especially to the children of Israel, the principles laid down there about the government of the world were valid for all time. Preaching on Exodus 12.26, C. J. D'Oyly told the congregation that these were the words of the Jewish children, but they were now being transposed to meet the present need. To those who doubted the eternal validity of God's word and subscribed to the notion that 'God does not deal with us and our generation as he did with Israelites of old', Charlton Lane swiftly added, 'St Paul clearly argues that He does'. Robert Blincoe was unequivocal about the relevance of God's word. He confidently assured his listeners that Jeremiah's words appealed to the British 'immediately' as they did to God's people of old. On one occasion, the rebels in Agra were taken by surprise when setting a trap; their plan was foiled by the sudden advance of the British column, and the Indians were caught in their own trap. Duff saw this, the Indians stewing in their own juice, as the 'literal verification of the Scripture saying, into the trap which they had so adroitly laid for others, they were made to fall helplessly themselves'.[111] He was of course referring to Psalm 57.6. Biblical texts were taken out of their historical past and endowed with a timeless meaning. The impression was that biblical verses written for the Jews were also written as an example for the British. What was happening in the Bible was truly and really happening in the present and especially to the British. The Bible was closely allied to and permeated every aspect of their life and thought. Biblical texts and allusions helped them to make sense of the situation of persecution.

The Humiliation Day sermons demonstrate two types of interpretation – literal and typological. Typology is a method of elucidating patterns of repetition, resemblances and parallels between current narratives or texts and earlier ones. It is a way of pointing out how an earlier event or narrative – the type, prefigured – is explained and verified by a later one. Typological interpretation succeeded in subordinating the Old Testament by anticipating Christ in the principal figures depicted in the Hebrew narrative. In the hands of the Victorian clergy, literal and typological methods were fused, and it was not always easy to separate them. Typological interpretation, as students of biblical interpretation know, is a legacy of the early church and not an innovation of the Victorian preachers. The early Church Fathers worked out two kinds of typology – mystical and historical. The former saw the kings of Israel as mystical

111 Duff, *The Indian Rebellion*, p. 161.

types who offered earthly models of Christ's heavenly rule, and the latter saw heavenly salvation made visible through the events of contemporary history.[112] It is the second type which was at work in these Victorian sermons. The typological interpretation permitted the preachers to apply the biblical verses to their own situation in a literal way. It was from the Old Testament that they drew most of their typological idioms. H. Hutton, choosing the Psalm 'Let the sighing of the prisoners come before thee' (69.11), saw an immediate connection between the text and the Europeans locked up in Lucknow and Agra as prisoners.[113] As the preachers expounded the biblical verses, they and the audience became Job, Ezra, David, Isaiah, and often collectively identified with the oppressed Jews. Their typological identification not only equipped them with a superior identity, and enhanced their status as righteous people, but also authorized them to frame their opponents, the Indian rebels, as murderers and harassers of God's prophets, nay God's own people. The preachers used the Bible to define and map their own world and to categorize the people of their time, good and evil, and then extracted specific biblical verses that celebrated or censured the behaviour and actions of those people. What it implied was that the British were good and the Indians bad because the Bible told them so. This kind of polarizing licensed them to fix in advance who were victims and who were victors, friends and foes, God's chosen and God's enemies. The literal-typological reading permitted them to maintain their identity and advance their political and theological agenda.

The hermeneutical approach of the Victorian preachers works in two phases. The preachers used biblical verses mostly in atomized form to appraise the events in India and depict them as similar to those experienced by the Israelites, as recounted in the Bible, and then draw out hermeneutical implications. The sermons were not simply dishing out direct injunctions from the Bible. The preachers were sophisticated in their homiletic practice. They appropriated the biblical chronicle and reframed the events happening in India to shape their audience's knowledge of these as world events. Once it was established that the world of the Bible was their world, and that the Bible referred to the events in India, the interpretation no longer depended on the literary and narrative context of the Bible. The application of biblical verses to contemporary

112 Henning Graf Reventlow, *The Authority of the Bible and the Rise of the Modern World*, tr. John Bowden (London, SCM Press, 1984), p. 140.
113 *The Times*, 8 October 1857, p. 6 col. 5.

events reinforced the idea that God's word recorded in the Bible could address with equal eloquence the present, as it had done the past. For their hermeneutical purposes, the historical and literary milieux in the Bible from which these verses emanated was secondary. The sermons suggested that time was irrelevant. They adopted a kind of transtemporal literalism which was not confined to a specific time. What occurred in the Bible had re-occurred for the benefit of nineteenth-century Christians. What was happening in India had already been prognosticated in the Bible. This kind of hermeneutics might have led the listeners to believe that the biblical writers knew the events of all times, and such a notion could enhance the reputation of the Bible as a faithful register of God's oracles. The preachers and their congregations were able to appropriate the verses literally, personally and contemporaneously. Their usage of biblical texts shows a remarkable ability to move between public and private, corporate and individual, formulaic and more spontaneous aspects of life. Biblical texts shaped, supported and validated their homiletic cause.

The appropriation of the Bible by these Victorian preachers was traditional and pre-critical. For them the theological aspect of the Bible was paramount rather than any historical investigation or critical study of it. This was the era in which apparent contradictions and moral predicaments in the Bible could be resolved by means of allegorical or mystical readings. Such readings helped to reinforce the notion that literal inspiration was a convenient and useful instrument which went a long way to mask the historical and ethical messiness of the Bible. After the middle of the nineteenth century, however, such an interpretative fudge was no longer possible.

These sermons were preached at a relatively serene time for the Victorian church. This was just before the hermeneutical grenades lobbed by the continental biblical scholars were to blast the quiet world of Victorian Christianity. Biblical critics were about to subject the Bible to an unprecedented historical inquiry never subsequently surpassed in its impact. Their investigation was to unsettle the cosy theological world of the Victorians by exposing the alleged purity and inerrancy of the Bible. The Bible was to become, in the hands of professional critics, a human document containing personal, historical, courtly and tribal narratives, and literary forms ranging from poetry to philosophy to myths. Three years after the sermons were preached, Victorian Christianity was to face interpretative 'mutiny' in the form of *Essays and Reviews*, which, among other things, claimed that the Bible could be treated like any other book.

German scholars, or as one of Congregationalist preachers of the time put it, 'men who cut up the Bible with German scissors',[114] who were responsible for causing turbulent religious unrest in Victorian England, were yet to make their mark. Higher Criticism, or what Spurgeon called 'the German poison',[115] soured the tranquil world of English discourse only in the late nineteenth century, and its energizing or enerverating impact was far-reaching only after 1890.[116] Mary Evans's (the future George Eliot's) translation of David Friedrich Strauss's *The Life of Jesus Critically Examined*, the founding text of biblical criticism, was available in English in 1846. Ironically, Strauss, whose views generated such an anguish among Victorian readers, continued to believe in the timeless quality of the Bible and its spiritual and ethical significance. True, there were a few exceptional incidents of critical engagement with the Bible in England, especially among the free churches. Samuel Davidson, the Congregationalist turned Presbyterian, was accused of abandoning the Mosaic authorship of the Pentateuch. The Anglican contact with German biblical scholarship, according to Glover, was 'rare in the early nineteenth century',[117] and 'the first important espousal of higher criticism by the Anglican Broad Church was in *Essays and Reviews* in 1860'.[118] The Colenso controversy, which I will consider in next chapter, was soon to follow. But they were on the whole untypical for mid-Victorian times. In the midst of modern discoveries and speculations, Maurice was certain where he stood: 'The Bible should be treated, not as a book which stands aloof, frowning upon all these inquiries, but as the *key* to the meaning of them'.[119] For him the Bible was the 'armour' with which to 'fight the hottest battles'.[120] Even as late as 1880 Albert Cave, in his unfavourable review of Robertson Smith's criticism of the Pentateuch, could claim that 99 per cent of biblical scholars in Britain were in favour of the trust-worthiness of Mosaic authorship, an indication of how churches could close ranks and band together, and reassert traditional notions about the Bible, and unfaltering loyalty to it.[121]

---

114 Willis B. Glover, *Evangelical Nonconformists and Higher Criticism in the Nineteenth Century* (London, Independent Press Ltd, 1954), p. 40.
115 Ibid.
116 Ibid., p. 36.
117 Ibid., p. 42.
118 Ibid., p. 44.
119 Maurice, *The Indian Crisis*, p. 35.
120 Ibid.
121 Glover, *Evangelical Nonconformists and Higher Criticism*, p. 36.

What I set out to examine here was the sort of sermons that were preached before the 'higher criticism' began to question the historicity and status of the Bible. The sermons painted a picture of a pre-critical innocence and an uncomplicated world of biblical authority.

Menace and mimicry

Let me bring this chapter to a close with a couple of remarks. The Indian rebellion provided the justification for imperial rule and for bringing India fully into the empire. The colonial discourse which emanated from the popular press and in parliament construed an image of the colonized as depraved and needing improvement and instruction, thus legitimizing conquest. The British crown took over from the East India Company. In Said's words, 'Europeans should rule, and non-Europeans be ruled. And Europeans *did* rule'.[122]

The rebellion began with a religious grievance, and religion continued to be contested even after the end of the revolt. From 1858 India came under the government of Queen Victoria. The Queen signed an Act on 2 August 1858 to assume responsibility for India, the proclamation being made on 1 November 1858. The Queen's proclamation made one allowance, namely no further interference in indigenous religions, perhaps a tacit acknowledgement of one of the principal causes of the revolt. In spite of the evangelicals' repeated demands for a firm commitment on the part of the British government to a policy of promotion of Christianity and requirement of Bible teaching in schools and colleges, the Queen's proclamation did not go far enough for them. It acknowledged the pre-eminence of Christian belief, but clearly distanced itself from any idea of enforcing that faith on her subjects who had qualms about it The famous sentence ran:

Firmly relying ourselves on the truth of Christianity, and acknowledging with gratitude the solace of religion, we disclaim alike the right and the desire to impose our convictions on any of our subjects. We declare it to be our royal will and pleasure that none be in any way favoured, none molested or disquieted, by reason of their religious faith or observances, but that all shall alike enjoy the equal and impartial protection of the law; and we do strictly charge and enjoin all those who may be in authority under us that they abstain from all interference with the religious belief or worship of any of our subjects on pain of our highest displeasure.[123]

122 Edward W. Said, *Culture and Imperialism* (London, Chatto & Windus, 1993), p. 120.
123 See Vincent A. Smith, *The Oxford History of India: From the Earliest Times to the End of 1911*, second edition (Oxford, Clarendon Press, 1923), pp. 728–9. Smith also has the full text of the proclamation.

The Begum of Hazrat Mahal of Oudh, one of the rebels, who refused the offer of a pardon and a pension and escaped to Nepal, issued her own counter-proclamation in answer to Queen Victoria's. Her riposte to Queen Victoria's position on religion is worth repeating:

In the proclamation it is written that the Christian religion is true, but no other religion will suffer oppression, and that the Laws will be observed towards all. What has the administration of Justice to do with the truth, or falsehood of a religion? That religion is true which acknowledges one God and knows no other; when there are three Gods in a religion, neither Muslims nor Hindus, nay not even Jews, Sun-worshippers, or fire-worshippers can believe it to be true. To eat pigs, and drink wine, to bite greased cartridges, and to mix pigs' fat with flour and sweetmeats, to destroy Hindu and Muslims temples on pretence of making roads, to build Churches, to send clergymen into the streets and alleys to preach the Christian religion, to institute English schools, and pay people a monthly stipend for learning the English services, while the places of worship for Hindus and Muslims are to this day entirely neglected; with all this, how can the people believe that religion will not be interfered with? The rebellion began with religion, and for it millions of men have been killed. Let not our subjects be deceived: thousands were deprived of their religion in the North West, and thousands were hanged rather than abandon their religion.[124]

It is appropriate that the last word should go to Hazart Mahal. Her counter-proclamation was a case of a colonial stereotype going against the scripted role. Hazart Mahal mimics Victoria's proclamation, but disrupts its authority by asking the perennial question with which interpreters have been wrestling: who has the power to interpret and decide on matters of religion? She appropriates the colonial document and turns it against the authority it came from. Instead of acquiescing, the colonized disconcerts the colonizer by demonstrating knowledge and power. Or, as Bhabha would have put it: 'mimicry is at once resemblance and menace'.[125]

124 For the full text of Hazart Mahal's counter-proclamation, see Edwardes, *Red Year*, pp. 171–3.
125 Homi K. Bhabha, *The Location of Culture* (London, Routledge, 1994), p. 86.

CHAPTER 3

Thorns in the crown: the subversive and complicit hermeneutics of John Colenso of Natal and James Long of Bengal

The path of the critical Interpreter of Scripture is almost always a thorny one in England.

Benjamin Jowett

It is the battle between sacred books and the direct eternal guidance of the Living God.

George W. Cox

This chapter is a follow-up to a promise I made in one of my earlier writings.[1] While looking at the interpretative outputs of dissident Protestant missionaries like John Colenso, who proved to be awkward to the establishment but endeared himself to the colonized by taking up their grievances, I came across James Long (1814–87), in whose works I noted remarkable parallels with Colenso.[2] To begin with, both sided with the oppressed – the Bengali indigo workers in the case of Long, and the Zulus in the case of Colenso. More remarkably, what was attractive to me was the way both of these Anglican missionaries marshalled and utilized the Bible for their Christian praxis. This chapter narrates and critiques their hermeneutical practices, and their often problematic entanglements with the colonial politics of the time.

At the outset, it should be said that in sheer volume of biblical work undertaken by these two missionary apostles Long is no match for Colenso. Colenso's output is enormous; his seven volumes on the Pentateuch run to more than five thousand pages, and the first volume went through several editions. Even more significantly, his work prompted a

---

1 See my *The Bible and the Third World: Precolonial, Colonial and Postcolonial Encounters* (Cambridge, Cambridge University Press, 2001), p. 111.
2 I owe a great debt to Geoffrey Oddie. It was in his writing that I first came across Long's hermeneutical practices. Since Oddie's interests and expertise lie elsewhere, he did not dwell much on Long's use of the Bible. See Geoffrey Oddie, *Missionaries, Rebellion and Proto-Nationalism: James Long of Bengal 1814–87* (Richmond, Curzon Press, 1999), especially pp. 44–5 and 70–1. Some of the quotations I have used here I located through his writings, though my use of them is different from his.

vigorous public debate. In today's world of academic star-rating, Long would have fared badly in the Research Assessment Exercise.[3] His writings would have been seen as theologically thin and inadequately footnoted; far worse, some of his hermeneutical ideas were expressed in non-academic media such as annual letters and reports to his parent body – the Church Missionary Society – and public addresses. In order to create some semblance of a level playing-field between Long and Colenso, I will look at one of the latter's little-studied works, the four volumes of Natal Sermons. These sermons were preached to settlers and not to the Zulus. The congregation consisted, as A. P Stanley, the Dean of Westminster, put it, of 'infidels, men who never entered a church before, working men in their shirt-sleeves'.[4] They were, nevertheless, no more than a variant on the educated public for whom he wrote his commentaries, and, indeed, he addressed them as if they were a congregation in a London church. The sermons were at times very heavy-going, with lengthy quotations from the writings of the early Church Fathers, Victorian scientists, continental theologians and English bishops. Colenso himself referred to these sermons as a continuation of his pentateuchal work. 'In four volumes of "Natal Sermons"', he wrote,

I have done my best to show that the central truths of Christianity – *the Fatherhood of God,* the *Brotherhood of Man,* and the *Revelation of God in Man –* are unaffected by these results of scientific inquiry, or rather are confirmed by the witness which the Pentateuch, when stripped of its fictitious character, gives of the working of the Divine Spirit in all ages.[5]

ENGLISH LITERATES AND BENGALI PEASANTS

Colenso and Long were engaged with two different constituencies. In his work on the Pentateuch and his Natal sermons Colenso was addressing the newly emerging educated middle-class in England and their South

---

3 For those who are outside the British academic world, the Research Assessment Exercise is a periodic evaluation of the research outputs of academics, akin to Michelin's *Good Food Guide.* Each department (like restaurants in the *Guide*) is given a rating on the basis of 'academic excellence'.
4 See Arthur Penrhyn Stanley, 'Postscript to a Speech delivered in the lower house of the convocation of the province of Canterbury, June 29, 1866': reprinted in John William Colenso, *Natal Sermons: Second Series of Discourses Preached in the Cathedral Church of St Peter's, Maritzburg* (London, N. Trübner & Co., 1868), p. 159. The remark of the Dean was not aimed at ridiculing the type of congregation to which Colenso was preaching but at showing the common appeal of his sermons, and the Dean went on: 'how welcome would be the sight in our cathedrals of even twenty artisans in their working dress!' p. 159.
5 John William Colenso, *The Pentateuch and Book of Joshua Critically Examined, Part* VI (London, Longmans, Green & Co., 1871), p. xv.

African counterparts, who were troubled and unsettled by the new scientific knowledge which was questioning the old beliefs. Long was focussing on rural Bengali peasants, who were at the receiving end of the European colonialism which was threatening to engulf their lives, customs and manners.

Colenso's aim was to appeal to educated people. For him, in 'an educated age' like his, 'an intelligent reader of the Bible' should know certain facts. What we call 'Canonical' scriptures had 'been brought together without any certain knowledge, in many cases, as to the author, or authors, by whom they were written'.[6] The attributions in the English Bible were not a sufficient reason for believing that the author ascribed to each biblical book was its the actual author. Colenso's contention was that it was erroneous to ascribe authorship of the first five books of the Bible to Moses, or to assume that 1 and 2 Samuel were written by Samuel, Job by Job, Esther by Esther, Matthew by Matthew, or the Pastoral Epistles and Hebrews by Paul. Colenso held the view that people should be 'taught to inquire, and read, and think for ourselves, as reasoning men, and not submit ourselves blindly to the yoke of authority'.[7] His target audience was the clergy of all denominations and the educated laity. He wanted them to be acquainted with the results of modern criticism, which was making inroads into English Christianity, so as to be able to 'reply to the questionings of some, to relieve the doubts and quiet the distrust of others, and to take part, in the pulpit and in the school-room, in laying the foundations of a truer knowledge, and therefore also a more just appreciation of the Scriptures'.[8] It was for this constituency that Colenso was trying to 'provide a commentary "in which the latest information might be made accessible to men of ordinary culture" and in which "every educated man might find an explanation of any difficulties which his own mind might suggest, as well as of any new objections raised against a particular book or passage"'.[9] With a view to educating, attracting, and influencing the thinking of educated people, Colenso went on to produce a series of lectures providing 'in a compact and readable form, the main facts elicited by that Criticism, unencumbered with Hebrew quotations and the mass of minute investigation'. He hoped that such a venture 'may

6 John William Colenso, *Natal Sermons: A Series of Discourses Preached in the Cathedral Church of St Peter's, Maritzburg* (London, N. Trübner & Co., 1866), p. 26.

7 Ibid.

8 John William Colenso, *The Pentateuch and Book of Joshua Critically Examined*, Part VII (London, Longmans, Green and Co., 1879), p. xx.

9 Ibid., p. xiv.

be found useful especially to Teachers in Day-Schools and Sunday-Schools, as well as to Parents among the more educated laity, who desire to impart to their children an intelligent knowledge of the real nature of these ancient books, which have filled all along, and still fill, so prominent a part in the religious education of the race'.[10]

Long's hermeneutical activities, on the other hand, were aimed at a very different public. He wanted to open 'the portals of divine truth to the masses'.[11] His audiences were the Bengali peasants who could not read even their own literature. In one of his annual letters, Long wrote to his missionary society: 'I have lots of scriptures lying by me in the house undistributed because I find in the villages I go to and those near to Calcutta a few of the people can read with intelligence, not 5 percent of the population can read their own books'.[12] His target audience were 'the Bengali boys and girls, peasant children who had been consigned by Brahminical pride and Muslim arrogance to the dungeons of ignorance and degradation'.[13] Long's aim was to democratize knowledge which had hitherto been the monopoly of higher classes who thought it was as 'useless to teach the common people to read as a cow to dance'.[14] Unlike Colenso, his method was not one of ruthless application of critical tools, but the employment of sapiential sayings which in his view were common to both biblical and Indian traditions. Long wanted to 'help Christian teachers, village preachers in the East to bring Christian truth before the minds of the common people in the Oriental mode by emblems, proverbs, thus engaging the attention, impressing the memory, strewing the path to abstract dogma with flowers'.[15] He was actively engaged with the masses and their modes of communication, rethinking how to disseminate Christian truths in ways easily accessible to ordinary people.

THE CHRISTIAN BIBLE AS BOTH FALLIBLE AND NUMINOUS

The Bible, for the Colenso of the Natal Sermons, was a fallible book written by 'frail and fallible men, compassed with infirmity and ignorance, men like unto ourselves'. For him, this 'is the very thing which helps

---

10 John William Colenso, *Lectures on the Pentateuch and the Moabite Stone* (London, Longmans, Green & Co., 1873), p. vii.

11 James Long, *How I Taught the Bible to Bengal Peasant Boys* (London, Christian Vernacular Education Society for India, 1875), p. 4.

12 Church Missionary Society (CMS). C11/0185/140 Annual letter 1856.

13 Long, *How I Taught the Bible to Bengal Peasant Boys*, p. 1.

14 Ibid.   15 Ibid., p. 4.

to strengthen and comfort us, when we see that it is One and the same Good Spirit, that was teaching them three thousand years ago, Who is teaching us now'.[16] The Bible, with its all imperfections, contradictions and inconsistences, and with all our ignorance of its history, and in spite of the work of modern criticism, still 'remains the Book of the pious heart, the Book of Books, which the overruling Providence of God has "caused to be written for our learning"'. There is 'no other Book which contains such variety of mental and spiritual food, for the necessities of living, labouring, suffering, and dying men'.[17] In the language of St Paul, Colenso remarked that 'whatever things were written aforetime were *written for our learning*'.[18]

For Colenso, however, salvation did not depend on believing the written word, nor was God's word confined to the Christian scriptures. The revelation of God's living word was available, as he was fond of repeating 'both in the Bible and out of the Bible'. For him, the essential thing was not faith in a written document. One 'may be very conversant with texts and creeds, yet may have but little real acquaintance with the truths themselves'.[19] The truth for Colenso was realized in enacting the will of the Father:

We know that our salvation cannot possibly consist in implicitly believing the historical certainty of this or that miraculous narrative, or in the unquestioning reception of this or that particular dogma, – but in a 'faith that worketh in us by love' to God and to our fellow men, – in 'doing the Will of the our Father in Heaven', – in listening to the Living Word, which speaks with us in God's name continually, in the Bible and out of the Bible, in the teaching of our Lord and his apostles, or in the secrets of our hearts, and in the daily intercourse of life.[20]

For Colenso, it was

not absolutely necessary, in order to have a living hope, that we should have this source of consolation, which we find in the Written Word; for we may gather it, as we have just heard, by 'patience', by 'patient continuance in well-doing' according to the Will of God – according to that which we know of His will, in our different circumstances. There were multitudes who lived the life of God on earth before there was a Bible: there are multitudes now, who, I doubt not, walk with God, even in heathen lands, though they have no Bible.[21]

16 Colenso, *Natal Sermons, Series* I, p. 65.
17 Ibid., p. 62.
18 Ibid., p. 61.
19 John William Colenso, *Natal Sermons, Series* IV (n.p., n.d.), p. 3.
20 Colenso, *Natal Sermons, Series* I, p. 197.
21 Ibid., p. 68.

God has spoken not only to the Hebrew race but to 'every nation under heaven – giving each nation its special gifts and its special work, for carrying out of the great scheme of His Providence'.[22] Colenso cited the example of the Galla of north-east Africa and the people of India, who had their own knowledge of the divine which 'shall not disappoint them, shall not "make them ashamed" in the day when the judgement of God shall be manifested'.[23]

What sustains people is the living word, 'the word which proceedeth from the mouth of God: Blessed are they which do hunger and thirst after righteousness; for they shall be filled! Blessed are the merciful; for they shall obtain mercy! Blessed are the pure in heart; for they shall see God! Blessed are the peacemakers; for they shall be called children of God'. These are, as far as Colenso was concerned, eternal words which 'shall never pass away'.[24] For Colenso, 'God is infinitely more glorified by justice and mercy and charity towards others, by the love of truth and purity of heart in ourselves, than by all the gorgeous worship, the multiplied prayers and praises, the temples and offerings . . . the rites and ceremonies, the vestments and decorations'.[25]

The Bible, for Colenso, was not a code of law which could be applied to all circumstances. For him, it was essentially a context-specific book produced by 'men who lived in the ages long ago, and in circumstances very different from ours'.[26] Contemporary situations were far too different from and more complicated than those of biblical times for any sort of direct and easy drawing of parallels. For him, the important task of hermeneutics was to appeal to the spirit of the Bible and the principles which govern its teaching rather than to the letter of the text. This was applicable to the words of Jesus as well:

His words are human words, and therefore subject to the limitations of our humanity – to the imperfections, to which all human utterances are liable, when used to express Eternal Truths. And, as his direct teaching was confined to the Jews, they were necessarily also cast, as it were, in Jewish moulds, and took the forms of the race and of the age in which he lived. It is the 'spirit' of His Teaching – the Light which shone in it – the Living Word that breathed in it – that shall not 'pass away'.[27]

22 Colenso, *Natal Sermons, Series* IV, p. 39.
23 Colenso, *Natal Sermons, Series* I, p. 69.
24 Ibid., pp. 28–9.
25 Colenso, *Natal Sermons, Series* II, p. 34.
26 Ibid., p. 63.
27 Colenso, *Natal Sermons, Series* IV, p. 179.

For Colenso, exegesis is not simply transplanting uncritically the ancient texts to the present but translating the essence of the word. In one of
his sermons Colenso told his congregation that 'the great work of the
Christian Teacher today is to translate the language of the devout men of
former ages into that of our own'.[28] In another sermon he reiterated the
same point: 'The words of the text require only to be translated into the
language and thoughts of our time, to convey to our minds a solemn
lesson of Eternal Truth'.[29] The basic tenets of Christianity – the Fatherhood of God, the Brotherhood of Man, and the revelation of God in man
– were not static 'through all the ages' but were 'becoming brighter and
brighter, more complete, more perfect'.[30] In other words, the word of
God was evolving and contextual.

Colenso was rejecting precedent and tradition in the light of modern
experience. He read the scriptures in a way that was predetermined by his
hermeneutical understanding: the experience of the fatherhood of God,
the brotherhood of man and the revelation of God in man, and how these
marks were evident in the world. The central criterion was to conform to
the 'perfect will of God, that desire to please the Heavenly Father and
surrender one's own will to God's will' which is 'manifested on all
occasions'.[31] He was working with a hermeneutic which was based not
on the literalness of the text but on an understanding of a gracious God
transforming lives in the present. The appeal to precedent and tradition
might have to be jettisoned in favour of the recognition that the same
Spirit which was at work in the earlier times is also at work currently. The
Bible was not be read as a book of rules and prescriptions that would
obscure the continuing revelatory power of God. It was a gateway to
God's new revelatory possibilities. For Colenso, revelation was an ongoing phenomenon: 'One and the same Good Spirit, that was teaching
them three thousand years ago, . . . is teaching us now'.[32] What is patently
clear in Colenso's hermeneutic is that the Bible is not a convenient
recourse in times of trouble and trial. It does not provide the 'certainty'
one is looking for at such times: 'We wish for "certainty". We want to
have either an infallible Bible or an infallible Church, – something to
which we may have recourse in our perplexities, – some infallible external
guide'.[33] God does not 'supply us with an infallible external authority,

---

28 Colenso, *Natal Sermons, Series* I, p. 39.
29 Colenso, *Natal Sermons, Series* II, p. 13.
30 Colenso, *Natal Sermons, Series* IV, p. 221.
31 Colenso, *Natal Sermons, Series* I, p. 315.
32 Ibid., p. 65.   33 Ibid., p. 67.

which shall supersede the necessity of our listening to that Living Word'.[34] What the Bible does provide us with is the assurance and comfort that the grace of God which was manifested in earlier times will also be manifest in our time. In a sermon with the title 'The Comfort of the Scriptures', Colenso told the congregation:

When we read the sacred records, these writings of the men of other days, – when we see how they have lived and died, have wrought and prayed, have stood up manfully and struggled with the power of evil within and without, have risen and fallen, and risen again . . . we may well have 'hope', with such experience of other men, in the ages long ago, confirming our own, assuring us that we are 'all of One', that the Living Word, the Eternal Son of God, was dwelling in them as He dwells now in us, 'Christ in us is the Hope of Glory'.[35]

Colenso was trying to impress upon his listeners that the ancient sacred record was a sufficient proof that God, who had guided his people under different circumstances, would also guide them now. Every generation was 'being trained to exercise this awful, yet glorious, responsibility',[36] namely to interpret afresh. Modern times needed new interpretations. No one generation could impose its understanding of God's word on another. Just as the Spirit guided the ancient people, so the same Spirit would guide modern people as well.

Colenso's aim was to eliminate the superstitious reverence accorded to the Bible, which he saw as a negative 'growth of the Reformation'. 'That slavish subjection to the mere letter of Scripture, which forbids us almost to investigate its history and origin, or even its true grammatical meaning, and often leads men to acts and principles of conduct in direct opposition to the spirit of it'. There are so many 'who make the Bible their idol, reject often in blind zeal the very essence of Christianity, and violate the whole spirit of Christ's teaching, while they profess to honour the Written Word, and reverence the Name and Person of Christ'.[37] Words, for Colenso, though a 'chief medium for imparting true knowledge, are but an imperfect means of conveying it'.[38] For him, the critical hermeneutical moment was the moment when the Spirit which acted in the past acts again in the present to make humanity the children of God rather than conforming to the old creeds:

As we, with the Bible in our hands, look back along the course of ages, and trace from the first lines of Genesis to the last of Revelation, through a thousand years

---

34 Ibid., p. 68.   35 Ibid., p. 69.   36 Ibid., p. 68.
37 John William Colenso, *Natal Sermons, Series* III (n.p., n.d.), p. 227.
38 Colenso, *Natal Sermons, Series* IV, p. 3.

of the world's history, the signs of a Divine Teacher, quickening, instructing, enlightening, the hearts of men, – as for two thousand years since then we have the evidence before us, in innumerable writings of our fellow men, that one and the selfsame Spirit has been all along and every where guiding true hearts, not indeed to a conformity of creed, but to a conformity of practice, becoming those who are children of God.[39]

Colenso's aim was to release both ecclesiastical authorities and ordinary people from what he called the 'thraldom of mere bibliolatry'.[40]

Unlike Colenso, who perceived the Bible as a fallible document containing fallible accounts of human lives, Long viewed the Bible as a numinous text full of poetic beauty and divine truth. He, too, like Colenso, was involved in searching the scriptures. But unlike Colenso, who was searching its pages with the toothcomb of modern criticism, Long was looking for sapiential nuggets embedded within them. Long's search, unlike Colenso's, which combined mathematical ruthlessness with moral urgency, was a gentle one, undertaken with the purpose of finding some reward at the end of the pursuit, as a 'miner searches for gold, or as people examine a will immediately after the death of the testator'.[41] Long employed a number of figurative terms to describe the Bible. The Bible as '*milk* to nourish the feeble minded, as *fire* to consume or enliven and as *gold* for its value and use, a seed on account of its hidden qualities, its power of spreading from a small beginning'.[42] On another occasion he described it as 'a *letter* from the father of mercies to his children at school, a *banquet* where all are invited, a *prism* which only glistens when in the light, a *portrait* of an absent friend, a *storehouse* of spiritual weapons, a *telescope* revealing the glories of the upper world', or, as in David's comparison, as 'silver tried in a furnace of earth seven times refined'.[43] It is seen as a road-map which shows the path to heaven, with Jesus acting as the 'pilot'. Such major doctrines as the 'Trinity and God's foreknowledge' were, in Long's view, 'strong meat which babes cannot digest'.[44] The image of the Bible as milk and the Bengalis as babies reinforces the colonial notion of the colonized as children in need of parental feeding which only the colonizer and Christianity could provide. Despite the New Testament provenance for the metaphor, Long's use of it inevitably in the

39 Colenso, *Natal Sermons, Series* III, pp. 278–9.
40 Colenso, *Natal Sermons, Series* I, p. 18.
41 James Long, *Scripture Truth in Oriental Dress, or Emblems Explanatory of Biblical Doctrines and Morals, with Parallel or Illustrative References to Proverbs and Proverbial Sayings in the Arabic, Bengali, Canarese, Persian, Russian, Sanskrit, Tamul, Telegu and Urdu Languages* (Calcutta, Thacker, Spink and Co., 1871), p. 147.
42 Ibid., p. 46.   43 Ibid., p. 193.   44 Ibid., p. 12.

context evoked the notion that they were helpless and unfit to think for themselves.

The Bible was significant for Long's work for two reasons: it contained proverbial sayings; and the customs and manners described in the biblical books were akin to those practised in India. He found both of these aspects useful when communicating the gospel message to Bengali peasants. His hermeneutical aim was to reposition the Bible, which had come to India with the British as a western book, as an eastern one: 'But the great point is – the charter of our salvation, the Bible, is an *oriental* book, thoroughly eastern, cast in a mould that no Saxon could have shaped'.[45] For Long, the Bible was

thoroughly oriental. So much so that I find numbers of passages easily intelligible to Bengali villagers which are to Calcutta Europeans an inextricable puzzle. In these days of a fierce and rampant Anglo-Saxonism, it is pleasing to find that the Bible, the book which has met with the widest circulation over any other book, is cast thoroughly in an oriental mould.[46]

For the missionary, it was a book which 'teems with similes, metaphor, and parables, but these mighty weapons lie resting in his armoury'.[47] Without the emblems and familiar illustrations, the Bible would have been a 'sealed book to the masses'. The Bible was imbued with an oriental spirit as this is 'exemplified in the lyrical odes of the Psalms, the proverbial writings of Solomon, the drama of Job, and Solomon's song; while of our Lord it is said that without a parable or simile spake He not to the people; he represented moral and spiritual truths by imagery drawn from nature, the relations of society, and the common occupations of men'.[48] Long did not view the Song of Solomon as a mere love song but as a disclosure of the soul of the devout and in the same league as those devotional writings of the East which treat the highest mysteries of religion in the same mystic and impassioned style.

Regarding Long's second reason, namely that, the Bible was significant because it referred to customs with which an Indian could easily identify, he said that these customs 'come home to the peasant's son in India with a force that a peer's son in England cannot realize'.[49] Examples of these

---

45 James, Long *Bible Teaching and Preaching for the Million by Emblems and Proverbs* (n.p., 1874), p. 1.

46 James Long, 'Address by the Rev. James Long at the Anniversary Meeting of the Family Literary' Club, in *The Second Anniversary Report of the Family Literary Club* (Calcutta, Sundaburson Press, 1859), p. 13.

47 Long, *How I Taught the Bible to Bengal Peasant Boys*, p. 1.

48 Long, *Scripture Truth in Oriental Dress*, p. iv.

49 Long, *How I Taught the Bible to Bengal Peasant Boys*, p. 4.

were: Moses, taking off his shoes on holy ground (Exod. 3.5); carrying one's bed; watering the seed with the foot in the paddy field; living under a palm tree as Deborah did; ceremonial raising up of idols; walking on the house roof as David did; women sewing pillows to arm-holes (Ezek. 13.18); Christ's coat without a seam; and keeping a perpetual fire burning on an altar (Lev. 6.13) – all were familiar to Indians. Long saw parallels between Indian and biblical wedding patterns. As in the Indian custom, a wife for Jacob was selected through an intermediate agent (Gen. 24.4). The elder daughter being given in marriage before the younger one is illustrated in Laban's refusal to marry his younger daughter to Jacob before his elder daughter is married (Gen. 29.26). Long's purpose in identifying oriental customs and manners in the Bible was to make an unfamiliar book familiar to Indians and, more importantly, to assure Bengali peasants that biblical religion was not alien: 'The orientalism of the Bible seemed to impress the natives with the idea of Christianity not being a merely English religion, and helped the young to realize to a great extent the value of the Bible'.[50]

MODERN CRITICISM AS THE PEOPLE'S TOOL

Colenso was one of the early users of modern criticism, which was having a slow but devastating impact on the English theological landscape. For him, the object of higher criticism was more than determining the historical validity of a particular narrative or ascertaining the exact meaning of a particular Hebrew or Greek term. The whole exercise for Colenso was deeply concerned with bringing relief to ordinary people who were affected by what he perceived as the Church's misreading of certain biblical passages. Critical investigation into the Bible was not merely a theoretical or a rational exercise, or a pursuit of the latest fashionable theory. For Colenso, the employment of critical tools was a utilitarian one, aimed at questioning the divine sanction which had been claimed in the course of history for various social evils – slavery, capital punishment, burning of witches, killing of heretics, marriages of affinity (those within prohibited relationships). Colenso's view was that once those biblical passages that had been utilized to justify contemporary evils were subjected to modern criticism, and when modern criticism had done its work, these malignant practices would 'in future be treated purely on their own merits as civil and social questions, without appealing to

50 Ibid.

supposed religious sanctions of the most stringent kind, which are now shown to be no authority whatever'.[51] For Colenso, these findings should be made known to the people because no good can come in the end of 'speaking lies in the Name of the Lord'.[52] Modern critical method was a liberative tool aimed at bringing succour to people who were shackled under ecclesiastical interpretations.

One of the ecclesiastical rules which came under heavy hermeneutical bombardment from Colenso was the severe regulation of Sunday observance, which restricted the freedom and enjoyment of the poor on Sundays. He delivered four sermons on this subject. These strict Sabbath regulations, in Colenso's view, were stacked against the interests of the poor. Under the guise of promoting Sabbath observance, these rules effectively deprived the poor of their 'rightful liberty'.[53] In one of his sermons Colenso referred to acts passed by Scottish Church authorities that strictly confined men, women and children to their houses except for attending churches: 'No street-lamps were allowed to be lighted on the darkest Sunday nights, because it was held that nobody had any right to be out of doors at such hours. The Assembly forbade any person taking a walk on the Sabbath, or looking out of a window, and therefore all the blinds were pulled down'.[54] He also listed English cases where ordinary citizens were denied the enjoyment of simple pleasures on a Sunday. The British Museum, the 'people's own property' was closed to them. Zoological gardens were closed to the lower classes but open to people who could 'afford to pay'. Hyde Park and the nearby Gardens were denied to the poorer section of the metropolis, but the 'rich and their splendid equipages', who had all the days of the week to visit them, were freely allowed. 'The glorious harmonies of Handel, Haydn, Mozart, or Beethoven' were not to be heard by the poor in the open air. He castigated bishops, the very same ones who challenged his theological position, who wrote to the directors of English Railway Companies urging them to cancel the cheap excursion trains on Sundays, thus barring the poor workers, their wives and children from escaping the crowded cities on Sundays and enjoying the 'blessings of the country, brought now within their reach by God's good gift of railways, where they might feel the soothing influences of Nature'.[55]

---

51 Colenso, *Lectures on the Pentateuch and the Moabite Stone*, p. 372.
52 Ibid., p. 18.
53 Colenso, *Natal Sermons*, Series 1, p. 226.
54 Ibid., p. 230.   55 Ibid., pp. 224–5.

His method was to 'cut away altogether' the grounds on which these rigid rules were based and which stripped away the diversion, recreation and enjoyment that the poor were hoping for after six days of rigorous and routine work. Armed with the latest ammunition, modern critical tools, Colenso was able to (a) demonstrate historically and exegetically that the fourth commandment as recorded in Exodus and Deuteronomy was untrustworthy, and that the books contained contradictory material; (b) expose the false morality of some of the regulations; and (c) point out the lack of apostolic warrant for such observances.

Colenso began where his considerable strengths lay, by pointing out that the biblical narratives on which Sabbath observance was based would not stand historical scrutiny. For him the fourth commandment, and for that matter all the ten commandments, were based upon an 'unreal imaginary foundation'.[56] He first debunked their Mosaic origin and their 'supposed Mosaic basis'. He told his congregation that the 'Ten Commandments in the present form, even as they stand in Exodus, were no part of the original narrative, but are a later insertion most probably . . . by the hand of Deuteronomist'.[57] He went on to establish that the author of Deuteronomy was certainly not Moses, and that it was written eight centuries after the Exodus had taken place. The words that were 'put into the mouth of Moses' were written by a person addressing the people of a quite different time.[58] What Colenso was trying to impress upon his listeners was the impossibility that Moses, who never came out of the Wilderness and who died in the land of Moab, could have delivered his last address on the other side of Jordan. In order to reiterate his point, Colenso demonstrated to his congregation the inconsistences between the Deuteronomic and Exodus accounts of the Decalogue (Exod. 20.11 and Deut. 5.15). Colenso told his listeners: 'See how in a moment the finger of Criticism points to the proof, lying plain before our eyes, that this story is an insertion of a later day than that of Moses, and most probably was not even a part of the original narrative of the Exodus'.[59]

Colenso also drew attention to a critical difference between the fourth commandment and the rest. The other nine commandments – honouring parents, abstaining from murder, adultery, theft, false witness and coveting – were formulated by intelligent men as a way of maintaining the best interests of society. But Sabbath observance was about ceremonial rites and related to the outward character of a person; it had nothing directly to do with the moral nature or the care and maintenance of society and

56 Ibid., p. 244.   57 Ibid., p. 257.   58 Ibid., p. 242.   59 Ibid., p. 255.

therefore was not essential to Christian faith. Although these differences would only be known to biblical critics, there was one variation which Colenso pointed out that even an ordinary reader would notice – the reason assigned for the hallowing of the Sabbath. In the Exodus narrative it is prescribed as the 'memorial of the rest of God' from the work of creation, while in the Deuteronomic account it was to be observed as a grateful act for the deliverance from Egypt.

Secondly, Colenso disputed the morality of the punitive measures taken against those who violated the Sabbath regulations. He was able to show that the cruel punishment meted out to a man who gathered sticks on a Sabbath, by stoning him to death, was theologically unacceptable and historically spurious. He pointed out that such a commandment would not have proceeded from the mouth of an 'Ever-Blessed God'.

Thirdly, Colenso was able to show from the practice of the apostles and from the writings of the early Church Fathers that there was no support for adhering to such rules. Colenso's contention was that the Christian Sunday did not replace the Sabbath, hence Christians were under no obligation to observe either the seventh or the first day: 'There is no ground whatever for supposing that the adoption of the Christian Sunday, in place of the Jewish Sabbath, rests upon apostolical authority. On the contrary, the apostles themselves, as we see by many instances in the Acts, kept with their countrymen the ordinary Jewish Sabbath'.[60] Surveying the works of the early Church Fathers, Colenso demonstrated that 'no writer of the first three centuries [had] attributed the origin of Sunday observances to any apostolic authority'.[61] Colenso's conclusion was that the fourth commandment, which was once binding upon the Jews, had now been 'abrogated altogether for *Christians*'.[62]

Questioning the validity of the Sabbath laws did not make Colenso an anti-Sabbatarian. He was not for the total abolition of all the rules surrounding Sunday observances. His view was that Sunday should be enjoyed by the working class without 'sacrificing its religious blessing'. Colenso hoped that 'the great works of human genius, the works of God-gifted men, and the wonders of creative wisdom, may be enjoyed in our Parks, and Gardens, Museums, and Galleries, without therefore emptying the House of God, or interfering with the proper rest of others'.[63] He was clear that Sunday should not be 'secularized' and that whatever was done on Sundays 'publicly or privately, to enlarge and elevate the enjoyments of

---

60 Ibid., pp. 251–2.   61 Ibid., p. 252.
62 Ibid., p. 248.   63 Ibid., p. 228.

the working class' should be 'done with a due regard to the Worship of Almighty God', and 'that the secular six days' work may be ennobled, purified and sanctified'.[64] His aim was to infuse what he called a Sabbatarian spirit and a Sunday spirit: 'a spirit of religious truth and thankfulness, of filial love and fear, and joy'.[65] Colenso wanted to make the working class good Christians and make them grateful to God. It was this spirit that he wanted to spread in the British empire.

Colenso put modern criticism effectively to use in order to demolish what he called the 'revolting doctrine, that warranted the practice of slavery'.[66] Exegeting Exodus 21, where the treatment of slaves is described, he was able to claim that in the light of modern criticism, clergy of all denominations would not be able to 'allow their flocks any longer to believe that a slave-holder can draw support for his practices from the actual utterances of the Living God'.[67]

Similarly, Colenso used his critical examination of biblical narratives to demolish the divine sanction the colonialists claimed for their pillaging and plundering of other peoples and their property. The example the colonialist cited for such action was that of the Canaanite war, in which the Canaanites were massacred as a part of a divine plan for a superior people to replace an inferior one. Although leading figures of the time such as Bishop Butler and Thomas Arnold held that such massacres were morally unacceptable under normal circumstances, the massacres were to be seen as acceptable because they were undertaken on behalf of God in order to pave the way for a much better people. One who took such a view was Thomas Arnold, who read the episode from a colonialist perspective and raised the ethical dilemma posed by such an action to a morally advanced people: 'The difficulty relates not to the sufferers in this destruction but to the agents of it; because to men, in an advanced state of moral knowledge and feeling, the command to perpetrate such general slaughter, – to massacre women, and infants, the sick and the decrepit . . . would be so revolting',[68] but 'men in the Christian stage of moral progress' see their part as 'executioners of God's judgements'.[69] In such cases the superior people 'act merely as men who fought for God, and not for themselves'.[70] In a perverted way, Arnold saw the task of the new

---

64 Ibid., p. 278.   65 Ibid., p. 235.
66 Colenso, *The Pentateuch and Book of Joshua Critically Examined, Part* VI, p. 619.
67 Ibid., pp. 207–8.
68 Thomas Arnold, *Sermons, with An Essay on the Right Interpretation and Understanding of the Scriptures* (London, B. Fellows, 1854), p. 398.
69 Ibid., p. 399.   70 Ibid., pp. 399–400.

disciples of the Son of Man as saving the interests of the advanced people rather than destroying the rights of the indigenous. This was a forerunner of the emancipatory imperialism we hear nowadays from the American and British administrations. In this view, imperialism is promoted as a humanitarian intervention whose aim is not to enslave people but to set them free. Following this argument, Sir Bartle Frere claimed that the raid and invasion by the Boers against the Zulus were based on 'a sincere belief in the Divine authority for what they did'. The Boers were spurred on by 'old commands which they found in parts of their Bible to exterminate the Gentiles and take their lands in possession'.[71] Colenso, using his customary combination of statistical analysis and theological liberalism, was able to demonstrate that such a pillage would not have been chronologically possible, arithmetically feasible or theologically acceptable. He went on to say that when compared to the accounts in the Bible, the tragedy of what happened in Cawnpore during the Indian 1857 uprising would 'sink into nothing'.[72] It was impossible for 12,000 Israelites to pillage property, destroy cattle, demolish cities and carry off 100,000 captives and 808,000 cattle without loss of a single Israelite. His claim was 'we are no longer obliged to believe, as a matter of fact' the story of the Midian war. What was more abhorrent to Colenso was the theological consequence of such acts: 'How is it possible to quote the Bible as in any way condemning slavery, when we read here, v. 40, of "Jehovah's tribute of" slaves, thirty-two persons?'[73]

Just as modern astronomy, geology, chemistry and natural sciences were being taught in the schools, Colenso wanted modern biblical criticism to be introduced in Sunday Schools. The modern sciences had infused new life into contemporary society, and Colenso felt that similarly the 'Science of Biblical Criticism is as needful to our true progress and highest happiness'.[74] For him the 'mass of traditional matter', the 'legends and legendary history' in the scriptures, the treatment of the scriptures as infallible, and 'obstinate adherence to things antiquated' were irreconcilable with the advanced knowledge of the times and might repel many from Christianity. Colenso spoke of modern criticism as a divine boon – a

---

71 George W. Cox, *The Life of John William Colenso, D.D. Bishop of Natal*, vol. 1 (London, W. Ridgway, 1888), p. 519.

72 John William Colenso, *The Pentateuch and Book of Joshua Critically Examined* (London, Longman, Green, Longman, Roberts, & Green, 1862), p. 144.

73 Ibid.

74 John William Colenso, *The Pentateuch and Book of Joshua Critically Examined, Part III* (London, Longman, Green, Longman, Roberts, & Green, 1863), pp. xxix–xxx.

boon granted by God to God's own children. 'It is a blessed gift'.[75] As
such, modern criticism in Colenso's view, should be received with 'joy
and thankfulness as God's gift, the gift of a dear Father to his children'.[76]
He saw modern criticism as an instrument performing the role of a
servant, serving God and the cause of truth. His repeated reference to
modern criticism as the 'servant of God' and 'servant of truth' was an
indication of this. What modern criticism did was to make the scriptures
'throughly humanized'.[77] Once modern criticism had done its job, what
the 'Scriptures may lose in revealing power, they will gain in human
interest'.[78] Colenso was so convinced of the divine role of modern
criticism, that he went on to say that the failure to embrace it 'must
be as great a *sin*' and to 'despise or disregard it, is to despise and disregard
the Bible'.[79]

After brutally exposing the fictitious nature of the Pentateuch as
history, Colenso proceeded to claim that 'we shall find in the Pentateuch
. . .', 'rich lessons of spiritual Truth, by which our soul may be cheered
and strengthened for the work of life'.[80] In spite of emasculating the
Pentateuch, the book retained for him the core and centre of religious
teaching: God is the one who creates and preserves; humankind is made
in the image of God; all that God made was good. For Colenso, critical
enquiry did not threaten Christian belief in a personal God or deny the
possibility to rejoice with the words of Psalm 8 and wonder at the creation
of this vast world. In fact, it enhanced it. In one of the sermons he said,
'Not indeed that an enlarged acquaintance with the Works of God in
Nature, when viewed in the Light of Reason, exhibits anything to contradict a living faith in a Personal God, which is the real sense our spirit's
life'.[81]

Although Colenso made use of modern criticism with devastating
effect in destroying literal reading of biblical events and accounts, this
did not mean that the potency of the text was diminished, nor was every
tenet of Christian faith discredited. For him the 'central truths of Christianity' remained safe and untroubled by scientific inquiry – the revelation
of God in and through the human Jesus, and that he came to manifest

75 Colenso, *Lectures on the Pentateuch and the Moabite Stone*, p. 366.
76 Colenso, *Natal Sermons, Series* I, p. 37.
77 Colenso, *Lectures on the Pentateuch and the Moabite Stone*, p. 315.
78 Ibid.
79 Colenso, *Natal Sermons, Series* I, p. 9.
80 Colenso, *The Pentateuch and Book of Joshua Critically Examined, Part* III, p. xxxi.
81 Colenso, *Natal Sermons, Series* III, p. 235.

'fatherly love' to humanity and to manifest that 'brotherly love' which should exist among the children of God's family: 'Whatever criticism may do with the documents relating to him [i.e. Jesus], – *must* do, as God's servant, as a minister of truth, – it will never take from us this pure ideal, which they have helped us to realize, – this image of a perfect man, perfectly obedient, perfectly loving, the perfect type of our Humanity, with which the Father is well pleased'.[82] This essence of Christianity – the Fatherhood of God and the Brotherhood of man and the revelation of God in man – according to Colenso 'will not die'. It will force its way 'again and again, like living waters, through the dark heaps of traditionary rubbish, the accumulating corruptions of ages, – an under-current some-times, hid from sight, bursting forth again still purer and clearer, more the creed of humanity, with every reformation, with every step of human progress'.[83] In one of his sermons Colenso further reiterated the point: 'Let the criticism do what it can, what it must, if it would be a servant of God, a servant of the Truth, it cannot strip us of this ground of our confidence in the Divine mission of the Son of Man'.[84]

Interestingly, Colenso did not see modern criticism as a threat to missionary advance. For those missionaries who complained that his advocacy of criticism would hinder the progress of mission work among the Zulus, and that it would 'unsettle their minds', his answer was that it was those very missionaries who came to Africa with a pre-critical Christianity, a message of eternal damnation and absolute confidence in the superiority of their religious tenets, who proved to be the barrier to the advancement of the Christian gospel in Africa. Colenso asserted that, 'on the other hand, it was modern criticism which had enabled the '"glad tidings", the message of their Father's love to reach them'.[85] Moreover, he claimed that, unlike those missionaries who were already full of doctrinal certainties, 'the heathen, to whom we send our Missionaries – who are not yet drugged with the results of past centuries of dogmatic teaching . . . are ready to open their hearts to us', and are willing to receive the message we bring to them as a word from the 'higher sphere'. Therefore '*what right* have we to begin our work among them, by laying down a basis of falsehood, and while professing to be servants of the God of Truth?'[86]

82 Colenso, *Natal Sermons, Series* IV, pp. 208–9.
83 Ibid., p. 222.
84 Ibid., p. 141.
85 John William Colenso, 'On the Efforts of Missionaries among Savages', *Journal of the Anthropological Society* 3 (1865), 271.
86 Colenso, *Lectures on the Pentateuch and the Moabite Stone*, pp. 368–9.

He even went on to say that it was a 'matter of bounden duty, not a matter of choice to communicate to our heathen converts those facts of Modern Science'.[87] He thought it was 'foolish and idle' and 'positively wicked and sinful'[88] to keep back from the Zulus those facts that were already known about the age of creation and the impossibility of the flood as narrated.

Colenso's use of critical method made misuse of the Bible more complex and difficult. Scholarship was now seen not as a barrier to ordinary people but as a vehicle to remove restrictions laid on them by church authorities. Colenso's use of modern criticism simultaneously desacralized and honoured the Bible. There was both rejection and acceptance of its narratival content. 'But the Bible, the old Bible, which some accuse us of attempting to destroy, to set aside, becomes more wonderful, more worthy of note, more precious, when viewed as the work of men like ourselves, as a part of human history, than if each word of it were an infallible utterance from the Eternal Throne'.[89] Once modern criticism had exposed 'unsound and delusive' readings of the Book, and once the Christians had gone through the 'painful and distressing' effect of such a discovery, 'as if the foundations of the universe were shaken', they would find that the Bible still contained the word of God; and the scriptures were still oracles of God: 'They will see that the foundations of their faith stand fixed and sure in the Eternal Rock of God's unchangeable Wisdom and Love'.[90]

In at least three respects the Bible remained a valid document for Colenso. Firstly, 'the scriptures teach about God and His doings: they speak messages from God to the soul: they are still "profitable for the doctrine, reproof, correction, instruction in righteousness": they are a gracious gift of God's Providence'.[91] Secondly, they provide comfort to those who are perplexed and harassed. When his congregation were troubled and confused he urged them to turn to the very Bible he allegedly discredited and maligned. He gave examples of the consolatory gems they contained. There is the Lord's Prayer 'with its simple petitions, which the child can understand', the Psalms which tell us 'how men lived

87 Colenso, 'On the Efforts of Missionaries among Savages', 277.
88 'On Missions to the Zulus in Natal and Zululand'; a lecture at the Marylebone Literary Institution, 23 May 1865; reproduced in Ruth Edgecombe (ed.), *John William Colenso: Bringing Forth Light. Five Tracts on the Bishop Colenso's Zulu Mission* (Pietermaritzburg, University Press, 1982), p. 230.
89 Colenso, *Natal Sermons*, Series III, p. 190.
90 Colenso, *Natal Sermons*, Series I, p. 38.
91 Ibid., p. 53.

and laboured and longed after God and were suffered to find Him', the examples of good men with all their 'patient faith, their noble self-sacrifice, their joyous confidence, their sure belief in the final triumph of God and His Truth' and above all there is the history of Christ himself 'with its calm serene trust in the ever-present help of His Heavenly Father, with its purity and goodness, its holy hatred of sin, its pitiful compassion for the sinner, its boundless love to God and Man, exhibited in life and sealed in death'.[92] He assured his congregation that they would be able to 'draw from the Scripture narratives the rich lessons' for their 'spiritual support and comfort' without 'being obliged to renounce the reasoning powers, with which their Heavenly Father has blessed them as part of His own Divine Image'.[93] For him, the critical analysis of a book that contained the records of the living faith of men centuries ago could not in any way undermine the living faith of humanity in God. Thirdly, the Scriptures provide hope:

When we read the sacred records, these writings of the men of other days, – when we see how they have lived and died, have wrought and prayed, and have stood up manfully and struggled with the power of evil within and without, have risen and fallen, and risen again, 'have fought the good fight, and finished their course, and entered into their rest', – we may well have 'hope' with such experience of other men, in the ages long ago, confirming our own, assuring us that we are 'all of One', that the Living Word, the Eternal Son of God, was dwelling in them as He dwells now in us, 'Christ in us the Hope of Glory'.[94]

Colenso saw his task as liberating the Bible from the hands of the church interpreters and placing it in the hands of lay readers, thus endowing them with enormous responsibility. For him this act was like taking away the keys which were with the scribes and Pharisees and giving them back to the people.

SUBALTERNS AND THE SAPIENTIAL TRADITION

Unlike Colenso, who was keen to promote the latest findings of modern criticism, Long found himself among Bengali peasants who, in his view, were 'utterly, unacquainted with any history except that of their gods and goddesses, or of the Prophet of Islam'. Biblical references to Roman and Jewish history presented peculiar difficulties, while the Bible's 'geographical allusions were a puzzle, as was also the biography of Christ, scattered

---

92 Colenso, *Natal Sermons*, Series II, p. 275.
93 Ibid., pp. 275–6.
94 Colenso, *Natal Sermons*, Series I, p. 69.

up and down in four different memoirs'.[95] In such a scenario Long felt it
was pointless to introduce the intricacies of modern criticism and its effect
on the Bible, but that he should begin with what they most understood
and appreciated, namely 'the emblems and illustrations of the Bible'
perceived with an intensity not understood by the cold phlegmatic
European. '"The children of the sun" are at home in the Bible'.[96]

Long was apprehensive about applying critical methods to the study of
the Bible. His view was that the German rationalistic thinking which had
penetrated biblical studies was more of a threat to Protestant Christianity
than the superstitious practices of Rome. In keeping with the evangelical
trend of the time, Long disapproved of a bishop of the Church of England
rejecting the historicity of the biblical narratives. When Long heard that a
London bookseller had sent fifty copies of Colenso's book to Calcutta,
presumably the first volume of the Pentateuch, Long wrote to his committee in London saying that 'Dr Colenso's work is likely to do some
injury among the natives of Bengal', and he hoped that Colenso would do
the honourable thing by resigning: 'Dr Colenso will resign'. Long added
that, if not, missionary societies ought to disown him.[97]

Long set out his hermeneutical aim in his preface to *Scripture Truth in
Oriental Dress:*

The simple object is to furnish *some* raw materials to those wishing to convey the
Doctrines of Christianity to the millions of India through popular preaching or
schools for the masses – to point out to natives of India non-Christian how
thoroughly Oriental the Bible is both in its subject and style, – and to open out
to European readers a new mine for illustrating Christian truths by Oriental
Proverbs and Proverbial sayings which enshrine the wit and wisdom of the
multitude.[98]

Long's method was determined by his understanding of Bengali peasants and their culture. Most of them, in his view, were 'ignorant of books'
and therefore they should be helped to keep awake during the missionaries' teaching. The answer he came up with was to follow the method of
Jesus – 'without a *parable* spoke He not unto them'. For Long, parables
brought out the beauty of truth through veiled imagery.

The utilization of parables meant the following in practical terms.
Firstly, Long presented biblical materials visually. His visual presentation
took two forms. One was to depict leading events in the Bible. Long used

95 Long, *How I Taught the Bible to Bengal Peasant Boys*, p. 1.
96 Ibid.
97 CMS c11/0185/89; 15 December 1863.
98 Long, *Scripture Truth in Oriental Dress*, p. i.

to hang portrayals of biblical stories in the classroom. The other was to explain biblical truths through indigenous visual aids. In one of his letters to his committee in London, Long explained his method:

Sometimes I sit down near a place abounding in thorns, then I take for my text – thorns the mark of the fall – at another time near a place infested with snakes, then I take as my subject the great serpent very old and how we may be cured of his poison. Some time ago I selected as a text "We are all as *water* spilled on the ground." They did not see at first the sense of the passage until I called for a vessel of water and, spilling it on the ground before them, asked them to gather it up off a *clay* floor. Villagers though ignorant of books know much of *things* and hence they are interested in such subjects. They at once saw its application to human life. At another time I wished to illustrate the unsatisfactory nature of the world from Solomon's picture of old age. I got an old man – 90 years old – as my text and a very good text he made.[99]

In a later writing Long explained how he linked the poison of the snake to the Book of Psalms 58.4, 5: 'They have venom like the venom of a serpent, like the deaf adder that stops its ear, so that it does not hear the voice of charmers or of the cunning enchanter'. For Long, the poison of a serpent was an allegory for sin: like the poison, sin inflames the fire of passion in people. It spreads quickly just as Adam's sin spread throughout the world. Like the wound of the cobra, sin is hardly noticeable in the beginning but when Eve ate the apple it poisoned the entire human race. Just as a snake bite is not painful but its effect is deadly, so also is the impact of sin. The serpent has a beautiful skin, as Absalom was beautiful, but he was disobedient to his father David and rebelled against him.[100]

Secondly, Long encouraged his students to chant and commit to memory biblical verses, a mode of practice popular in the East: 'the boys and girls, Mussulman and Hindu, learn it by heart, chant it, as intonation is a universal practice in the East'.[101] 'Simple chant' reminded Long of 'Gregorian'.[102] Long had a book compiled of 365 emblems, one for each day of the year, and his pupils had to commit these to memory. The idea was that memorized texts learnt early in life become firmly embedded in one's psyche.

Thirdly, Long taught the Bible orally. He again drew inspiration from the indigenous practice of oral telling of Hindu stories, and the potential power of *kathaks*, or reciters. At the popular level, the majority of Hindus

99 CMS c i /o185/136 Annual Report 1858.
100 Long, *Scripture Truth in Oriental Dress*, pp. 96–7.
101 Long, *Bible Teaching and Preaching for the Million*, p. 6.
102 Long, *How I Taught the Bible to Bengal Peasant Boys*, p. 3.

experienced their sacred writing through professional storytellers and reciters. The recitation of Hindu *Puranas* and *ithihasas* had a deep impact on the common people. Long exploited the indigenous method in order to disseminate biblical truths: 'Oral teaching is the mode by which Hindus and Mohammedans make the common people acquainted with their religion, and they understand well the principle of picturing by words. The Hindus have a *Kathak,* or reciter, whose recitations and illustrations of Hinduism are very poetical and telling on the common people'.[103] The oral narration involved semi-dramatization as well. Long's intention was to 'dramatize Scripture narratives as all great preachers and teachers have done'.[104] He found the oral and performative method well suited to Bengali peasants who lacked the basic background to the history of the Bible: 'The Children have little time at school to gain an acquaintance with the leading history and facts of the Scriptures from the book itself; these have, therefore, to be given in the form of narrative without book, which is more accordant with the oriental mode, and decidedly more impressive'.[105] Elsewhere Long wrote: 'I found teaching the *history* of the Bible orally was more impressive, and enabled one to give the leading events of Scripture in a shorter space of time'.[106] He quoted approvingly a bishop who examined his students on the Book of Acts and Daniel and found their answers 'accurate' and 'intelligent', which in the bishop's view was the 'effect of a system of oral instruction'.[107]

Long's fourth method was to juxtapose biblical proverbs with Eastern proverbs. In a letter he wrote to his committee in London, he explained the method thus: 'I find also the interlarding of preaching with Bengali proverbs in illustration has a good effect. But after all it is difficult with all the stiffness of the Anglo Saxon and the assumptions of a conquering race to get to the level of the people and so to sympathise with them'.[108] In a way that anticipated Said's contrapuntal reading, Long was suggesting that 'on the principle of diamond cut diamond', proverbs 'require a commentary on the plan of corresponding or illustrative proverbs, European and Asiatic'.[109] His aim was to provide a commentary on proverbs 'formed mainly by parallel or illustrative proverbs'. Here are some examples of his juxtapositions. As a way of explaining Jesus' words 'How

---

103 Ibid.   104 Ibid., p. 4.
105 Long, *Bible Teaching and Preaching for the Million*, p. 6.
106 Ibid.
107 Ibid.
108 CMS c1/0185/136 Annual Report 1858.
109 Long, *Bible Teaching and Preaching for the Million*, p. 8.

often would I have gathered your children together as a hen gathers her brood under her wings, and you would not' (Matt. 23.37), Long juxtaposed a Kannada proverb, 'Will a man pet and bring up a parrot and then throw it into the fire?'[110] The Bengali aphorism 'The yogi begs not in his own village' was seen as equivalent to the saying of Jesus that a prophet is without honour in his own country. Another Bengali proverb, 'The sieve says to the needle that you have a hole in your tail', was treated as a counterpart to the utterance of Jesus, 'Cast the mote out of thine own eye' and links it up with 'the kettle calling the pot black'.[111] Similarly an Indian tribal Badaga saying, 'In trying to save a drop of ghee, he upset the ghee pot', was used to illustrate the Matthean saying 'For what will it profit a man, if he gains the whole world and forfeits his life?' (Matt. 16.26).[112]

If Colenso marshalled the heavy armoury of historical criticism, Long was applying literary forms – parables, proverbs and illustrations – as a way of unlocking biblical treasures: 'Knowledge must be imparted to them in a way suited to their capacity and modes of thought and the book of nature must be ransacked for illustrations to the Book of Revelation'.[113]

Long gave a number of reasons for his privileging of proverbial sayings. Firstly, it was the method employed by oriental teachers like Solomon, Buddha and Christ, as 'media of popular instruction in the form of *sutra* or aphorisms'.[114] He also claimed support from the history of the Church, citing the examples of Chrysostom and Bishop Latimer. For Long, 'the parables of Christ are equally acceptable to the children of the sun as to the cold Saxon'.[115]

Secondly, nearly thirty years of missionary experience in India had convinced Long that the 'mere facts of the Bible, without the morals and doctrines connected with them' are 'of little profit; but to make abstract dogmas interesting and intelligible they must be clothed in the beautiful drapery of emblem, metaphor, proverb'.[116] Sapiential sayings were seen as accessible interpretative material for theological doctrines: 'Poetry and parable form in India the vehicles of knowledge'.[117] Similarly, while

110 Long, *Scripture Truth in Oriental Dress*, p. 263.
111 Ibid., p. 246.
112 For more comparisons, see James Long, 'Bengali Proverbs', in *Calcutta Christian Observer*, 28 April 1860, pp. 179–85.
113 Long, *How I Taught the Bible to Bengal Peasant Boys*, p. 1.
114 Long, James, 'On Eastern Proverbs, Their Importance and the Best Mode of Making a Complete Collection, Classified with the Native Interpretations', Oriental Congress, Berlin, September 1881, p. 4.
115 Long, *Bible Teaching and Preaching for the Million*, p. 2.
116 Ibid.
117 Long, *How I Taught the Bible to Bengal Peasant Boys*, p. 2.

biblical history and geography needed a certain degree of knowledge and education to understand them, 'parables, proverbs, and emblems speak in a universal language, drawn from God's great book of nature, open to all to read'.[118] More significantly, when reasoning failed, proverbs often settled an argument among orientals: 'A Proverb often hits the nail on the head, when a train of reasoning would be of little avail, – particularly with Orientals'.[119]

Thirdly, sapiential sayings, in Long's view, emanated from and reflected the perception of ordinary people. In the *Calcutta Christian Observer*, he wrote that proverbs were 'a key to village life and rural lore. They show that, independent of books, there is much common sense among the common people, and their faculties of observation have not lain dormant'.[120] It was the method of Bengali women. 'The masses of the East', Long claimed, 'think differently and Bengali women can fight each other, not with the fist, but by pitching proverbs at one another'.[121] Long castigated the preference of the orientalists of his day, who spent much time studying the kings and conquerors, coins, architecture and antiquities of the people, which do 'not give an insight as the proverbs do, into the internal history, manners, belief, opinions and language of the masses'.[122] Long admitted that proverbial sayings contained the frivolous, the superstitious and the absurd, but they were 'words of the wayside' and 'they relate to the masses, to those whose views and opinions in these days of extended suffrage are cropping up, and gradually controlling upper strata of society'.[123] Though these proverbs come from people who are low 'in the scale of society', their use of proverbs 'shows the hold those primitive outpourings of the soul take of the human mind in all stages of civilizations'.[124]

Fourthly, proverbs appeal to the 'Anglo-Saxon mind' as 'the great universal voice of humanity'. They act as 'universal law'.[125] They reflect the experience of individuals and communities everywhere.

Fifthly, Long had a preference for proverbial sayings because they have a timeless quality about them and they are constantly in circulation. They

118 Long, *Bible Teaching and Preaching for the Million*, p. 2.
119 Long, 'Bengali Proverbs', p. 179.
120 Ibid.
121 James Long, 'On the Importance and Best Mode of Making a Collection of Oriental Proverbs', Oriental Congress, Leiden, September 1883, p. 2.
122 Ibid., p. 1.
123 Long, *How I Taught the Bible to Bengal Peasant Boys*, pp. 1–2.
124 Long, *Bible Teaching and Preaching for the Million*, p. 8.
125 Long, 'Bengali Proverbs', p. 179.

existed before books and 'have from the dawn of hoary time been current among the people, and have been preserved as their inheritance and heirloom when everything else – customs, land, religion – have changed, and even if they die out in one country they are preserved in another'.[126] They tend to survive and outlive history, empires and conquerors. Proverbs are handed down from 'remote ages through the memory of people', and 'elucidate in many points the social conditions, feelings and opinions of the masses, besides throwing light on various questions of philology, archaeology, and history'.[127] Moreover, reflecting the orientalist view of the time, Long was of the opinion that in countries like India, where the Hindus were anti-historic and there was difficulty in tracing the past, proverbs provided 'history not merely of kings and conquerors, but of the people in their innermost thoughts, in the domestic hearth'. He went on to claim that he had found 'in the Bengali proverbs numerous references to old customs, old temples, historical characters, which have long since passed away unrecorded either in MSS or books'.[128] The archaisms preserved in the proverbs, in Long's view, had philological value and they provided clues to the origins of nations.

More alarmingly, Long's next two reasons for advocating proverbs as a mode of pedagogy reveal his collusion with colonial designs, not only fitting in with the colonial motive but also helping to further the colonial cause. Proverbs are seen as weapons against Brahminical power and presence. In chapter 2, on the Indian rebellion, we saw a sample of colonial antagonism towards Brahminical influence and power. Missionaries always found Brahmins a great hindrance to their missionary progress. Marginalizion of proverbial sayings in brahminical literature played into Long's hands. He claimed that Brahmin pundits treated proverbs as 'relating to the baser sort'[129] and despised them as vulgar. In the colonial game of playing one against the other, proverbs were seen as people's knowledge, which was sneered at by Brahmins, and thus it became a powerful tool to woo the non-elite and castigate the Brahmin elite.

But more importantly for Long, the study of proverbs supported the colonial cause: 'In order to govern the masses well we must know them, – a difficult acquisition. In this respect, proverbs afford some clue through

126 Long, 'On Making a Collection of Oriental Proverbs', p. 2.
127 Ibid., p. 6.
128 James Long, 'Oriental Proverbs in Their Relations to Folklore, History, Sociology with Suggestions for Their Collection, Interpretation, Publication' (15 February 1875), p. 3.
129 Ibid., p. 2.

the labyrinth, reflecting as in a mirror the natural spirit and social position of a people, throwing light on dark places in their history and geography'.[130] After the Indian uprising and native chiefs had been won over by the colonial administration, Lord Canning wanted to know how to assess the mood and the mind of the ordinary people and turned to Long. Long urged Canning to look at the vernacular press and at indigenous proverbs, because 'proverbs in popular use are also of value in gauging the depths of popular sentiment'.[131] Studying the native wisdom was to learn from the enemy how to manage them: 'But in order to maintain that European superiority, and on the principle of *fas est ab hoste docori* [*sic*], I believe it would be most useful for Europeans of all *classes* to see themselves now and then in the mirror of the Native press'.[132]

Long also saw his task of rescuing proverbs in apocalyptic terms. He envisaged a world which was fast disappearing, and an important task before this happened was to rescue the wisdom tradition of the people. In one of his papers he claimed that Hindu society was at a crossroads and that the old order preserved by the pundits and *kathaks* or storytellers, and their way of handing over the traditional lore were fading away. Modern western education was rapidly sweeping across the continent and making traditional folklore redundant: 'Now is therefore the time to collect what remains of the living proverbs, which are connected so much with local history, and the domestic life of the people'.[133] In a paper read at the Oriental Congress at Leiden, Long was even more desperate: '*Now or never*, therefore, must be our motto to rescue the proverbs and folklore of the East from oblivion'.[134]

Finally, what was the actual function of proverbial sayings in the hermeneutics of Long and Colenso? In Long's case, they fulfilled three roles. Firstly, they introduced the biblical world – a world that would have otherwise been alien to Bengali peasants. The level of familiarity of the indigenous proverbs would have been strong enough to enable Long's audience to appreciate a large number of biblical references. It was an effective way of driving home the message of the Bible. Seeing the biblical world through familiar indigenous proverbs meant that the Bible was no longer seen as a strange book. Secondly, sapiential sayings helped to

---

130 Long, 'On Making a Collection of Oriental Proverbs', p. 2.
131 Long, 'Oriental Proverbs in Their Relations to Folklore', p. 2.
132 James Long, 'The "Nil Darpan" Controversy-Statement', in *The Friend of India*, 27 June 1861, p. 712.
133 Long, *How I Taught the Bible to Bengal Peasant Boys*, p. 7.
134 Long, 'On Making a Collection of Oriental Proverbs', p. 3.

'clinch an argument': 'Solomon's Proverbs show the views of Scripture on this subject, and have ever been an arsenal richly stored with weapons for bringing down moral truth to the level of the popular understanding'.[135] On another occasion, he put it this way :' A proverb often hits the nail on the head, when a train of reasoning would be of little avail, – particularly with Orientals'.[136] Thirdly, Long's attitude, especially his hermeneutical reason for placing these proverbs side by side with the canonical writings is not easy to ascertain, but one can hazard a guess that his appropriation of proverbial sayings is analogous to the Church of England's attitude to the Apocryphal books. The sixth of the Thirty-Nine Articles says that these could be 'read for the example of life and instruction of manners, but yet doth it not apply them to establish any doctrine'. In other words, the apocryphal texts are read not for doctrinal instruction but for moral example. Proverbial sayings had a similar function in Long's hermeneutic. He wrote: 'All orientals are fond of apologue, fables, and figurative language, and love to clothe ethical and religious truth in graceful and pleasing drapery of metaphor, thus engaging the attention, impressing the memory, and strewing the path to abstract dogmas with flowers; even dictionaries have been composed by them in verse'.[137] Long did not mine proverbial sayings for doctrinal purposes but as examples of life which could be used for instruction. As he put it, 'they are their legitimate inheritance, and as such are a suitable menstruum' for 'ethical instruction'.[138]

Colenso, who spent much time looking at the great historical accounts of the Hebrews, did not pay much attention to the wisdom tradition. When he did have an opportunity, he employed his customary critical approach to analysing the sapiential books. Unlike Long, who treated the wisdom literature at the redacted level, Colenso subjected it to his routine historical and literary analysis. He claimed that the Book of Proverbs consisted of seven parts, and, more significantly, he found it to be wanting because it did not contain the laws of Israel. He relied on the work of Kuenen to determine the date of composition of these various parts. Colenso noted that references to law occurred twelve times in the Book of Proverbs, broadly in the sense of 'instruction as of a father or mother' but there was 'no allusion anywhere to 'the Law of the Pentateuch'.[139]

135 Long, *How I Taught the Bible to Bengal Peasant Boys*, p. 3.
136 Long, 'Bengali Proverbs', p. 179.
137 Long, *Scripture Truth in Oriental Dress*, p. i.
138 Long, *Bible Teaching and Preaching for the Million*, p. 3.
139 Colenso, *The Pentateuch and Book of Joshua Critically Examined*, Part VII, p. 462.

There was 'no sign throughout of any acquaintance with the Levitical Legislation of the Pentateuch, nor even any especial reference to the Ten Commandments, such as we should expect to find in a work of this nature, if these commandments had been the ancient recognized foundation of the national code of morals'.[140] Out of ninety-seven Natal Sermons that Colenso preached, he chose only once the proverbial sayings of Jesus as his text (Luke 9.34–5), but even here he used the text merely as a metaphor, to explicate how the acts of Christians are slowly but surely advancing the welfare of the people and making the 'whole world sweet'. The wisdom tradition functions at three levels for Colenso. Firstly, Colenso agreed with Long that it had potential pedagogical value. Jesus' continual use of it was an example of this. It was the method of Jesus: 'Our Lord, we know, constantly made use of this faculty, when he addressed his disciples or the multitude, not in plain discourse, but in parables'.[141] Secondly, parabolic speech is a convenient vehicle for conveying eternal truths. Colenso placed parabolic speech within the realm of imagination. It is through imagination that eternal truths are clothed in a form that the 'human mind may more distinctly grasp'.[142] He taught in parables 'a method the very opposite of creeds, and catechisms', as a way of drawing out the minds of his hearers rather than imposing beliefs upon them.[143] Thirdly, it provides continuity with the past: 'The wise maxims of that olden time, contained in the Book of Proverbs, link the present age with the past, and show that the human race has been essentially the same during the last 3000 years of its History'.[144]

RECONFIGURING JESUS: SON OF MAN AS HEN AND ROCK

Colenso's view of Jesus was a minimalist one. He rarely used traditional Christological titles to describe Jesus. One title which predominated in his writings was the Son of Man. Occasionally he used the title 'Prophet of Nazareth' but, for Colenso, Jesus was always a Son of Man. In Jesus, humanity had the 'plainest manifestation of the Divine compassion'.[145] He was the 'perfect image of the Divine Man. That image of perfect beauty and holiness – of Perfect Man'.[146] Apart from calling Jesus Son of

140 Ibid.
141 Colenso, *Natal Sermons*, Series 11, p. 176.
142 Ibid.
143 Colenso, *Natal Sermons*, Series iv, p. 86.
144 Colenso, *Natal Sermons*, Series i, p. 62.
145 Colenso, *Natal Sermons*, Series iv, p. 69.
146 Colenso, *Natal Sermons*, Series i, p. 315.

Man, Colenso was very reluctant to speak about him and hardly provides any clue as to how he understood this title.

Applying the same historical rigour to the New Testament documents as he did to the Hebrew scriptures, Colenso came to the conclusion that there was hardly anything to know about Jesus. Jesus' life was 'obscured with the mass of traditionary matter, which makes it difficult to make out distinctly the features of the original narrative'.[147] Colenso challenged the popular notion that Jesus lived a life similar to that of any ordinary person, hence he provided examples for facing the practical duties one undertakes in one's life. In Colenso's view, Jesus was hardly a good guide. In one of his sermons, he said people often point to Jesus as a good guide for the various duties of life. But, he asked, what do we really know of him? We know 'scarcely anything' about his childhood and boyhood, and of his youth 'nothing'. On how he behaved as a son or a brother, we have 'very little' information. As a husband or a parent Jesus had left us with 'no example'. He had not provided us with 'patterns' for students, businessmen, artisans, domestic servants, village labourers or soldiers. He had never been a 'pauper in the poorhouse', or a prisoner in the 'dungeon of the oppressor'; he had not been in the ward of a hospital with 'lingering disease' or been a 'patient racked with pain'. In other words, he had offered hardly any models as to how to face the day-to-day situations that people encounter. His active ministry was only for three years, and 'that Example in any case is properly suited for boys, young lads, or men, and not for girls, maidens, or women'.[148] Colenso found Jesus' message culture-specific and conveyed in the idiom of the time: 'His direct teaching was confined to the Jews, they were necessarily also cast, as it were, in Jewish moulds, and took the form of the race and of the age in which he lived'.[149]

The scarcity of 'models of conduct' does not mean that Jesus' life was 'less valuable'. For Colenso, the shining example of Jesus did not lie in mundane and minutely detailed prescriptions for living. Jesus' life was 'not a mere *copy* which we are closely to follow in all our different relations of life'.[150] The following of Jesus meant not merely imitating certain acts, but appealing to the '*Spirit* of his life – to the *principle* which ruled it', namely, the willingness to 'conform to the perfect Will of God, that desire to please his heavenly Father, that surrender of his will to God's Will,

---

147 Colenso, *Natal Sermons, Series* IV, p. 220.
148 Colenso, *Natal Sermons, Series* I, p. 315.
149 Colenso, *Natal Sermons, Series* IV, p. 179.
150 Colenso, *Natal Sermons, Series* I, p. 316.

which he manifested on all occasions'. It is this spirit and this principle that should provide us with actual guidance and prompt us to say to ourselves, in different situations, 'In this way Christ would act or would have acted'.[151] Colenso's view was that Christians find themselves in a 'thousand different situations and relations, in which our Lord, as his life is recorded in the Gospels, never found himself'. In such circumstances, one has to appeal to the spirit of Christ – the spirit of filial trust, obedience and devotion. Christ becomes an example 'because he came not to do his own will, but the will of the Father who sent him, – because he sought not his own glory, but in all that concerned him was simply obedient, leaving his cause in God's hands, – because he bore witness for the Truth all on occasions, regardless of consequences'.[152] All religions speak of the 'existence of an Unseen Power'. But the 'central and essential truth of Christianity' is that this Unseen Power 'in its moral nature, is revealed in human life and action, in that of Jesus'.[153]

One can discern certain parallels in Colenso's approach to the Bible and presentation of the person of Jesus. Both are products of fallible humanity. The Bible was a human book; so also was Jesus human and restricted by human limitations: 'His words are human words, and therefore subject to the limitations of our humanity – to the imperfections to which all human utterances are liable, when used to express Eternal Truths'.[154] More significantly, what was crucial was the spirit and the principle which both the Bible and Jesus represented. It was not simply a matter of appealing to the letter of the text, but to its spirit. It was same with the teaching of Jesus. It is the '"spirit" of His Teaching – the Light which shone in it – the Living Word that breathed in it – that "shall not pass away"'.[155]

Colenso also differentiated between the religion of Jesus and institutional Christianity with its creeds, rituals and rites: 'We hear nothing from the lips of Jesus about creeds and articles as necessary to salvation – and nothing about forms of worship, rites and ceremonies, as binding on his followers'.[156] Jesus' injunctions were restricted to a few teachings about how to pray, how to baptize, and how to celebrate the Lord's Supper. Jesus' religious practice included visiting the house of worship and joining

151 Ibid., p. 315.
152 Ibid., p. 317.
153 John William Colenso, *Three Sermons Preached in the Cathedral Church of St Peter's, Maritzburg* (Pietermaritzburg, P. Davis & Sons, 1883), p. 11.
154 Colenso, *Natal Sermons, Series* iv, p. 179.
155 Ibid.
156 Colenso, *Natal Sermons, Series* 11, p. 33.

in common worship, of praying and giving thanks, both privately and publicly, to God. Jesus tells us nothing about systems of church government – about priests and deacons, bishops and metropolitans, synods and councils – but he reminds his followers that the Son of Man came not to be ministered unto but to minister. This does not mean that creeds and forms of church government are unimportant. But to Colenso they were not '*essentials*' in 'the religion of Jesus'. The true Christians, for Colenso, were 'those who were 'meek' and 'merciful', 'pure in heart', 'peacemakers', those who were 'hungering and thirsting after righteousness', whom Christ calls 'blessed'. Colenso's point was that doctrinal differences and questions about the forms of church order should not be used as excuses for not keeping the 'last emphatic command' of Jesus: 'By this shall all men know that ye are my disciples, if ye have love to one another'.[157]

Long saw Jesus essentially as a teacher who imparted wisdom to ordinary people through simple pithy sayings. He lamented that the life of Jesus was presented as an example to follow but that his most important example in teaching the poor in similes and parables was overlooked. In his numerous teachings and lectures, Long repeated tirelessly the verse from Mark to ram home his point – 'without parable spake he not unto the multitude' (Mk 4.34). Commenting on the profusion of the lives of Jesus, Long observed that 'now, while many lives of Christ have been published, there is not one that gives prominence to this characteristic of His ministry, not even Dr Farrer's excellent one'.[158] Long regretted that 'while many books have been written on our Lord's life and character, none yet have dwelt on Him as an oriental guru or teacher in the oriental way, by fables, apologues, proverbs, and emblems'.[159] Long made use of traditional Christological images to describe Jesus. This was in keeping with the Indian way of describing the deities in figurative speech drawn from nature. Long depicted Jesus variously as a 'Rose',[160] a 'lily', a 'hen',[161] a 'root' or a 'rock',[162] explaining the reason for his choice of images. Although almost all the metaphors he used had a long Christological history, his explanations were original, locating them afresh in the experience of his Indian readers. Jesus was a rose because the rose is 'noted for its fragrance, and the name of Christ is like ointment poured forth;

157 Ibid., p. 34.
158 Long, *Bible Teaching and Preaching for the Million*, p. 8.
159 Ibid., p. 2.
160 Long, *Scripture Truth in Oriental Dress*, p. 78.
161 Ibid., p. 41.   162 Ibid., pp. 79–80.

like the roses of Ghazipore which, when distilled and pressed, yield the fragrant rose-water used at feasts'.[163] Jesus was compared to a lily among thorns, because like a lily he was fragrant, white, pure, fruitful and beautiful in world of pain and cruelty. The lily is the queen of flowers, the only flower that 'bloomed without a thorn, a worm or a canker in it; such was the youth of Christ; it bloomed in the barren desert of Judea as amid the filth of Jerusalem; like the rays of the sun, it could enter dirt without being defiled'.[164] For his Indian readers, Long provided an indigenous equivalent for the lily: the lotus. Jesus was symbolized as a mother hen who shelters and clucks to warn her young. He showed compassion for them. His weeping over Jerusalem was a sign of this. As a mother hen, he nourished them by his great 'drop of blood'. The image of a hen had its limitations, as Long explained, since the hen forgets the young when they are grown up. Christ, in Long's view, never gives up his own. Jesus was identified with a root because like a root he diffuses life into branches. Like a root '*hidden* under the earth, so Christ's divinity is veiled in flesh, keeps the tree *firm* in storms, and draws *nourishment*, for the tree by sending suckers into the soil which spread laterally to get food'.[165] Jesus as a rock provides a 'solid', 'strong' and 'durable' foundation. Like rock caves he offers shelter 'so the Christian like the dove has his nest in the clefts of the rock'.[166] Jesus' wisdom is like a diamond found in rock. He is pure water which comes from a rock. Again, as with the hen metaphor, Long was quick to point out the limitations of the image. Unlike the rock, Jesus is not barren and does not crumble. Other references to Jesus which have biblical connections include Jesus Christ as the Bread of Heaven because all spiritual nourishment comes from him.

In addition to these metaphors, Long referred to Jesus as a carpenter, and this had an interesting personal significance. When he was jailed as a result of his involvement with the indigo workers, Long regarded his suffering as an honour, especially because it was 'suffering for Him who was preeminently the friend of the working classes and a carpenter himself'.[167] For Long, the religion of Jesus was summed up in Jesus' words 'the poor have the Gospel preached to them'.[168] Long sincerely hoped that only the 'religion of the carpenter's Son' had any hope for

163 Ibid., p. 146.   164 Ibid.   165 Ibid., p. 197.   166 Ibid., p. 80.
167 CMS c1/0185/139 Annual letter 1867.
168 James Long 'Address of the Reverend James Long to the Court', in *Trial of the Rev. James Long,
    for the Publication of the 'Nil Darpan'; with Documents Connected with Its Official Circulation,
    Including Minutes by the Hon. J. P. Grant, Statements by W. S. Seton-Karr, and Resolution by the
    Governor-General of India in Council* (London, James Ridgeway, 1861), p. 21.

'these degraded millions'.[169] Despite this significant excursion, Jesus was essentially for Long, an 'oriental guru, after the Eastern manner'.[170]

Long and Colenso were both involved in colonial politics and both significantly took up the cause of the colonized. Colenso interfered on behalf of two Zulu chiefs who were unfairly treated by the colonial administration. The treatment accorded to them has all the hallmarks of colonial high-handedness and racial prejudice. In the case of Langalibalele, this uppity native failed to obey colonial orders and had to be punished as a deterrent, even if the charges against him were trumped up. In the case of Cetshwayo, this Zulu chief had to be maligned in order to legitimize the redrawing of the map of the Zulu nation in the interests of European needs. Long became embroiled in the plight of the Bengali indigo workers, and the immediate cause which landed him in trouble was his lending a hand to translate a Bengali play, *Nil Darpan*. The play was a savage satire on the indigo planters but, in the words of Long, 'in simple homely language, [the play] gives the annals of the poor; pleads the cause of those who are feeble'.[171] The struggles of Long and Colenso on behalf of the Bengali peasants and the Zulus have been recorded eloquently elsewhere and need not detain us here. What is significant for our purpose is that the interference of both men in colonial politics was a direct result of their hermeneutical pre-understanding – the right interpretation of the word is the enactment of it. If raising historical questions about the authenticity of biblical narratives earned the wrath of some of the Anglican establishment, Colenso's championing of the cause of the Zulus alienated him from even those who supported him through the Pentateuch crisis. The letter Colenso wrote to J. N. Wheeler, a member of one of his congregations, made clear his hermeneutical intentions – word and deed are intertwined:

I am very sure that you would not be the man to wish me to preach, Sunday after Sunday, what I do not practise – to tell my people to take up, when the occasion comes, heavy burdens of duty on behalf of their fellow-men, when I myself

---

169 James Long, 'Peasant Degradation an Obstacle to Gospel Propagation', Church Missionary Meeting, Calcutta (8 April 1856), p. 4.
170 Long, *Bible Teaching and Preaching for the Million*, p. 2.
171 James Long's 'Introduction' to *Nil Durpan: The Indigo Planters' Mirror. A Drama Translated from the Bengali by a Native* (Edinburgh: Myles Macphail, 1862), p. 2.

shrink from touching such work with my own hands, though here it has been laid in the providence of God at my very doors. Year after year since I returned to Natal from England I have been *saying* this and that from the pulpit.[172]

For Colenso, Micah's message, which was spoken all those years ago, was still valid for colonial Natal. In a soul-searching sermon he preached on the Day of Humiliation, Colenso asked his congregation whether, as an English nation, they were true to Micah's words – doing justice, loving mercy and walking humbly before God.

As I have already mentioned, Long drew inspiration from the example of the motto of the great founder, Jesus: 'The poor have the Gospel preached to them.' It was this saying which prompted Long to become involved with the problem of the indigo workers. In the statement he made to the court he said: 'Should I not have been a traitor to the religion I professed, whose great Founder's motto is "The poor have the Gospel preached to them", had I not availed myself of all legitimate opportunity to bring the wants and sufferings of the ryots, and the feelings and views of Natives generally, to the notice of men who had the power of remedying them?'[173] Many years before liberation theology reconfigured Christianity as a political religion for our time, Long identified the basic tenet of Christian faith as political. It is political in the sense that

in the early ages it assailed the slavery of the Roman Empire, in the middle ages it afforded an asylum to the serfs against the oppression of the feudal chiefs; at the period of Reformation it brought freedom to the peasant's home; in modern days it has abolished slavery in the West Indies; and it has protested against American slavery, and is now throwing its mantle of protection round the aboriginal tribes throughout the world.[174]

Both Colenso and Long, in their defence of the indigenous, put the blame squarely on the English for their atrocious behaviour, whereby they brought discredit both on the gospel and on their nation. In a letter Colenso wrote to Sir Bartle Frere, he said: 'But, above all, I mourn the loss of our character among the native tribes of South Africa, as an honourable nation, a just and truth-loving people, upon whose plighted word the Zulu king and people have been for so many years implicitly relying'.[175] In his address to the court before sentence was passed, Long echoed Colenso:

172 George W. Cox, *The Life of John William Colenso, D.D. Bishop of Natal*, vol. 11 (London, W. Ridgway, 1888), pp. 373–4.
173 Long, 'Address of the Reverend James Long to the Court', p. 21.
174 Ibid.
175 Cox, *The Life of John William Colenso, D.D.*, vol. 11, p. 501.

As a missionary, I have a deep interest in seeing the faults of my countrymen corrected; for after a residence of twenty years in India, I must bear this testimony – that, of all the obstacles to the spread of Christianity in India, one of the greatest is the irreligious conduct of many of my own countrymen. Thousands of natives have said to me, 'We judge of the Christian religion by what your countrymen do, not by what they say; by the life, not by the doctrine'.[176]

For Long, his trial and imprisonment were occasions to demonstrate the true face of Christianity. He wrote:

My trial and imprisonment . . . will, I trust, show the importance of Missionaries keeping themselves free from race prejudices, and the natural pride of the conqueror, and will show natives that *genuine* Christianity recognizes the principle of Catholicity in raising its followers above the prepossessions of race and country. And may the Christian public in England be awakened to the following truth – that the preaching of Missionaries in India will not have its full effect on the natives as long as the lives of many Englishmen in India indicate to the native mind that Christianity is a fine theory, beautiful in a book but not realized in practice.[177]

For Colenso and Long, the power of the gospel resided not in neat church dogmas but in the everyday practice of Christian life. While castigating the un-Christian activities of their erstwhile missionary colleagues, Long and Colenso had no doubts about the civilizing value of colonialism and Christianity. Given the option, though, they chose to legitimize Christian faith rather than colonialism. Colenso saw not only the Zulus but also his own countrymen as victims: 'How much wretchedness there still is in our motherland, unremedied, unsoothed, alas! uncared for! Advanced civilization, and its sure consequence a crowded population, seems to have brought heathen darkness, and misery which savage lands know nothing of, close to the doors of those who inherit the intellectual light, the wealth and culture, of all the ages'.[178] Both Colenso and Long envisioned an intimate world of the Christian household, which was seen as a supreme alternative to the world beyond the family. Their aim was 'to bring every wanderer home to the family of God'.[179]

Colenso's attitude to the Zulus was a complicated one, veering from admiration for their critical skills to labelling them as people with

176 Long, 'Address of the Reverend James Long to the Court', p. 21.
177 *Proceedings of the Church Missionary Society for Africa and the East. Sixty-Third Year 1861–1862.* London: Seeley, Jackson, and Halliday, p. 93.
178 Colenso, *Natal Sermons, Series* III, p. 304.
179 Ibid., p. 262.

childlike minds. He was appreciative of the critical streak in Zulu culture. It was his Zulu translator, William Ngidi, whom Colenso called his African philosopher, an 'intelligent native' and 'one with the docility of a child but the reasoning power of mature age', who posed to him a series of awkward questions which challenged both the accuracy of the Bible and the morality of the biblical God. These were the very questions which had plagued him during his parochial days in England. But, as he recalled, he 'contented' himself 'with silencing, by means of specious explanations' or drew 'from it practical lessons of daily life, without examining closely into the historical truth of the narrative'.[180] Now these questions came to him afresh through the intellectual challenge of a Zulu, though, on the other hand, Colenso felt that it would be a century before the Zulus would be ready to receive the complex nature of Christianity. For 'this generation', in his view, it was sufficient to teach them to pray, as 'taught by Christ Himself, in the Lord's prayer and in the Sermon on the Mount', and introduce them to such parts as were suited to them: 'the devotional Psalms, the simpler prophetical messages, the more edifying portions of the Old Testament history, the account of the life and death of Jesus'.[181] 'Such teachings', Colenso claimed they would 'imbibe . . . as mother's milk'. The Zulus, like children, needed the 'sincere milk of the Word'[182] to nourish them and enable them to grow.

Contrary to the prevalent attitude of the time, Colenso and Long did not think that the Zulus and the Bengalis were inherently backward people. This relative openness towards Zulu and Bengali culture did not prevent them from seeing that these cultures were deficient in themselves for nurturing a perfect moral and Christian life. Their hope was that imperial rule combined with Christian values would lift these peoples to a condition which the Europeans themselves had reached. When Long claimed that the poor had the gospel preached to them, his concern was more than the economic poverty of the peasants. It was their spiritual and cultural poverty which bothered him. It was this kind of poverty which made the Bengali peasants poor in the sight of missionaries such as Long and allowed them to become a suitable target for Christianizing activity. The conclusion these two Anglicans reached was that it was in the interests of the 'natives' to become Christians. Since conversions were few and far between and coercing the natives to join the Christian faith

---

180 Colenso, *The Pentateuch and Book of Joshua Critically Examined*, pp. vi–vii.
181 Colenso, 'On the Efforts of Missionaries among Savages', 276.
182 Ibid.

would go against their liberal stance, the alternative Long and Colenso came up with was to place them under Christian rule where the adminis-trators and company employees were expected to set a Christian example through their care and noble behaviour towards those who were in their charge. In one of his sermons Colenso drew attention to the responsi-bilities of the European: 'And thus every white man, who teaches the natives industry and cleanliness, and the arts of civilized life, may be in fact, as many a white man is, a true minister of God's love to his fellows'.[183] When the English failed to live up to these expectations, Long and Colenso did not hesitate to criticize them openly. 'The real obstacle to the spread of the Bible' in India, in Long's view, 'was the insulting tone of many Europeans towards natives and the atrocities practised by them'. In a letter he wrote to his committee in England after the 1857 Indian uprising, he described how, at the re-taking of Lucknow, the city was plundered by Christian soldiers and 'native females committed suicide to escape being violated by these Christian soldiers'.[184] He had heard often from 'Thousands of Indians' that 'we judge of Christian religion by what your countrymen do, not by what they say; by the life, not by the doctrine'.[185] Long's solution to these appallingly negative pictures of Christianity was to enable the masses to 'search the Scriptures for them-selves and thereby to learn that Christianity in the *book* was very different from what the lives of too many of its professors in India would indicate it to be'.[186] Similarly, Colenso was scathing in his attack on the English for their atrocious behaviour. In a sermon he preached on the Day of Humiliation after the great disaster at Isandhlwana, he said that the vengeful acts of the English were 'loathsome and abominable in His sight, a pandering to one of the basest passions of our nature, bringing us Christians below the level of the heathen we fight'.[187]

Colenso and Long, in both their Christian praxis and their exegetical practices, generally condemned the racial attitudes of the English and their despicable manners towards the 'natives'. In this respect they were exceptional. Although they were critical of the English, however, neither of them entertained an idea of English national character which was not

183 Colenso, *Natal Sermons, Series* III, pp. 264–5.
184 CMS C11/0185/45 9 April 1859.
185 Long, 'Address of the Reverend James Long to the Court', p. 21.
186 C.M.S.CI1/0185/45; 9 April 1859.
187 John William Colenso, 'What Doth the Lord Require of Us?': A Sermon Preached in the Cathedral of St Peter's, Maritzburg on Wednesday, March 12, 1879', Reprinted in Natalia 6 (1879), 21.

tied up with colonies and colonialism. Their understanding of the British character was intertwined with imperial ambition.

CONCLUDING REMARKS

Colenso and Long were not typical Victorian missionaries who came to wield power among those to whom they ministered. They were middle-class people who took upon themselves the responsibility of ruling the country and the colonies on a basis of Christian ideals. They subscribed to the view that in spite of different cultures, humankind under the father-hood of the Christian God was one human family, who shared common values and a single vision of life based on those values, which were equally applicable across cultures. Those who had an awareness of this had the duty to enlighten others. They did not fail to flaunt the superiority of the missionaries. Colenso encapsulated the mood of the time: 'We stand on a far higher level, intellectually and socially, with respect to those whom we seek to convert. We possess superior knowledge, superior power, which makes the intelligent Christian Missionary of our days almost a being from another and a higher sphere in the eyes of his flock'.[188] Such a claim was always accompanied by a sense of humility. In another sermon, he claimed that this task had made the British a humble people – 'men chosen of God, elect spirits, higher, purer and therefore humbler than the rest'.[189]

It is very apparent that Colenso and Long were unusual missionaries. Unlike the majority of Christian proselytizers of the time, they did not preach the 'dogma of eternal hell' for the heathen. Their sermons and writings did not paint a picture of 'crude notions of atonement' or 'Tartarus of fire', but were filled with 'Goodness, the Righteousness and the Fatherly Love of God'.[190] In spite of projecting a hell-free gospel message, Colenso and Long conceived of missionaries as 'heralds of civilization' who 'bring blessing to those among whom they toil'.[191] They wanted to cast Christianity as a very English type of faith – accommodating and reasonable.

From a postcolonial perspective, the reading strategies of Colenso and Long fall within the category of what I have described elsewhere as

---

188 Colenso, *Natal Sermons, Series* III, p. 262.
189 Colenso, *Natal Sermons, Series* IV, p. 3.
190 Colenso, *Natal Sermons, Series* III, p. 264.
191 Ibid.

dissident reading.[192] This is a kind of oppositional discursive reading practice undertaken by some colonialists. Prompted by both pangs of guilt and humanitarian motives, the intention of dissident discourse is to humanize colonialism and soften its avaricious and predatory motives. Fully located within and coopted by the colonial apparatus, what it, at best, did was to undermine it from within by raising concerns over the abuses of colonial power. As a moral critique of colonialism, dissident reading exposed the political chicanery and cultural violations of imperial practice but never questioned the imperial mission itself. As a discourse it did not aim to dismantle the whole edifice of colonialism but effectively questioned its territorial and cultural expansions. The hermeneutical endeavours of Colenso and Long amply demonstrate the marks of dissident reading.

While nineteenth-century biblical criticism in Europe and the debate surrounding the Bible had been determined by Christian culture and had been largely driven by intellectual and ecclesiastical questions posed in Europe, Long and Colenso were able to place the Bible in a wider multicultural context and reread it from the perspective of the critique offered by Zulu and Bengali cultures. It was a time when the colonized were seen as 'uncivilized people, ready like children to receive new impressions' and their cultures were treated as 'ancient and dying'. Long and Colenso utilized these very decadent and fossilized cultures to open up the Bible. Colenso pioneered cultural exegesis by employing Zulu concepts to illuminate the Epistle to the Romans, and utilized indigenous Zulu terms for God rather than importing or inventing others. He saw parallels between Zulus and biblical Jews in their life and practice but he somehow overlooked the proverbial tradition, one of the persuasive communicating avenues prevalent in Africa. Colenso's under-appreciation of the African sapiential tradition may have been due to his acknowledgement of the innate intellectual ability of the Zulus to question their received wisdom, as exhibited by his translator William Ngidi.

Colenso's interpretative activity was a sterling example of a hermeneutical principle which was being mooted in Victorian England, especially by Benjamin Jowett in *Essays and Reviews*, namely the right of scholars to treat the Bible as any other book and apply the same critical standards to it as to any other book. Colenso embraced the maxim fully and applied it ruthlessly and compellingly. His intention was to preserve the authority of

---

192 See R. S. Sugirtharajah, *Postcolonial Criticism and Biblical Interpretation* (Oxford, Oxford University Press, 2002), p. 44.

the Bible. His solution was to employ critical tools to replace problematic narratives with the texts which he believed to be genuine and to encapsulate the word of God as he understood it.

Reflecting the prevailing confident mood of the time, Colenso was able to speak about the 'certain results of modern criticism'[193] and the 'grand results of Modern Science'.[194] Such claims will be received with some scepticism today. Like most ideas that emerged with modernity, they are undergoing vigorous reappraisal. The lesson Colenso has for us today lies not in the clinical precision with which he demolished the historical claims made for some biblical accounts, but in his concern to make his findings available to ordinary people. As we saw earlier, his concern was for the common reader. His gravest miscalculation, that brought upon him the accusation of heresy, was not what he discovered or what he said but how and to whom he said it. His main audience were the ordinary readers, and he wrote for them in English. Colenso was not the first one to question the historicity of the Pentateuch narratives in England. There were two Anglican divines, Archbishop Whately and Thomas Burnet, the Master of Charterhouse, who had already shown the 'impossibility of holding the traditionary view' with regard to events like the creation and fall, and the flood. Burnet's tract was published in 1692 but it was written in Latin. Colenso's 'fault' was that he wrote in a language which the working classes and artisans of London could read. Colenso himself commented that the whole unsavoury episode could have been avoided had the writings of Whately and Burnet been available in English. Of Burnet, he wrote that if the views of this able divine had been published in the English tongue, so as to be ' "understood of the people", it is probable that we should not now, a century and a half afterwards, be still discussing the historical reality of these ancient narratives'.[195] It was even suggested by Sir Charles Lyell that the entire regrettable controversy could have been averted had Colenso published his expositions in '*Latin* so as to be confined to a circle which could be safely entrusted with such novelities, without there being any danger of unsettling the creed of the multitude'.[196] Colenso's crime was, as Sir Charles put it, 'freely communicating such knowledge to such a class of students'.[197]

193 Colenso, *Natal Sermons*, Series I, p. 242.
194 Colenso, *Natal Sermons*, Series III, p. 235.
195 John William Colenso, *The Pentateuch and Book of Joshua Critically, Examined, Part* IV (London, Longman, Green, Longman, Roberts, & Green, 1864), p. xvi.
196 John William Colenso, *The Pentateuch and the Book of Joshua Critically Examined, Part* V (London, Longmans, Green & Co, 1865), p. xliii.
197 Ibid.

In the appropriation of the Bible, Long and Colenso complemented each other. They exemplified two ways of arriving at possible meanings – literary and historical. For both, the survival of the Bible depended on its potential to provide meaning and value to people when they are overwhelmed by despair and distress. The ways in which Colenso and Long handled the Exodus narrative showed how they placed a high premium on the spiritual need of the people. Both saw the typological value of the narrative and regarded it as an event that happens in everyone's life. Long wrote: 'In reading of the journey of the Hebrews from Egypt to Canaan by the way of the wilderness, we see a pattern of our life, and of all the trials we are to undergo as Christians in our progress through this world to the kingdom of heaven'.[198] Although Colenso viewed the narrative as fictitious, he knew very well that the historical validity or invalidity of the Exodus, or for that matter of the flood or the patriarchal history, is irrelevant and a distraction when one is discussing the meaning of life and death. He concurred with Long that what is crucial in one's life is the recurring theme of endless searching wanderings: 'So thoroughly, however, have we all from our childhood been imbued with this story, so thoroughly has it penetrated our everyday language, that pious persons often speak or sing of their weary wanderings in this wilderness-life'.[199] Where Colenso differed from Long was with his ruthless application of critical methods. Colenso was able to show that the despicable practices, such as slavery and cruel treatment of slaves, exploitation of people, and Sabbatarian rules, found in the biblical narratives, did not have divine sanction and hence should not be imposed on hapless people.

Hermeneutically Long and Colenso were far apart in two regards. First, for Colenso, the word of God has to be heard afresh in every age, and every generation has to fashion it anew. The Bible for Colenso was not a blueprint or prescription but an open-ended oracle of God which always has to be discerned anew. The appeal to biblical precedent or textual evidence has to be abandoned in favour of the recognition that the same spirit which was at work in ancient times is also at work in contemporary events. In Colenso's hermeneutical scheme, the Bible is pre-eminently an important book but this does not mean that it possesses the revelatory authority for questions facing today's world. The Bible is there as a reliable reminder, to guarantee the living and ongoing presence of God's activity in the world. What is more, God's revelatory word is not confined

198 Long, *Scripture Truth in Oriental Dress*, p. 69.
199 Colenso, *Lectures on the Pentateuch and the Moabite Stone*, p. 285.

to the Book alone. For Long on the other hand, the Bible embodies God's word and it is written there for all generations. For him, the laws of the Bible are immutable: 'The Bible laws are in their essence in ten *precepts* and two *golden* rules; human laws are repealed, others are substituted, but God's law is the same; it is not "the glorious uncertainty of the law" as with human laws'.[200] Secondly, unlike Colenso, Long was not interested in questioning the historical acts of God. For him, God teaches through ordinary things – through signs, tokens and types. Long supported this method by citing biblical examples: Ezekiel's symbolic action of drawing on a tile to announce the siege of Jerusalem (4.3); Jeremiah's breaking of the pot to denote Nebuchadnezzar's fury; his parable of the broken jar to proclaim the impending doom (19.1); his use of baskets of figs to debunk the claim to superior virtue of those who escaped the deportation (24.1–8); and Jesus' pointing to a child to illustrate the Kingdom of God. (Matt. 18.1–6). For Long, God speaks 'in a universal language, drawn from God's book of nature', thus open to all and easy to understand.[201] Long initiated a strategy to explain the Christian gospel which by-passed and at times went beyond the familiar Semitic and Hellenistic images, a strategy which was to be taken up later by some Indian Christian theologians in the colonial period who argued that God's presence could be discerned through non-Judaic sources. The chief among them was Panippedi Chenchiah, whom we shall look at in the next chapter.[202] Since then, unfortunately, no Indian Christian theologian has followed this up.[203]

Long repeatedly claimed that the Bible was not a western but very much an eastern or an oriental book. This was not because the biblical texts were composed in the East by orientals or were extensively influenced by oriental religious and philosophical ideas, but because he believed the Bible was easy for the oriental mind to understand. Its contents resonated with Eastern ways of thinking, acting and being. When he claimed that the Bible was an 'Oriental' or an 'Eastern' book, he was not alone in making such a claim. Benjamin Jowett of *Essays and*

---

200 Long, *Scripture Truth in Oriental Dress*, p. 185.

201 Long, *Bible Teaching and Preaching for the Million*, p. 2.

202 See his discussion on the place of the Christian Old Testament and Judaism, D. A. Thangasamy (ed.), *The Theology of Chenchiah with Selections from His Writings*, Confessing the Faith in India Series No. 1 (Bangalore, The Christian Institute for the Study of Religion and Society, 1966), pp. 154–73.

203 The exception is my tentative attempt to use wisdom as a way of doing theology; see R. S. Sugirtharajah, 'Wisdom, Q, and a Proposal for a Christology', *The Expository Times* 102:2 (1990), 42–6.

Reviews also espoused such an idea. For Jowett, the Bible was a 'book written in the East', and because it was an eastern book it was likely to be misunderstood in the West 'because it speaks the language and has the feeling of the Eastern lands'.[204] Where Jowett would have distanced himself from Long was in his attitude to the Bible's innate authority. Jowett's view was that the 'Book of Scripture' should not be given to people 'to be reverenced like the Vedas or the Koran, and consecrated in its words and letters',[205] advice which Colenso not only would have endorsed but also put into practice effectively. For Long, on the other hand, the Bible had an innate authority, although there were for him two words of God: 'One written on paper, the Bible, the other written by the spirit on the heart'.[206]

While orientalists, missionaries and early Indian converts like K. M. Banerjea, Nehemiah Goreh and Upadhyay were delving into the written Sanskrit texts and juxtaposing them with biblical narratives, Long was basing his hermeneutics on the oral tradition of the masses. Where Banerjea and others were looking for correspondences and equivalences for vedic concepts like *prajapati* (Lord of Creatures) and *Cit* (consciousness) in the Bible, Long was trying to place the wisdom tradition of the Bible alongside oriental proverbial sayings which enshrined 'the wit and wisdom of the multitude'.[207] His preference for wisdom literature both contributed to and restricted his hermeneutical intentions. Instead of going for the historical acts of God as a starting point, as most interpreters do, Long opted for the wisdom tradition, which not only provided an alternative to the historical mode of God's revelation but was also accommodative of a variety of popular cultures. The significance of wisdom is its ability to borrow freely and to mix and match material creatively from different cultures, and Israel's wisdom is no exception. So too was the Indian tradition, as Long was well aware. The strength of wisdom is that it is fluid, multicultural and open. The inclusive nature of the sapiential tradition, however, did not prevent Long from claiming the centrality of Christ in the redemptive plan of God. What he came up with was not Jesus as a sage representing multiculturalism and religious pluralism, but an ethnic figure – '*white and pure*' – representing the European races.[208]

204 Benjamin Jowett, 'On the Interpretation of Scripture', in *Essays and Reviews. The Sixth Edition* (Longman, Green, Longman, & Roberts, 1861), p. 367.
205 Ibid., p. 427.
206 Long, *Scripture Truth in Oriental Dress*, p. 193.
207 Ibid., p. i.   208 Ibid., p. 205.

Long's method reinforced the popular orientalist notion that India lacked acute, logical, rational minds. He overlooked the often neglected orientalist 'discovery' of India's indigenous traditions of reasoning and logic. T. H. Colebrooke, an orientalist and a mathematician, in a paper read at the Royal Asiatic Society in February 1824, entitled 'The Philosophy of the Hindus: On the Nyāya and VaiSesika Systems', based on the Nyayasutra,[209] was able to demonstrate that India too possessed rational and scientific traditions which were akin to Greek thought. Unlike most learned papers, Colebrooke's Royal Asiatic presentation was not consigned to the academic dustbin. It became an influential and accessible text. Jonardon Ganeri claims that Colebrooke's essay became the 'standard reference for the next fifty years' and Colebrooke, through his influence and his contacts with eminent logicians of the time, was 'able to generate a great deal of interest . . . not only among Orientalists, but also within the English philosophical community'.[210] Long's insistence on India's symbolic and figurative thinking, and his convenient disregard of the Colbrookian thesis, puts him with those orientalists, such as William Jones and Max Müller, who envisioned an India which was essentially intuitive, non-logical and eternally spiritual, and he thus unwittingly played into the hands of the colonialists, who saw the lack of science education as a justification for the colonial presence.

The identification of Colenso and Long with the cry of the oppressed does not mean that they were at the forefront of the anti-colonial struggle. In all fairness, they were not in favour of the ending of the empire. They were proud of the achievements of the British. Long listed remarkable reforms that the British had achieved in India: open courts, trial by jury, local assemblies, decentralized administration, peasants' rights, national education and railways. These internal reforms and developments were signs that Britain was the 'mother of a great empire'.[211] The most Long would concede was Indian self-governance under European superintendence: 'I myself believe thoroughly in the truth of Lord W. Bentinck's maxim "India must be managed by Native agency under European superintendence"'.[212] Even the nationalists of the time did not envisage anything more. Both believed in the value of the empire and saw it as a

---

209 One of the principal texts of the Nyaya school, composed between 200 BCE and 150 CE. For Colebrooke's article (pp. 26–58) and other essays on Indian logic, see Jonardon Ganeri (ed.), *Indian Logic: A Reader* (London, Curzon Press, 2001).
210 Ibid., p. 5.
211 James Long, *Russia, Central Asia, and British India* (London, Trübner and Co., 1865), p. 42.
212 Long, 'The "Nil Darpan" Controversy-Statement', p. 712.

trust given to the British. In spite of stepping out of line with the colonial administration, idealistic notions about imperialism and paternalistic tendencies are evident in their writings. Colenso spoke about the

duty which we owe, as English Christians, towards the inferior races under our charge; to say that surely the rule of a nation like ours over so many weaker communities means something more than the amount of property, of material wealth, she can squeeze out of the subject peoples; that if England extends her sway over the earth to inforce justice, to practise mercy, to show care and pity for the weak and helpless, to redress the wrongs of the downtrodden and oppressed, and to raise her dependents in the scale of humanity, there is then a reason for the existence of her vast colonial empire.[213]

Colenso believed that 'a powerful nation like ours has a right and a duty to inforce [changes], if need be, upon our Zulu neighbours' but what he disapproved of was the manner of enforcing them: 'It seems to me that if we cannot inforce the changes we desire in a better way than this, we have no right to try and inforce them at all'.[214] Long, too, held the view that stronger nations had a duty towards weaker ones: 'There are certain stages in society when the Government of enlightened foreigners is better for a nation than that of her own rude chieftains'.[215] The myth of the superior people conquering the inferior races is still prevalent. Robert Cooper, an influential figure who was close to the British Prime Minister Tony Blair, was able to write, a century and a half after Long and Colenso, advocating re-colonization: 'The weak still need the strong and the strong still need the orderly world'. The means to achieve this was by resorting to 'force, pre-emptive attack, deception . . . when we are operating in the jungle, we must also use the laws of the jungle'.[216] Long viewed the suppression of the Indian uprising of 1857 not only as a 'victory of the British Lion' but also 'as a boon in restoring order, putting down anarchy' and, more importantly, as a condition of 'developing the resources of India'.[217] What horrified them both was the atrocious behaviour of the colonial administration, which brought hardship to the indigenous people. The horrors they witnessed – the killing of Zulus,

213 Colenso's letter to the Dean of Westminster December 17, 1874, in Cox, *The Life of John William Colenso, D.D.*, vol. 11, p. 394.
214 Ibid., p. 501.
215 James Long, 'Address by the Rev. J. Long at the Anniversary Meeting of the Family Literary Club', in *Third Anniversary Report of the Family Literary Club with the Anniversary Address by the Rev. James Long* (Calcutta: C. H. Manuel & Sons, 1860), p. 17.
216 Robert Cooper, 'The Post-Modern State', in *Re-Ordering the World: The Long Term Implications of 11 September*, ed. Mark Leonard (London: The Foreign Policy Centre, 2002), pp. 16–17.
217 Long *Russia, Central Asia, and British India*, p. 41.

plundering of their cattle, appropriation of their lands, in the case of Colenso; the land settlement which deprived Bengali peasants of their lands, the inhuman behaviour of Christian soldiers during the 1857 Indian uprising, and the arrogant attitude of English civilians in India, in the case of Long – were all attributed to lapses in the otherwise exemplary behaviour and motivation of the British. These lapses were put down to the personal highhandedness of a few colonial officers or the incompetence of ambitious colonial administrators and could be set right once they were brought to the attention of the British public and raised with the higher echelons of power and authority in the empire. It was like the American administration blaming the atrocities at Abu Ghraib jail in Iraq on a few rotten apples among the ranks of its soldiers. What Colenso and Long did not realize was that what they thought of as lapses were in fact the very fabric of colonialism. True, Long and Colenso were critics of the predatory nature of imperialism, but, like many liberals of today, they admired and encouraged a humanitarian and interventionist empire. Or, as the current advocate of such an interventionist colonialism, Michael Ignatieff, has put it, these two Anglicans were supporting a 'redemptive exercise of temporary imperial rule'.[218]

The strength of their writings was to provide a paradigmatic text for the European colonialists, and to set them an agenda to fight against their own imperial desires and colonial expansion and to give up their bigotry and self-righteousness. The hermeneutical acts of Long and Colenso, measured against the norms of their time, were dysfunctional, and at the most were irritants to the authorities. They did not unsettle the colonial system nor did their resistance-hermeneutics cause any dislocation. They were moral critics of imperialism, but nonetheless they colluded with it.

---

218 Michael Ignatieff, *Empire Lite: Nation Building in Bosnia, Kosovo and Afghanistan* (London, Vintage, 2003), p. 111.

CHAPTER 4

Texts and Testament:
the Hebrew scriptures in colonial context

The Manusmriti, the Old Testament, and scores of other holy texts
could do with judicious editing and interpretation.

David Davidar

In truth, the Jew does not walk from the Old Testament to the New.
What was done was that the Christian walked backwards from the
New Testament to the Old.

P. Chenchiah

When a Christian from Manchester asked Gandhi to read the Bible, he
accepted his advice and got himself a copy. This is how Gandhi recollected
his experience:

I began reading it, but I could not possibly read through the Old Testament. I
read the book of Genesis, and the chapters that followed invariably sent me to
sleep. But just for the sake of being able to say that I had read it, I plodded
through the other books with much difficulty and without the least interest or
understanding. I disliked reading the Book of Numbers. But the New Testament
produced a different impression, especially the Sermon on the Mount which
went straight to my heart. I compared it with the *Gita*.[1]

Godfrey E. Phillips, in his enquiry into the use of the Old Testament in
the mission field, captures another example of this uneasiness about the
Old Testament, this time experienced by a Chinese Christian:

Intending missionaries or evangelists waste their time if they spend a lot of it
studying the Old Testament. It would be better for them to spend the time on
Sociology or Psychology . . . The Old Testament teaching given in theological
colleges in China is, in the experience of most of the students, devoid of interest
or value for their after work. Reading the Old Testament is like eating a large
crab; it turns out to be mostly shell, with very little meat in it.[2]

---

1 M. K. Gandhi, *Christian Missions: Their Place in India* (Ahmedabad, Navajivan Press, 1941), p. 16.
2 Godfrey E. Phillips, *The Old Testament in the World Church: With Special Reference to the
Younger Churches* (London, Lutterworth Press, 1942), p. 23.

This chapter has two foci. The first section looks at how orientalists and missionaries handled the Old Testament in the colonial context, the former using their newly discovered Asian texts as a means of verifying the historicity of biblical creation narratives, and the latter treating the Old Testament as a document of progressive revelation. It also draws attention to how a model of the chronological progress of divine revelation advocated by missionaries was hindered and complicated by the canonical arrangement of the Old Testament, and how they tried to solve this by aligning with an unusual ally – historical criticism, or higher criticism as it was then known – an ally of which most missionaries of evangelical leanings were suspicious and which they detested. The second section narrates how those at the receiving end viewed the Old Testament, especially a Vellala Saiva Hindu, Arumuka Pillai, and a Shudra Christian, Arumainayagam Suttampillai. Both appropriated it as a convenient hermeneutical tool to redefine their identity and used it as a hermeneutical shield to withstand the onslaught of missionaries on their culture and community. Most revealingly, this section demonstrates how neither Arumuka Pillai nor Arumainayagam Suttampillai[3] regarded the Hebrew scriptures as an archaic document and as having served its purpose, but as a document relevant to their immediate interpretative needs and resonating with their hermeneutical ambitions. The chapter ends with a glance at the depiction of empires and their fate in the Old Testament, and the warning this offers to those with an ambition to establish a new imperium.

PITTING GENESIS AGAINST THE PURANAS

When the Hebrew scriptures arrived with the missionaries in South Asia, as part of the Christian Bible, they were to confront the biggest threat to their authority. Unlike the challenge the Hebrew Bible was to face in the West in the latter part of the nineteenth century, when higher criticism, as we saw earlier (chapter 3), unleashed a series of questions which began to undermine its historical veracity and moral worthiness, in South Asia it met a different set of challenges in the form of ancient Asian religious texts. These Asian sacred texts substantially disrupted the claim of the Hebrew scriptures to religious uniqueness and divine inspiration and dislodged the Christian missionary assertion that the Hebrew scriptures

---

3 His title Suttampillai means monitor and is sometimes spelt Sattampillai.

were the oldest deposit of God's revelation. In Asia the missionaries had to contend with religions which had textual traditions older than the Hebrew scriptures, while the scriptures' reliablity as a source of history became doubtful.

William Jones,[4] one of the pioneer British orientalists in the eighteenth century, had no such doubts: 'Either the first eleven chapters of Genesis, all due allowances being made for a figurative Eastern style, are true, or the whole fabrick of our national religion is false; a conclusion which none of us, I trust, would wish to be drawn'.[5] Unlike Islam, which emerged after Christianity and did not threaten the antiquity of the Christian scriptures, the presence of Asian religions older than the one described in the Hebrew scriptures seemed to challenge the claim that the Jewish narratives contained the oldest record of human history and, much worse, they would be seen as a derivative from much older Asian religions. The notion that all the people of the earth had some inclination to divine truth embedded in them made the Christian enterprise complicated and vulnerable. In a way this was a hermeneutical conundrum which had been bothering Christians ever since they left the European milieu, a largely monocultural and mono-religious milieu. Faced with this unanticipated threat, a solution was sought in two ways. One way was to reconcile Asian chronological traditions with the biblical chronology. For William Jones, this rested on the work of the seventeenth-century scholar John Ussher, the Archbishop of Armagh (1581–1656), who had fixed a chronology of the world which went unchallenged until the rise of higher criticism in the nineteenth century. In his calculation, the creation was about 4004 BCE, the flood 2349 and the exodus 1491. These dates had been included in the margins of the King James Version since 1701.[6] The other way was to uphold the notion of a single monotheistic origin of all the peoples of the

4 Sir William Jones (1746–94) served in India as a judge. He was engaged in the orientalist enterprise of collecting, studying, codifying and translating Sanskrit texts. It was his translation of Kalidasa's *Sakuntala* which introduced the Sanskrit play to a European audience. Literature related to Jones's contribution to scholarship is too extensive to list here. I have benefited from the works of Thomas R. Trautmann and Sharada Sugirtharajah. For an introduction to Jones's life and work, see Garland Cannon, *The Life and Mind of Oriental Jones: Sir William Jones, the Father of Modern Linguistics* (Cambridge University Press, Cambridge, 1990). For Jones's biblical work, see Thomas R. Trautmann, *Aryans and British India* (University of California Press, Berkeley, 1997), pp. 44–59. For Jones's treatment of Hindu tradition, see Sharada Sugirtharajah, *Imagining Hinduism: A Post Colonial Perspective* (London, Routledge, 2003), pp. 1–37.

5 William Jones, 'On the Gods of Greece, Italy, and India', in William Jones, *The Works of Sir William Jones in Six Volumes* (London, G. G. and J. Robinson, 1799), p. 233.

6 Alan Richardson, *The Bible in the Age of Science* (London, SCM Press, 1961), pp. 41–2.

world, as depicted in the Book of Genesis. The single-origin theory proved to be a double asset. It vindicated the historicity of the Hebrew scriptures and also explained the similarities of these traditions. The person who crystalized these views was William Jones. He was not the first person to espouse the ideas; they had been propounded before. The Jesuits in China, faced with the older Confucian history, which had an enviable written record, reduced it to fit in with biblical history.[7] The common origin of the human race was 'the simplest of the historical explanations habitually used by Christians'.[8] Jones reworked this idea and packaged the Puranic history within the biblical framework, and in the process repositioned the Christian Bible within the oriental context. For his generation, it was Jones who articulated these issues convincingly and gave an erudite explanation.

Jones was confident about the validity of Mosaic chronology and the authority of the Hebrew scriptures. For him, 'the most ancient history of that race, and the oldest composition perhaps in the world, is the work in *Hebrew*'.[9] His claim was that the first eleven chapters of Genesis 'are merely a preface to the oldest civil history now extant'.[10] His reason for upholding the inspired nature of the Hebrew scriptures was shaped by the Christian apologetic, which placed a great premium on the fulfilment of prophetic predictions: 'The connection of the Mosaick history with that of the Gospel by a chain of sublime predictions unquestionably ancient, and apparently fulfilled, must induce us to think the Hebrew narrative more than human in its origin, and consequently true in every substantial part of it'.[11] In his view, 'the truth and sanctity of Mosaick History' was not affected by any resemblances found in the older 'idolatrous' nations of Egypt, India, Greece and Italy.[12]

With a concern to reinforce Christianity, Jones's hermeneutical tactic was to redraw the chronological map of the world. He summarily dismissed outright the cumbersome and long-drawn-out Indian history which did not fit in with his timeframe. He arbitrarily fixed a universal

7 P. J. Marshall and Glyndwr Williams, *The Great Map of Mankind: British Perceptions of the World in the Age of Enlightenment* (London, J. M. Dent and Sons Ltd, 1982), p. 118.
8 P. J. Marshall (ed.), *The British Discovery of Hinduism in the Eighteenth Century* (Cambridge, Cambridge University Press, 1970), p. 37.
9 William Jones, 'Discourse the Ninth on the Origin and Families of Nations', in *Works*, p. 133.
10 Ibid., p. 136.
11 Ibid.
12 Jones, 'On the Gods of Greece, Italy, and India', *Works*, p. 276.

deluge as the starting point of human history because it was documented in various ancient writings:

The sketch of antediluvian history, in which we find many dark passages, is followed by the narrative of a *deluge*, which destroyed the whole race of man, an historical fact admitted as true by every nation, to whose literature we have access, particularly by the ancient *Hindus*, who allotted entire *Puránа* to the detail of that event, which they relate, as usual, in symbols or allegories.[13]

Hence the parallel flood narrative in the Puranas[14] was seen as a proof of the authenticity of the biblical flood, and in Jones's view it became a convenient marker for the beginning of all history. Thus Hindu yugas[15] before the flood were either squeezed into the Ussherite timetable, or considered as metaphorical. For Jones, it was impossible to believe 'that the *Vedas* were actually written before the flood'.[16] The *Bhagavata Purana*[17] has a story similar to that of the Genesis flood narrative. In the Puranic version, Manu, the ancestor, was told of an imminent flood, and, as in the Genesis story, he was saved along with seven sages by Lord Vishnu incarnated in the form of a fish, the survivors finding shelter on the top of a mountain. The Genesis narrative, too, had eight people being saved: Noah and his wife, his three sons, Shem, Ham and Japheth and their wives (Gen. 7.13). When the flood abated the new creation dawned. Jones's contention was that Manu was none other than Noah disguised by Asiatic fiction. He differentiated this Manu in the *Purana* from the Manu, the progenitor of human race, who is identified with Adam:

Whatever be the comparative antiquity of the *Hindu* scriptures, we may safely conclude, that the Mosaick and Indian chronologies are perfectly consistent; that MENU son of BRAHMA, was the A'dima, or first created mortal, and consequently our ADAM; that MENU, child of the Sun, was preserved with *seven* others, in a *bahitra* or capacious ark, from an universal deluge, and must, therefore, be our NOAH . . . and that the dawn of true *Indian* history appears

---

13 Jones, 'Discourse the Ninth on the Origin and Families of Nations', in *Works*, p. 134.
14 Literal meaning 'stories of old'. These Hindu narratives, mostly in verse form, contain legendary and mythological versions of history and of the creation and destruction of the universe. There are eighteen Puranas going back to Vedic times.
15 According to Hindu cosmology, the world goes through a cycle of four yugas, or ages. The first age, the perfect one, is followed by gradual moral and physical degeneration.
16 Jones, 'On the Gods of Greece, Italy, and India', in *Works*, p. 245.
17 The story of Lord Vishnu's various avataras ('descents') especially that of Lord Krishna. Vishnu (preserver) is the second member of the Hindu triad, the other two being Brahma (creator) and Shiva (destroyer of evil).

only three or four centuries before the Christian era, the preceding ages being clouded by allegory or fable.[18]

Jones sought a solution to religious diversity by subscribing to the monogenesis theory of the time validated by the Book of Genesis. He claimed confidently that '*Egyptians, Indians, Greeks,* and *Italians,* proceeded originally from one central place, and that the same people carried their religion and sciences into *China* and *Japan*: may we add, even to *Mexico* and *Peru?*'[19] Even more confidently he located the origin of the common place as Iran: 'It is no longer probable only, but absolutely certain, that the whole race of man proceeded from Iran as from a centre whence they migrated'.[20] He also advanced the notion that the original revealed religion was monotheistic and that idolatrous ideas crept in later. He dismissed the idea that Moses would have borrowed from other sources:

There is no shadow then of a foundation for an opinion that Moses borrowed the first nine or ten chapters of *Genesis* from the literature of *Egypt*: still less can the adamantine pillars of our Christian faith be moved by the result of any debates on the comparative antiquity of the *Hindus* and *Egyptians*, or of any inquiries into the *Indian* theology.[21]

Jones found in Indian narratives an able ally but at the same time the narratives inhibited his enterprise. On the one hand, the Puranic flood narratives could be read as an independent verification of the biblical flood, thus buttressing the truth of the Bible. The external sources validated the historical accounts of the Bible and bolstered the image of the Bible. On the other hand, the endless cycles of time in Indian texts thwarted Jones's idea of neat biblical linear time advancing towards a final telos. The history recorded in Genesis became the benchmark for discerning and determining other histories, and those which did not fit in had to be squeezed in, erased or dismissed as wild allegorical imaginings.

The Bible as a deposit of historical accuracy and biblical prophecy as prediction were to be doomed when they came under heavy attack in the nineteenth century, and the same fate befell Jones's researches and his flawed theory of a common humanity emerging from Persia.

---

18 William Jones, 'A Supplement to the Essay on Indian Chronology', in *Works*, pp. 326–7.
19 Jones, 'On the Gods of Greece, Italy, and India', in *Works*, p. 274.
20 Jones, 'Discourse the Ninth on the Origin and Families of Nations', in *Works*, p. 137.
21 Jones, 'On the Gods of Greece, Italy, and India', in *Works*, p. 277.

MISSIONARY IMPOSITIONS

While an orientalist like Jones had tried in the eighteenth century to firm up the historicity of the Hebrew Bible, and by extension the history of humankind, with the help of the sacred texts of Asian religions, nineteenth- and twentieth-century missionaries found the Old Testament both an asset and an awkward proposition to deal with. It provided them with complicated signals. On the one hand, it became a convenient bulwark against what they perceived as pagan practices prevalent among the natives, but, on the other hand, the canonical arrangement of various books, their repetitive nature and endless genealogies proved to be troublesome. More specifically, the haphazard placement of different Old Testament writings threw a spanner in the works of progressive and linear theology advocated by missionaries.

In the former case, the missionaries in the colonies benefited from some remarkable resemblances between the beliefs and practices of biblical Jews and those of 'the uncivilized races'. They noticed how closely certain definable phases through which the Israelites progressed were evident in the religious features of the colonized. In the nineteenth century, influenced by German idealism and Darwinian social evolutionism, Christian theologians mooted the idea of an evolutionary progress in the Hebrew religion. It was propounded that, beginning with the lowest level of animistic practice, the Israelites steadily graduated to a more sophisticated monotheistic and moral understanding of faith which prepared them to grasp the ultimate manifestation of God in the form of Jesus Christ. The Hebrew scriptures were seen as a record of progress, providing examples of the different stages of the evolutionary model of the Hebrew religion. Henry Lapham, a Baptist missionary who worked in Sri Lanka, then Ceylon, in the last two decades of the nineteenth century and later taught at Selly Oak in Birmingham, identified roughly four progressive stages through which the faith of the Jewish people advanced, animistic, polytheistic, humanistic and legalistic.[22]

Lapham's fourfold linear march goes like this. In the early stages, the beliefs and customs of the Israelites exhibited many animistic practices, which continued even after the time of Moses. These practices included reverence shown to sacred trees (Gen. 12.6; Deut. 11.30; Judg. 4.5; 6.11; 9.37), sacred springs (Lev. 14.5; Num. 19.17), sacred stones (Gen. 28.18;

---

22 Henry A. Lapham, *The Bible as Missionary Handbook* (Cambridge, W. Heffer and Sons, 1925), p. 46.

31.45; 35.14), and the practice of divination and frequent use of fetishistic images (Judg. 8.27; 17.4). Later, in the eighth and seventh centuries before the Common Era, the Hebrews were idolatrous and polytheistic, with numerous altars which came under no central supervision. These practices were the survivals of Canaanite religion. The introduction of the Canaanite god, Baal, by King Ahab, and the Ammonite god, Moloch, by Manasseh, were supreme examples of polytheistic idolatry. The literary period, after the exile and during the third or fourth centuries before the Common Era, was humanistic. The books which embodied this humanistic phase were Proverbs and Ecclesiastes.[23] These books do not refer to priests, temples, prophets or to mystic fellowship with God. The Lapham legalistic period, in which Scribism and Pharisaism thrived, followed during the two centuries before the advent of Christ. The chief figures who influenced the promotion of legalism were Ezekiel and Ezra.

Lapham identified in Asian religions a similar four-stage process. He found that animism, though not an organized religion, was practised in varying degrees in all the religions of Asia. He identified Hinduism as polytheistic, Confucianism and Buddhism as humanistic. These last two traditions were not seen as revealed religions, but based on natural religion. He labelled 'Mohammedanism' legalistic. What was important about the Old Testament, for Lapham, was its documentary and revelatory value. It provided encouragement to those who toiled hard among the plethora of gods and obnoxious religious practices:

To one labouring under this bewilderment it comes as a glad surprise to discover that we have in the Old Testament the record of how God Himself led a people right on from semi-animistic beliefs and practices such as the Jews had when Moses took them in hand, to a fullness of preparation for the Truth of God incarnate, the final and living Word of God.[24]

Its virtue lay in its narration of how a people of lesser spiritual acumen was led to a higher spiritual status. In mapping out the religious landscape of the Asian religions, Lapham found the Old Testament a convenient tool to educate the missionary: 'The supreme value of the modern study of the Old Testament to the missionary is that it shows him God as missionary to animists, polytheists, humanists and legalists. It brings him to the feet of God the missionary, and bids him take his seat there on the footstool and learn'.[25]

23 Ibid., p. 94   24 Ibid., p. 49.   25 Ibid., p. 50.

A later, mid-twentieth-century missionary in India, Godfrey Phillips, saw things differently. 'Why trouble modern Aryans and Dravidians with such relics of an early Semitic religion?'[26] For him, the revolting sights he and other missionaries saw in everyday India – the sacred bull, the lingam, the pillars, the stones for the dead, devadasis (sacred prostitutes), the serpent cults, sacrificial propitiation, personified deities, worship of sun and moon, priestly institutions, formalized worship, the mother-goddesses and many other accessories of worship – were similar to the practices that existed in ancient Israel. One missionary's comment on the African situation was seen as equally true of India: 'We live in Old Testament times out here in many ways'.[27]

This whole range of images, customs and rituals, according to Phillips, was pre-Aryan and not indigenous to India, but imported and 'superimposed' by traders and settlers from the Mediterranean and Asia Minor, emanating from the very region from which the Old Testament emerged. Phillips remarks: 'We find ourselves strangely stirred by thinking that a large part of the religion of South-Western Asia which preceded the events out of which came the Old Testament scriptures is alive today in Indian villages to which neither Old nor New Testament has yet penetrated'.[28]

These resemblances enabled missionaries to say that current Indian religious practices equated to a stage that the biblical Jews had gone through, and the implication was that if the Jews could break away from prevailing pagan practices and graduate from a lower to a higher level of spirituality, so could modern Indians. These momentous changes were, as the missionaries saw it, enshrined in the scriptures. Phillips claimed that

to one set of people in that area, the Hebrews, certain things happened which, interpreted by inspired leaders, gradually led them from this primitive religion to ethical monotheism, and confronted them with the one, living, holy God . . . This Old Testament literature is the literary deposit of that whole process. In other words it enshrines the record of how God leads ordinary man from the place where the simple Hindu villager now stands, to such knowledge of Himself as prepares him for the advent of Jesus.[29]

The missionary perception was that people 'who start where the Jews started, can come to know the living God as the Psalmists and Prophets

26 Phillips, *The Old Testament in the World Church*, p. 134.
27 Cited in Brian Stanley, *The Bible and the Flag: Protestant Missions and British Imperialism in the Nineteenth and Twentieth Centuries* (Leicester, Apollos, 1990), p. 168.
28 Phillips, *The Old Testament in the World Church*, p. 37.   29 Ibid., p. 134.

knew Him'.[30] Although missionaries claimed that Israelite and Indian religious practices had certain noticeable affinities, they maintained a hierarchy of degeneracy. Israel's spiritual decadence was somewhat superior; for example, the practices that went on in Solomon's temple and those in the Kali temple in Calcutta might look ghastly to modern onlookers 'but the bloodshedding in the first was linked with something capable of infinite growth, the doing of the will of God so far as it was understood, whereas that in the other is joined to a whole complex of ideas which point not to an ethical future but to an animistic past'.[31]

By saying that 'the revolting practices' which modern missionaries witnessed in India were similar to those that 'Jeremiah faced',[32] missionaries were able to fix India and her religions as unchanging and static, and were able to present popular forms of Hinduism as Baalism. In other words, like Baal and Baal worship, which were confronted and defeated at Mount Carmel, Hindu gods and Hindu religious practices must be opposed and vanquished.

The prevailing missionary thinking of the time was that the religious practices of the natives were a defiance of the monotheistic ideal and a failure to acknowledge the lordship of the one God revealed through Jesus. The conspicuous expression and confirmation of resistance to a single God was the worship of many gods and goddesses, and visitation to several sacred places. In the Old Testament, missionaries found a jealous God, 'an effective protest against religious mixture'.[33] This is a God who cannot be worshipped along with others; his people must face the '"either-or" of true religion'. Missionaries told Indian converts from the lower castes that they could not 'worship Jehovah and at the same time worship gods very unlike Jehovah'.[34] The stern warning from the Old Testament from the outset provided legitimacy for missionaries, prohibiting any form of syncretism or pantheism. Such intermingling of gods and interchange of religious practices were seen as a serious threat to the practice of a purer religion. Those who worshipped other gods were seen as transgressing the ten commandments. The Old Testament injunctions enabled missionaries to stigmatize all religious manifestations as heathenish except those of Protestant Christianity.

Another aspect of the Old Testament which proved useful to missionaries was its ruthless teaching about those who backslide. Missionaries witnessed many religious waverers. The Old Testament is uncompromising

---

30 Ibid., p. 38.   31 Ibid., p. 87.   32 Ibid., p. 38.
33 Ibid., p. 44.   34 Ibid., p. 135.

in its teaching about people who rejected the salvation that God had bestowed on them. The Old Testament is vague about how the Gentiles are brought to the household of God. Unlike the New Testament, the Old Testament is not explicit about mission. We do not encounter a Paul-like figure roaming around converting the Gentiles. The Old Testament is unequivocal about the kind of fate that awaits those who fail to accept the ideal of ethical monotheism. It is this hardline attitude towards those who are unable to make up their minds that attracted the missionaries to the Old Testament.

'One of the functions of the Old Testament', claimed G. E. Wright, the biblical archaeologist and Old Testament scholar, was to provide 'an enlightenment from the faith of Israel' which has enabled the church to realize that the entry into the kingdom of God 'cannot be found among the religions of the world, but solely in the faith of Abraham and his seed of which we are heirs in the Church by Jesus Christ'.[35] The unequivocal condemnation of idolatrous practices which undermined the monotheistic ideal was interpreted as giving the missionaries a licence to deal with India's religious practices.

TAMPERING WITH THE TESTAMENT

While missionaries celebrated the Old Testament as evidence of God ushering a people into spiritual development, the haphazard canonical arrangement thwarted their evangelical belief in progressive revelation. The sequence of the Old Testament books as they occurred in the Bible, missionaries believed, presented 'the difficulty of making the historic revelation which is crowned by the incarnation stand out plainly as its vital message'.[36] One of the solutions mooted was to rearrange the books chronologically. The idea was to offer a comprehensive anthology of stories and messages which embodied the gradual revelation of spiritual truth. This proposed lining-up of the biblical books, they thought, would not only bring out the natural evolution of its basic doctrines but also the historical integrity of the various books. Such a rearrangement would give the prophets their rightful place. In advocating this rearrangement, Henry Lapham wrote: 'For the orderly way in which the revelation of God is given makes more clearly manifest than ever the divine superintendence and control of the long process'.[37]

35 G. Ernest Wright, 'The Old Testament: A Bulwark of the Church Against Paganism', *Occasional Bulletin from the Missionary Research Library* 14:4 (1963), 4.
36 Phillips, *The Old Testament in the World Church*, p. 106.
37 Lapham, *The Bible as Missionary Handbook*, p. 45.

The missionaries also thought that the 'natives' would, like Gandhi, have found it difficult to grasp the basic meaning of the Old Testament in the order in which it stood. Similarly, Geoffrey Phillips opined that when, for example, the 'older churches' found it difficult to grasp the writings of the Hebrew prophets, the 'younger churches' would find the prophetic message, so vital to the whole revelation, 'unintelligible'.[38] The solution was to make available native-friendly, truncated Bibles. It was suggested that these shortened versions of the Bible should carry brief notes, easy paragraph captions, and that the text should distinguish between poetic and prose writings.

Another apprehension the missionaries had was that the 'natives' might misuse the Old Testament. A classic case was that of the Gikuyu converts in Kenya. The Gikuyu, whose social organization was based on polygamy, were shattered to see how this institution which harmonized their communal activity had been undermined by the missionaries' insistence on monogamous marriages. Well aware of the polygamous status of significant and exemplary biblical figures, they approached missionaries for guidance and enlightenment. The missionaries, however, paid no attention to their queries because they assumed that an African was 'suited to receive what was chosen for his simple mind, and not ask questions'.[39] The Gikuyu were left on their own without any help from the missionaries, and Jomo Kenyatta, the Kenyan leader, who was involved in the Kenyan anti-colonial struggle and who later became the prime minister, told a story of how they refused to play the role of passive recipients and how they overturned the imposed reading of the missionaries. They looked again at the white-man's authority, the Bible, and decided to select the names for their baptisms from among the biblical characters who practised polygamy. Many went for names like Jacob (Gen. 29.15–30), Solomon (1 Kings 11.1–4), David (2 Sam. 12.24) and Abraham (Gen. 16.4). They believed that by following these illustrious biblical figures they were doing the right thing and not committing the sin of adultery. According to them, polygamy was permitted by God as long as they practised God's ways. They were astonished, therefore, to see missionaries condemning them 'for fulfilling that which is sanctioned and condoned in the Ibuku ria Nga (the Bible)'.[40] The missionaries

---

38 Phillips, *The Old Testament in the World Church*, p. 106.
39 Jomo Kenyatta, *Facing Mount Kenya: The Tribal Life of the Gikuyu* (London, Secker and Warburg, 1968 [1938], p. 271.
40 Ibid., pp. 272–3.

considered such a reading a mischievous use of the Old Testament, and, more pertinently, repellent to the morality that they advocated.

There was another reason for the abridged or rearranged Bibles. Missionary administrators felt that, with so many native languages to deal with, it would be a great financial strain to translate the whole of the Bible in each case. The practical solution was to offer a judicious selection of stories. Phillips proposed that these stories would 'teach the simpler kind of African his most practical lessons regarding sin, morality, and God's saving dealings with men'. He added, 'if they are skilfully woven together – and this is essential – they can show him God's gathering together of His own people and continuous preparation of the world for Christ'.[41] He went on to say that 'later on, possibly after many generations, when the Church has grown strong, able to undertake the translation and the cost of publication, and when the progressive character of revelation has been generally understood, the Church itself can decide whether or not to translate the whole into its local vernacular'.[42]

In their attempt to rearrange the Hebrew scriptures, missionaries found an unusual ally in historical criticism. Contrary to common belief, many of the evangelical missionaries did not see higher criticism as a destructive tool. In the approving words of R. F. Horton, who was Chairman of the Congregational Union and had an interest in the world church, it 'proved to be a restorative' agent.[43] They were not threatened by its negative impact on the Christian faith:

Think what modern scholarship has done for the Pentateuch in unravelling the perplexing problems which those first five books presented to the thoughtful reader. Think what it has done for the books of Daniel and Jonah and for the prophecies of Isaiah. It has made prophets live again. Before, they were abstractions, shadowy figures in a scheme of apologetics. Now they are living souls, real actors in the drama of life, very human, very lovable, very courageous, and, above all, pioneers and pathfinders in the spiritual pilgrimage of mankind.[44]

The missionaries extended a cautious welcome to modern criticism and found it a useful although annoying accomplice. Conservative British Old Testament scholars of the time, such as T. K. Cheyne, S. R. Driver and George Adam Smith, were able to demonstrate that the dreaded modern

---

41 Phillips, *The Old Testament in the World Church*, pp. 121–2.
42 Ibid., p. 121.
43 Robert F. Horton, *An Autobiography* (London, George Allen and Unwin Ltd, 1917), p. 95.
44 Francis Wrigley, *The Old Testament in the Light of Modern Scholarship: Abbreviated and Arranged for Use in Home, School and Church* (London, Independent Press, 1932), p. x.

biblical criticism could be evangelical-friendly. George Adam Smith even sanctified it with Christological approval: 'textual and historical criticism takes its charter from Christ Himself'.[45] These conservative scholars were able to demonstrate that even the faith-shattering scientific enquiry into the origin, authorship and content of the biblical books was consistent with 'reverent belief in Divine Inspiration, the supernatural guidance of Providence in the history, the Divinity, Miracles, and Resurrection of the Lord Jesus Christ, and, in general, a broad and free, but genuine and complete acceptance of evangelical Christianity'.[46] Horton, in his autobiography, was able to claim that the damage done to the text by the extravagances of German biblical scholarship had given way to 'sober criticism' which had 'now finally taken its place as the only criterion by which we are to know *what that book*, which we as Christians accept as the final court of appeal and the authoritative law-book of our religion, as literature is'.[47]

One of the results of higher criticism was the dating of the different books of the Old Testament. This, in Lapham's view, had 'placed missionaries under special obligation'[48] to arrange these books in chronological order. The perceived understanding was that modern scientific enquiry had enabled the missionaries to see 'in Christianity the missionary message for the world, which had been prepared by a natural historical development, and which is therefore guaranteed by the science and by the widening thought of our time'.[49] Historical method had shown the missionary evolution of Israel from the beginning. Lapham approvingly quoted Horton's Carey Lecture of 1913:

It is one of the advantages of the critical method applied to the Old Testament that by the arrangement of the books in their chronological order, and the discovery of the development of revelation in them, we have found in the prophetic literature the germ and development of the missionary idea. By such a re-arrangement as scholarship now makes we see the prophets move up and on, as if in an ordered development, toward the Christian revelation and the Person of Christ.[50]

45 George Adam Smith, *Modern Criticism and the Preaching of the Old Testament: Eight Lectures on the Lyman Beecher Foundation, Yale University, USA* (London, Hodder and Stoughton, 1901), p. 28.
46 This is a quotation from an anonymous review of Alfred Cave's *Inspiration of the Old Testament* in *London Quarterly Review* 71 (1889). Cited in Willis B. Glover, *Evangelical Nonconformists and Higher Criticism in the Nineteenth Century* (London, Independent Press Ltd, 1954), p. 206.
47 Horton, *An Autobiography*, p. 95.
48 Lapham, *The Bible as Missionary Handbook*, p. 45.
49 Robert F. Horton, *The Bible: A Missionary Book* (Edinburgh, Oliphant, Anderson and Ferrier, 1904), p. 126.
50 Lapham, *The Bible as Missionary Handbook*, p. 45.

The missionaries were confident that the scientific method brought out 'the missionary significance of Israel, and showing the steps by which the older religion widened into the new'.[51]

Missionaries believed that they had a new tool in the scientific method, which had been unavailable previously. Modern criticism made plausible the progressive manifestation of God in history. The scientific handling of the historical data of the Bible yielded positive 'results that it would be foolish to ignore',[52] claimed Horton.

Thus from the critical handling of Old Testament history comes the astonishing result, that Israel was gradually led under prophetic guidance from a primitive obscurity of Semitic immorality and idolatry, through a chequered history of trivial wars and insubstantial dynasties, into the fiery furnace of the Captivity, from which it emerged, like Job from his affliction, to realize a greatness which it had never known in the past. Between that return from exile and the coming of Christ, the history of that prepared people is the incubation of the Messianic idea. Apparently engaged in glorifying and stereotyping its past, Judaism was really waiting with bowed head for the expectation of Israel. And that proselytising impulse which we can discern in the last century BC, as if Judaism were just on the point of blossoming into a missionary religion, is the last and proper outcome of its long development, and the natural link with that Christian revelation to which it had been pointing.[53]

Higher criticism thus further strengthened the theological conviction of the missionaries that the New Testament was the crowning glory of the Old. This was the heyday of higher criticism, and the scholars, as we saw in chapter 3, were confidently talking about the assured results of modern criticism. On the basis of these assured results, a systematic biblical theology emerged, its main business being to trace the historical development of the Christian faith. In conservative missionary circles these assured results further reinforced their belief in inspiration, providing a mysterious hand in the gradual march towards the divine revelation in Jesus.

There were already in existence a number of shorter or abridged Bibles designed for school and home use in Britain and America. These shorter versions had another hermeneutical purpose, that is, to reassure Christians in those countries who were perplexed by modern criticism. Kent's *Shorter Bible, The Little Bible,* and *The Old Testament in the Light of Modern Scholarship*, abbreviated and arranged by F. Wrigley, were some

---

51 Horton, *The Bible: A Missionary Book*, p. 115.
52 Ibid.   53 Ibid., pp. 124–5.

of them. Translation of these into various native tongues was discounted because these shorter Bibles were aimed at potential or lapsed western Christians who had some notion of the Christian faith, and it was thought that the Bibles would not appeal to colonial converts who were totally new to the Christian faith.

There was also another group of western thinkers who advocated slimmer, chronologically rearranged, and narratively recast Bibles. Among them were Matthew Arnold, R. G. Moulton, James George Frazer and Ernest Sutherland Bates.[54] These scholars were not necessarily moved by missionary or religious concerns but were enchanted by the pure literary beauty of the English prose of the Bible. James George Frazer, of *Golden Bough* fame, encapsulated the mood:

> But how many read it not for its religious, its linguistic, its historical and antiquarian interest, but simply for the sake of the enjoyment which as pure literature it is fitted to afford? . . . The passages of greatest literary beauty and interest – those on which the fame of the book as a classic chiefly rests – are scattered up and down it, imbedded, often at rare intervals, in a great mass of other matter, which, however interesting and important as theology or history, possesses only subordinate value as literature. It seemed to me, therefore, that a service might be rendered to lovers of good literature by disengaging these gems from their setting, and presenting them in a continuous series.[55]

These western scholars wanted to eliminate confusing details, inappropriate materials and endless repetitions, to highlight the literary aspects of the Bible. R. G. Moulton lamented: 'But, though the Bible is proclaimed to be one of the world's great literatures, yet if we open our ordinary versions we find that the literary form is that of a scrap book: a succession of numbered sentences, with divisions into longer or shorter chapters, under which all trace of dramatic, lyric, story, essay, is hopelessly lost'.[56] Quiller-Couch went on to suggest that the Bible should be printed in order to distinguish prose from poetry in the original text: 'I should print the prose continuously, as prose is ordinarily and properly printed: and the poetry in verse lines, as poetry is ordinarily and properly printed'.[57]

---

54 For a careful analysis of those who advocated the Bible as literature, see David Norton, *A History of the Bible as Literature*, vol. 11: *From 1700 to the Present Day* (Cambridge, Cambridge University Press, 1993), pp. 272–98.

55 James George Frazer, *Passages of the Bible: Chosen for Their Literary Beauty and Interest* (London, A. & C. Black, 1927), pp. v–vi.

56 Richard G. Moulton, *A Short Introduction to the Literature of the Bible* (London, D. C. Heath, 1900), p. 9.

57 Arthur Quiller-Couch, 'On Reading the Bible (11)', in *The English Bible: Essays by Various Authors*, ed. Vernon F. Storr (London, Methuen & Co. Ltd, 1938), p. 115.

Although missionaries toiling in the colonies and scholars working in the metropolis were advocating the rearrangement of the Bible from different hermeneutical perspectives, their hermeneutical goal was the same – to affirm the progressive revelation of God which culminated in the manifestation of Jesus. Sutherland Bates put it thus: 'To afford a consecutive narrative from the creation to the exile, supplementing this by a selection from the Apocryphal 1 Maccabees in order to complete the story down to the times of Jesus'.[58]

The proposal for a shorter or rearranged Bible unwittingly raised a question about another cherished belief of the evangelicals, namely the unchanged and unchanging nature of the Biblical canon. This supposedly timeless narrative was subjected to the modernizing demands of the time, reshaped, reformulated and reordered. Paternalistic concern coupled with evangelical fervour determined what sort of Bible the natives should have. True, missionaries did utilize historical criticism but at the same time they were well aware that too much attention to historical details might blur the significance of the Old Testament. Philips articulated the point thus: 'But in the large part of the Old Testament we tend to be more occupied with the historic religious literature of a remarkable people than with the developing plot of a story unfolding towards Christ as its true meaning and climax'.[59]

The indigene talks back

The interpretation of the Old Testament by missionaries did not go unchallenged. One of those 'natives' who resisted was the Indian theologian, Pandipeddi Chenchiah (1886–1959). He was particularly directing his challenge to Godfrey Phillips and Marcus Ward. Like Phillips, Ward, in his book *Our Theological Task*, was arguing for the indispensable nature of the Old Testament for Indian Christian theology. Like other resistant voices, Chenchiah hit them with the argument where it really hurt the missionaries. He resorted to the very instrument the missionaries used for legitimizing their claims, the Bible. He cited the decision of the Council of Jerusalem against circumcision for Gentile converts. For him, such a decision implied that Paul felt that the whole Old Testament was unnecessary for Christians who had come from a non-Jewish background:

---

58 Ernest Sutherland Bates, *The Bible Designed to Be Read as Literature* (London, William Heinemann Ltd, 1937) p. xvii.
59 Phillips, *The Old Testament in the World Church*, p. 84.

St Paul has settled the controversy once for all. He never maintained that the Old Testament was obligatory on the Gentiles. The Law for the Gentile was not Mosaic law, but a law written in their hearts. The ordinances of Moses are an integral part of Judaism and did not bind them. The point of the whole controversy between St Paul and St Peter was whether a Christian need be a Jew in faith in order to be a Christian. The early Church joined St Paul in saying 'No'.[60]

Chenchiah found it puzzling that Europeans were more solicitous of the Old Testament than St Paul had been.

In Chenchiah's opinion, ideas like incarnation, indwelling of the Holy Spirit in human beings, the union between the Father and the Son and a similar union between the Christ and the believer are 'repugnant to the genius of Judaism' and will not mean anything without the Hindu background.[61] He claimed that the Pauline and Johannine constructions of Jesus would be intelligible only to those who were raised in Hellenistic and Hindu religious traditions. He found the Old Testament unhelpful in understanding the incarnation because it was 'in spirit and in explicit teaching . . . 'inimical to any conception of incarnation'.[62] This does not mean that the Old Testament did not have any valuable insights. He found the Psalms very spiritual, the prophetic message a proto-communism, and the exodus motif a helpful paradigm for the national movement. In spite of these positive observations, Chenchiah felt that it was not necessary to hold on to the Old Testament as 'an integral part of the Christian message'.[63] He reckoned that it was scarcely necessary for an understanding of the Christian faith.

Chenchiah was not convinced by the traditional argument that Jesus was the fulfilment of the Old Testament: 'The attempt to force Jesus into the framework of the Old Testament has pressed out the new elements in Christ and distorted and deformed his shapely figure'.[64] He also disputed the claim that one needs to know the Old Testament in order to understand the New. In one of his articles in the *Guardian*, he challenged Phillips: 'Prof. G. E. Phillips should know better with all his experience as a missionary. Any villager can understand Jesus, and many have, without knowing anything of the Old and for that matter anything of the New. Why should a Hindu understand the complicated Pauline theology to follow Jesus?'[65] His constant question to missionaries was: 'Why should

60 D. A. Thangasamy (ed.), *The Theology of Chenchiah with Selections from His Writings*, Confessing the Faith in India Series No. 1 (Bangalore, The Christian Institute for the Study of Religion and Society, 1966), p. 162.

61 Ibid., p. 160.   62 Ibid.   63 Ibid., p. 158.

64 Ibid., p. 163.   65 Ibid., p. 159.

there be only one path to Jesus and not two, one from Old Judaism and other from Old Hinduism?' He taunted them: 'Why in the name of reason and good sense should not God's dealings with my race be my Old Testament even as God's dealing with the Jew was the Old Testament of Jewish Christian?' He went on: 'I can pick up material for an Old Testament in Hinduism, making selections in the light of what Jesus said and did. That was exactly what early Christians did and later Hindu converts ought to do'.[66] As he put it memorably: 'In truth, the Jew does not walk forward from the Old Testament to the New. What was done was that the Christian walked backwards from the New Testament to the Old'.[67] Or, in his inimitable way, he teased the missionaries: 'Why should it be necessary to understand the Old Testament to grasp the Sermon on the Mount?'[68] In a way Chenchiah was echoing a hermeneutical concern which K. M. Banerjea, an earlier convert, had raised with the missionaries. Did our rishis get 'Mosaic instruction' in order to understand the significance of sacrifice?

In arguing for detaching Jesus from his Jewish environment, Chenchiah was not denying the contribution of Judaism. Chenchiah's attitude to the Old Testament should not be seen as a case of anti-Semitism. He pointed out that India's relations with the Jews were more cordial than Europe's. He could not understand how westerners who were championing the Old Testament in India were persecuting the Jews in Europe. India on the other hand, Chenchiah recollected, had an honourable record by providing asylum to Jews going back to the days of Nebuchadnezzar. His point for the missionaries was that one 'cannot love the Old Testament and hate Jews'.[69] He did not want to assume the role of teaching Jews their own religion. Phillips even denied the Jews the possibility of understanding their own sacred text: 'Jews themselves could not understand it, for its true meaning is only revealed in the light of Christ to whom it points'.[70] He reminded the missionaries that 'after all, the Old Testament is their religion, not that of Christian European. They may be credited to know the genius of their faith, the meaning of their own prophecies, the face of their own Messiah'.[71] For Chenchiah, the contribution of Judaism lay not where missionaries put it 'in its theology but in its sociology, not in its view of God but in its view of man and his future'.[72] In his view, the Old Testament is valuable but it should not be 'woven into the fabric of Christian theology'.[73]

66 Ibid., p. 162.
67 Ibid., pp. 161, 162.
68 Ibid., p. 159.
69 Ibid., p. 162.
70 Ibid., p. 82.
71 Ibid., p. 161.
72 Ibid., p. 163.
73 Ibid., p. 164.

What Chenchiah was advocating was similar to what happened to the Indian epic the *Ramayana*. When the *Ramayana* reached various countries in Asia, it took its own form, content and style. The Introduction to the *Thai Ramayana* describes this metamorphosis thus:

True, the story is of Indian origin, but the clothes they now wear are characteristic of Thais of former days. The story has been so developed and adapted to the Thai character that no Thai thinks of it as a thing of foreign origin . . . The details of the description and the events were changed so as to fit Thai reasoning and surroundings . . . Indian characteristics to the story have all but lost their meaning. The story has taken the imagination of the Thai people or rather, the Thai beliefs have been so well incorporated into the story, that the Thai people believe that such things have really happened in the past'.[74]

Chenchiah's contention was that a similar hermeneutical rebirth should happen to Christianity. It should move out of its Jewish habitat and forge a new identity. He acknowledged Christianity's indebtedness to Judaism but insisted 'that Christianity should stand on its own legs and build on its own foundation'.[75]

Although missionaries were used to citing the Hebrew scriptures as a potential warning against borrowing materials from surrounding areas, what they did not realize was that the hermeneutical starting point for Christians in Asia, Africa and Latin America was not Israel. Their categorization of Asian religions, especially Hinduism, as polytheistic, iconocentric, cyclical and ahistorical, and of Judaism as monotheistic, iconoclastic, linear and historical, are too simplistic and fail to take into account the multiplicity of competing movements and trajectories that lie within these traditions. The labels such as Hinduism, Buddhism and Confucianism are in themselves problematic in that they try to impose a homogeneity on religions which are fraught with internal diversity and competing doctrinal and ritual claims. The mode of discourse employed by missionaries in their dealings with other religions was framed and determined by the need to spread and propagate the Christian faith. They were more interested in asserting the truth-claims of Christianity than in developing cross-cultural links with these various Asian religions. Their concern was to maintain correct doctrinal positions rather than to immerse themselves in the everyday rituals, devotions and pietistic activities of the people.

---

74 King Rama I, *Thai Ramayana: Masterpiece of Thai Literature Retold from the Original Version* (Bangkok: Chalermint, 2002), pp. 2–3.
75 Thangasamy (ed.), *The Theology of Chenchiah*, p. 164.

SAIVIZING THE HEBREW SCRIPTURES

The rest of the chapter will focus on the writings of two people, both Tamils, one from Sri Lanka, and the other from India. Arumuka Navalar was a high-caste Vellala Saiva Hindu from Jaffna, whereas Arumainayagam was a low-caste Shanar Christian from Tinnevelly. Both looked favourably upon the Hebrew scriptures and used them as an effective instrument in their dealings with missionaries. Arumuka Navalar moblized them to defend Saivism against missionary attack on temple and worship practices, whereas Arumainayagam employed them to cleanse European cultural elements from Christianity and to claim social respectability and exalted status for his community, which was despised by some missionaries.

Arumuka Pillai (1822–79),[76] a prominent Saiva reformer from Jaffna, Sri Lanka, saw the Hebrew scriptures as endorsing worship practices similar to those prescribed in the Saiva scriptures. He utilized his knowledge of the Hebrew scriptures to show that, far from being heathenish, the worship of Siva fundamentally resembled the worship prescribed in the Hebrew scriptures. He reminded his readers that these scriptures were followed by Jesus, and by Paul and the apostles after Jesus' death. Drawing on Judaic sources, Navalar was able to reassure the Saivas[77] of Jaffna that they need not be ashamed of their own tradition and temple practices.

Arumuka Pillai was generally known by his honorary title, 'Navalar', 'the Eloquent' or 'the Learned'. Not only did he single-handedly revive Saivism in Jaffna and South India but he also played a significant role in slowing down the progress of missionary work in mid-nineteenth-century Jaffna. His literary and educational work played a huge part in preventing high-caste Vellala Hindus from embracing one or other of the Christian

---

76 Arumuka Navalar was a major force in Tamil nationalism and Saivite rejuvenation in Sri Lanka. For his contribution to Saiva revival, and for his educational and Tamil literary works, see R. F. Young and S. Jebanesan, *The Bible Trembled: The Hindu–Christian Controversies of Nineteenth-Century Ceylon* (Vienna, Institut für Indologie der Universität Wien, 1995); Dennis D. Hudson, 'Arumuga Navalar and the Hindu Renaissance among the Tamils', in *Religious Controversy in British India: Dialogues in South Asian Languages*, ed. Kenneth W. Jones (Albany, State University of New York Press, 1992), pp. 23–51; Dennis D. Hudson, 'Winning Souls for Siva: Arumuga Navalar's Transmission of the Saiva Religion', in *A Sacred Thread: Modern Transmissions of Hindu Tradition in India and Abroad*, ed. Raymond Brady Williams (Chambersburg, Anima Publications, 1992), pp. 23–51; Dennis D. Hudson, 'A Hindu Response to the Written Torah', in *Between Jerusalem and Benares: Comparative Studies in Judaism and Hinduism*, ed. Hananya Goodman (Albany, State University of New York Press, 1994), 55–84; Dennis D. Hudson, 'Tamil Hindu Responses to Protestants: Nineteenth-Century Literati in Jaffna and Tinnevelly', in *Indigenous Responses to Western Christianity*, ed. Steven Kaplan (New York, New York University Press, 1995), 95–123.

77 Devotees of Siva.

denominations that were operating in the peninsula. Like many of the colonial subjects of the time, he was educated in a missionary school and, in his case, ended up teaching there. Peter Percival, the principal of Wesleyan Mission School (later Jaffna Central College), where Navalar studied, asked him to stay on to help him in editing treaties and especially with the translation of the Bible into Tamil. The resultant version, which is known as the 'Tentative Version' or the 'Navalar Version', failed to win the approval of missionary translators, especially in South India, because it 'fell flat on the market'.[78] Promoted by the missionaries, South Indian Christians were reluctant to use the version produced in Jaffna. The main reason was that Navalar's translation deviated from the Fabricius[79] version, which had been in circulation for more than seventy years. This had, according to S. Kulandran, who wrote a monograph on the history of the Tamil Bible, 'acquired a certain status, if not sanctity' among the Tamil Christians.[80] The Navalar version is probably the only Bible version which has the name of a non-Christian associated with it. His involvement with the translation introduced him to the detailed intricacies of the biblical religion. His having worked in a Protestant environment for eight years and his intimate knowledge of the Bible must have convinced Navalar of the similarity between the temple-based ritualistic worship which was at the centre of the Hebrew scriptures and the Saiva temple practices prescribed in the Saiva scriptures. Such a realization awakened his Saiva consciousness.

It was the taunting of converted high-caste Christians and missionaries which prompted Navalar to launch his sustained rebuttal. This was a time when the vilification of Saivism escalated. This aggressive mood was exemplified in a new bimonthly bilingual periodical, *Utaya Takakai – The Morning Star*, started by two Tamil Christians. The purpose of the periodical was clear – Tamil culture, and along with it Saivism, was becoming decadent, and Tamil salvation lay in imitating the western

---

78 S. Kulandran, *The Word, Men and Matters (1940–1983): Being a Rescript in Five Volumes of the Writings of the Rt Rev. Dr S. Kulandran, Bishop of Jaffna Diocese C.S.I. 1947–1970)*, vol. 1, ed. D. J. Ambalavanar (Chunnakam, Institute for the Study of Religion and Society, 1985), p. 271.

79 Philipp Fabricius was a German missionary who came to India in 1740 under the Tranquebar Mission. His Tamil version of the New Testament appeared in 1774, and the Old Testament in 1777.

80 S. Kulandran, 'The Tentative Version of the Bible or "The Navalar Version"', *Tamil Culture* 7 (1958), 248. For the controversy surrounding the Tentative or Navalar version between the Jaffna and Madras Auxiliaries of the Bible Society, see *A Brief Narrative of the Operation of the Jaffna Auxiliary in the Preparation of a Version of the Tamil Scriptures* (Jaffna, Strong and Asbury Printers, 1868).

sciences and knowledge introduced by the missionaries. Characterized by the Protestant preoccupation with the scriptures, these Christians constantly teased Saivites, Muslims and Catholics to open up their texts for public inspection and analysis. Their failure to take up the gauntlet was attributed to the weakness and obscurity of these religious texts. Of all these three traditions – Saivism, Islam and Roman Catholicism – it was Saivism which was singled out as the epitome of degeneracy:

> There is nothing in the peculiar doctrines and precepts of the Siva religion that is adapted to improve a man's moral character or fit him to be useful to his fellow men . . . If the world were to be converted to the Siva faith no one would expect any improvement in the morals or the happiness of men. Every one might be as great a liar and cheat – as great an adulterer – as oppressive of the poor – as covetous – as proud, as he was before – without sullying the purity of his faith.[81]

Naturally Jaffna Tamil Saivites were up in arms. According to Dennis Hudson, who has done extensive work on Navalar, Hindu movements and Tamil Christianity in northern Sri Lanka and southern India, the Saivas, assembled in a monastery near a Saiva temple in Jaffna, came up with a series of measures to combat the Christian onslaught. Unlike converted Christians, Saivites did not show any antagonism towards their fellow Tamils who had strayed from their religious tradition. In fact, there was a general sympathy towards them and they were looked upon with great pity. Their conversion was put down to their failure to grasp the basic tenets of Saivism. To prevent any more of these conversions, two courses of action were taken: one was to educate the Jaffna Tamils in the basic knowledge of Saivism, and the other was to propagate Saiva truths. It was decided to start a Veda and an Agama school to educate Tamils about their own religious and cultural heritage, and to disseminate Saiva teaching to the public at large. To achieve the latter, it was decided to acquire a printing machine 'which would effectively shut the mouths of the missionaries and stop their abuse'.[82]

Navalar's hermeneutics have to be seen in the light of this uneasy religious atmosphere prevalent in Jaffna at that time. Navalar wrote a letter to the *Morning Star* and signed it as a son of Saiva and lover of good doctrine. He pointed out the conspicuous parallels he detected between the ritual practices in Saiva temples and the temple at Jerusalem. Ten years after the publication of the letter, Navalar expanded these ideas and

---

81 *Utaya Tarakai – Morning Star* 2, (1842), p. 287 quoted in Hudson, 'Tamil Hindu Responses to Protestants', p. 98.
82 *Morning Star* 2 (1842), p. 271.

brought out a booklet in Tamil entitled *Caivatusanaparikaram* (pronounced as *Saiva-dushana-parikaram; Remedy for Invective on Saivism*),[83] in which he put forward his case more vigorously and in much detail.

The strength of Navalar's hermeneutics lay in providing convincing parallels from the Christian Old Testament for every Saiva practice which was ridiculed by the missionaries. When the Saivas were accused of being heathenish and polytheistic, Navalar pointed out that the missionaries themselves indulged in such practices because they worshipped three gods – Jehovah, Christ and the Holy Spirit. He cited incidents from the Hebrew scriptures which were tantamount to the adoration of many gods: Abraham 'bowed himself toward the ground' and served three divine messengers who appeared at the oak of Mamre (Gen. 18.1–5); Joshua 'fell on his face to the earth' and worshipped the captain of the host of the Lord (Josh. 5.13–15). In contrast, whereas Navalar was unequivocal about the oneness of Siva,[84] he did not see any contradiction between the oneness of Siva and his many manifestations, which were not many gods, as the missionaries had misconstrued. He conceded that Saivas did worship other gods, but these were diclosures of the one and the same Siva. When missionaries ridiculed the fact that Siva had consorts, Navalar drew attention to the Song of Songs, where the woman and her suitor expressed love and desire for each other. Navalar allegorized the suitor as Christ wooing his bride: 'The Christ the human being was attracted to a woman, praised her beauty and had intercourse with her and got separated from her and as a result she experienced agony and constantly went in search of him'.[85] Navalar asked the missionaries why they accepted these dalliances described in their own scriptures and never condemned them.

When missionaries found that there were so many temples and holy places, it shocked their Protestant sensibilities. Navalar found a biblical precedent for them. For him, different holy places were like residential palaces of a king, made available for the Saivas to worship and to receive blessings. He culled thirteen passages from the Hebrew scriptures to draw attention to practices similar to those in Saiva temples. He started with the earliest of holy places: the ground where Moses was asked to remove his shoes (Exod. 3.5), the mountain and hill where God resided (Mount Zion), places where God had to be worshipped (Bethlehem and Bethel),

---

83 The text I am using is published by Victoria Jubilee Press, Madras, 1890.
84 Siva is the third member of the Hindu triad.
85 *Caivatusanaparikaram*, p. 19. All translations from this text are my own.

and God's final and permanent abode in Jerusalem, built by Solomon, where he dwelt for ever (1 Chr. 23.25). Navalar's claim was that, if the Saiva texts extolled the building and consecrating of dwelling places for transcendent beings as meritorious, the Hebrew scriptures too supported such ventures. He cited the cases of Moses, who was commanded by God to build a dwelling place, and David, who embarked on such a project, which was eventually completed by his son Solomon. Similarly, when missionaries dismissed the public reading and exposition of Saiva texts and the Puranas in temples and monasteries as a futile exercise, Navalar drew their attention to similar practices encouraged in the scriptures of the missionaries. He cited Nehemiah; 9.3 1 Thessalonians 5.27; and Colossians 4.16.[86] One text that Navalar forgot to remind the missionaries about was 1 Timothy 4.13. Here the writer outlines the marks of a preacher: to teach, preach and be able to read the scriptures aloud in public. Navalar's dispute with the missionaries was that if it was acceptable for one religious community to read aloud and explain its texts to its adherents, why was it wrong for a different religious community to engage in such an activity.

Navalar was able to locate a biblical parallel for the Siva lingam, another theological sore point for the missionaries. The image looked like a phallic symbol to the missionaries, who saw it as a perfect example of the spiritual decadence associated with idol worship. But for Saivas it was an abstract symbol of Siva, expressing his creative power. For Navalar, the Jewish ark of the covenant, the ancient symbol of Jehovah, was a counterpart to the Saiva lingam. He cited fifteen passages to support his claim, the chief textual corroboration coming from the passage which described the final location of the ark, after its wanderings from Sinai to Solomon's temple at Jerusalem. To rub it in, Navalar pointed out that David 'sacrificed oxen and fatlings' and danced before the Lord with all his might' (2 Sam. 6.12–14), and Solomon, too, sacrificed countless goats and cattle and performed ritual acts before the ark. Navalar's contention was that the missionaries, who found symbolic meanings in such ritual practices as the eating of bread and drinking of wine, dismissed the image of Siva as a mere stone. One person's sacred image is another person's stone!

Navalar also took up the issue of the anointing and feeding rituals associated with the Siva lingam. According to the Saiva scriptures, it is meritorious to offer milk, fruit and balls of cooked rice to the transcendent being. Navalar presented parallel passages from the Hebrew scriptures,

86 Ibid., p. 42.

for example the Lord's instruction to Moses: 'And thou shalt set upon the table shewbread before me alway' (Exod. 25.30). Just as fragrant libations were used to anoint the lingam in the *abhiseka* ritual, Moses had been asked to prepare the anointing oil according to a specific recipe, which included spices such as myrrh, cinnamon, sweet calamus and cassia. Navalar equated the daily food-offering ritual of *naivedya* with the Bread of the Presence and referred to the passage from the Book of Leviticus where Aaron and his sons were to make food offerings on behalf of the people of Israel. He pointed out that the stipulations regarding the loaves, their number and size and how they were to be arranged on the table, and the use of frankincense were, from the Saiva point of view, essentially gifts for God (Lev. 24.5–9).

Navalar was able to find biblical correspondences for all the important performative activities related to Saiva worship. For the lighting of the dipa (lamp), he cited the divine directions to Moses about regular and continual kindling of lamps (Exod. 27.20–1; Lev. 24.1–4). For the Saiva practice of singing and dancing, he referred to levitical and priestly musicians who were appointed by David and were skilled in using musical instruments such as lutes, lyres and cymbals (2 Chr. 15.14). For equivalents to the observance of auspicious days and times prescribed in the Saiva scriptures, Navalar pointed to the calendar of holy days and seasons in Leviticus (Lev. 23) and recalled the words of the husband of the Shunammite woman who wanted to visit Elisha: 'wherefore wilt thou go to him today? It is neither new moon, nor sabbath' (2 Kings 4.23); and the directive of David to the sons of Levi that they had to be on duty continually every morning and evening, and on sabbaths, new moons and feast days (1 Chr. 23.30–2).

For the Saiva ritual of bathing in rivers for the absolution of sins, Navalar was able to cite parallel examples from the Hebrew scriptures. The Saiva scriptures declare that those who bathe at holy places in the River Ganges, and at the Bridge of Rama at Rameswaram, according to the rites and with love, were absolved of their sins and cured of their diseases. Navalar cited the case of Naaman who bathed in the river Jordan to be cleansed of his leprosy (2 Kings 5).[87] His message to the missionaries was simple and direct: they did not know what they were talking about. As conquerors of this nation, they went about insulting Saiva religion:

---

87 He also cited examples from the New Testament, examples where the invalids, the lame and the blind were led into the Pool of Bethesda to be healed. He also referred to the healing power of water when the newly baptized were absolved of their sins.

You have not understood even the least truth. You rather cherish the view that what I hold is all that I will achieve. You have all the time disparaged us and our religion. At least in the future do not make a habit of this and thus waste the days of your life. Your salvation will be achieved by gaining true knowledge'.[88]

Navalar's relentless use of passages from the Hebrew scriptures made it certain that the missionaries would not dare to use the Bible again to tarnish the image of Saivism. The citation of Hebrew texts was Navalar's answer to the editors of the *Morning Star*, who were mocking the scriptures of the Saivites. Missionaries who under normal circumstances would have pounced on Navalar became quiet. The Thirtieth Annual Report of the Jaffna Tract Society described this reluctance to speak out as a 'dignified silence'.[89] There was a grudging admission by one Wesleyan missionary that the effect of Saivite–Jewish juxtapositions turned the tide 'in favour of Saivism against Christianity'.[90] It was left to another Vellala convert, Daniel Carroll Vishvanatha Pillai, to confront Navalar. His *Subhradipa*, which appeared three years after Navalar's booklet, ignored the crux of Navalar's thesis, namely his Saivite–Jewish parallels, and focussed on the Pauline notion of salvation by faith and praised the selfless service of the missionaries who had done so much more than the Jewish and Saiva ascetics whom Navalar so admired. Ironically, Daniel Carroll Vishvanatha Pillai's enthusiasm for the new faith waned and he returned to his Saiva tradition.

Navalar's use of the Christian Old Testament consisted of paraphrases of texts and allusions. This might be due to the fact that his writings were addressed to Hindus who did not bother with the actual text. Rarely was a full text quoted. When he did provide a full quotation, it came from the version he had helped to translate. Texts were loosely arranged to support his stance. Although Navalar himself was an erudite Saiva commentator, there was no attempt to exegete the passages from the Hebrew scriptures. By merely citing texts Navalar implied that the missionaries who were sneering at Saivism were in fact scorning pertinent elements which were

---

88 *Caivatusanaparikaram*, p. 39.
89 There was a response in the *Morning Star* when Navalar wrote his first anonymous letter. The reply was published in four issues (9.2. 1843, 23.3. 1843, 9.3. 1843, and 23.3. 1843) under the title 'Remarks on the Pretended Resemblance between the Rites and Ceremonies of the Mosaic Dispensation and Those of the Shivas'. These responses trivialized Navalar's biblical comparisons, and their basic question was if, as Navalar claimed, God was unchanging, why then were Judaistic practices not more evident in the Christian religion? See R. F. Young and S. Jebanesan, *The Bible Trembled*, p. 117, and also p. 137.
90 Hudson, 'A Hindu Response to the Written Torah', p. 45.

intrinsic to the Christian faith. What, in effect, Navalar did was to force
the missionaries to rethink the canonical authority of God's revelation.

Navalar's hermeneutics exposed the vulnerability of the Protestant
faith when pitted against a highly sophisticated temple-centred Saiva
religion. In keeping with the evangelical mood of the time, missionaries
placed a high premium on the doctrinal aspect of their faith, a faith firmly
based on a book which itself contained elements of cultic worship and
temple-based rituals and practices. The missionaries' understanding of
that book was a selective one, which steered clear of any of the rituals
mentioned in the book. It was those very omissions which became an
effective instrument in Navalar's hands.

The misunderstanding between the missionaries and Navalar arose
as a result of how these two interpreted the notions of action and belief.
For missionaries, who came out of the Protestant tradition, salvation was
through faith. The New Testament taught them that salvation was a
gift from God and that it was by faith alone. Good works in themselves
did not redeem a person; rather, they were by-products of salvation,
symptomatic of a person who had been saved. The outward works were
a barometer of one's inner spiritual well-being. But what mattered to
Navalar was *carya* (temple service) and *kriya* (ritual service) fuelled by
anpu (love). For adherents of Saiva faith these were the driving forces of
Saiva bhakti. Navalar's thinking was shaped by the Saiva Nayanmars
(servitors). For them, the love for Siva is expressed through concrete cultic
actions:

Love for Siva, it seems, does not develop without attention to the details of cultic
service, nor is it expressed except through such service and usually in the midst of
one's daily householder life. Attention to the *linga*, for example, may mean a
commitment to supply oil for lamps in a specific temple, or to grind the
sandalpaste for a specific linga, or to prevent the temple services from being
disrupted or its articles from being polluted.[91]

The *Periapuranam*, one of the Saiva scriptures, which narrates the lives of
sixty-three Saiva saints, records instances of the extreme lengths to which
these saints will go to show their unswerving love to Siva. A notable case
in point was a Nayanar's cutting off of his own father's leg when
the father's action prevented the son from performing puja to the Siva
lingam. The liturgical honouring, and commitment to service of Siva

91 Dennis D. Hudson, 'Violent and Fanatical Devotion among Nāyanārs: A Study in the *Periya
   Purānam* of Cēkkilār', in *Criminal Gods and Demon Devotees: Essays on the Guardians of Popular
   Hinduism*, ed. Alf Hiltebeitel (New Delhi, Manohar Publications, 1990), p. 377.

were more important than personal liberation. R. Rangachari, in his introduction to his English translation of *Periapuranam*, observes: 'Their goal was not "liberation", the ultimate end of life, but loving service to the Lord was all that they ever craved'.[92] For missionaries who were raised on minimal ritual practices, such acts were signs of extreme fanaticism, and they could not comprehend the external expressions of a Saiva devotee. For them, such acts were malign manifestations of one's inner spiritual decadence.

Unlike missionaries who viewed both the Hebrew and Hindu texts as underdeveloped, ineffectual and obsolete, Navalar treated them as having a timeless character.

He used Saiva signifiers to decode biblical texts. He grappled with the ritual significance of the Christian Old Testament and maintained that the Hebrew scriptures had a permanent and enduring value for the Christian faith. He did not see the Old Testament as a preparation for the New Testament, to be dispensed with on the arrival of the gospel in the form of Jesus. The missionaries' claim that the potency of the Hebrews' ritual acts had become otiose with the advent of Jesus was unacceptable to Navalar. As far as he was concerned, these rituals prescribed in the Hebrew scriptures had to go on for ever. He cited nearly fifty passages from Genesis, Numbers, Exodus and Leviticus, the last two supplying the bulk of the texts, in order to underline the eternal validity of these statutes. If Jesus declared ineffectual what Jehovah had commanded, then Jesus surely must be greater than his father and a rival to him. But Navalar pointed out to the missionaries that the four gospels provided proofs that Jesus participated in the rituals. He cited the example of Jesus' own circumcision, his going to the temple with his parents, his visits to the temple during festivals, and his telling the cleansed leper to show himself to the temple authorities to fulfil the laws of Moses. Navalar also refused to accept the claim of the missionaries that the crucifixion of Jesus had put an end to the old rituals. If so, he asked the missionaries, why did Paul continue with those ritual practices after the death of Jesus? Paul circumcised Timothy and kept the vow that he himself had promised to fulfil (Acts 18.18). In his letter to Romans, Navalar claimed that Paul exempted only circumcision, and, as far as the letter to the Hebrews was concerned, the writer's message was that only ceremonial sacrifices had been superseded and not the rituals. These had to be continued. Navalar implied that the missionaries had fabricated a religion which had no basis in the Bible. Unlike the missionaries, who portrayed Judaism as a passing phase, Navalar did not see Judaism or Saivism as transitory stages. For him, Saivism and Judaism contained relevant messages from which both missionary Christianity and Christianized Hindus had deviated.

Unlike Raja Rammohun Roy and Thomas Jefferson, Navalar did not bring out abridged or edited texts but produced a virtual Hebrew scripture assembled around texts which venerated ritual practices. In effect, his comparative hermeneutics made intelligible by means of biblical terms and references what missionaries found alien and incomprehensible in the Saiva tradition. Biblical customs were likened to those of the Saivites; these biblical Jews became 'implicit Saivites'. This was a complete reversal of the conventional hermeneutics, which tended to project Indians, Africans and Native Americans as implicit, or incognito Israelites.

Indian nationalists in the subcontinent, reeling under the heavy on-slaught of the missionaries' attack on Hinduism, usually reacted in two ways. One was to see Hinduism as a faith that had declined from its own pristine purity, and the other was to acknowledge the religious wealth and resourcefulness of Hinduism but at the same time accept that it needed new energy to survive in a hostile Christian missionary environment. Hindu reformers such as Raja Rammohun Roy and Dayananda Saraswati belonged to the first category. They were engaged in purifying Hinduism of its later accretions and going back to the untainted original. Navalar belonged to this second category. He did not see Saivism as a decadent religion which needed reform from the outside. Unlike the nationalists, who extolled philosophical Hinduism in response to the missionaries' attack on popular Hinduism, Navalar defended the latter. He did not demarcate Hinduism into 'high' or 'low' 'popular' or 'philosophical'. For him, it was one entity. He was the defender of people's Hinduism. He wanted to mount his defence on behalf of the learned as well as the ordinary people. His main concern was that the Saivites who had lost touch with their own religion should be helped to understand their tradition. Navalar did not see the coming of missionaries in terms of revitalizing a decrepit religion, as was commonly the case, but in terms of chastising Saivas and arousing them from their religious apathy. For him, the missionaries were agents of Siva, 'the eternal, joyful and holy Supreme Being who created, protects and rules all the worlds'.[93] It was

93 Navalar's anonymous letter to the *Morning Star*, quoted in Hudson, 'Tamil Hindu Responses to Protestants', p. 99.

Siva who had brought those missionaries from the West, but they were not aware of this hidden divine purpose, namely to energize the Saivas. In Siva theology, Saiva belongs to all the world, as this text affirms:

> Obeisance to You Civan who owns the southern country
> Obeisance to You, O God, from people of every country.

Navalar differed from Hindu reformers of the colonial period in one other respect. Hindu reformers such as Dayananda Saraswati were keen to win back converted Christians to the Hindu fold, but Navalar did not urge Tamil Christians to give up their new faith and return to Saivism. Nor was he was keen on bringing everyone to the Saiva faith. His hermeneutical enterprise was directed to both Christians and his fellow Saivites. He reminded the Christians that, on the basis of the textual evidence he had produced from their very own writings, they should give up their negative engagement with Saivism and respect its rituals rather than ridicule them. To the Saivas, his message was that they should know their own scriptures. This would protect them from the predatory tendencies of native Christians and foreign missionaries. He saw his task as re-educating Tamil Saivas in their own tradition rather than imposing the Saiva ethos on others. This tolerance could be attributed to the Saiva belief that Siva accepts worship done to other gods as done to Siva, provided it is done with a devout heart. One of the Saiva texts put this quite explicitly: 'The God who is above all other Gods (Siva) will deign to accept the worship of the one who worships the god-of-his-choice by leading a life of righteousness, by getting rid of anger and other vices, whose mind thinks of God, whose mouth repeats mantras, whose hand picks flowers to worship Him.'[94]

For Navalar, the Saiva scriptures mandated practices which were similar to those prescribed in the Hebrew scriptures. For him, both these texts made the temple and the liturgical and cultic activities paramount. It was a weakness of the missionaries that they failed to appreciate the depth of temple devotion found both in Judaism and Saivism.

AN 1857 UPRISING OF AN ECCLESIASTICAL KIND

Arumainayagam Suttampillai's (1823–1919) mobilization of the Hebrew scriptures has to be seen against a background of European dominance, missionary paternalism and native agency. His reading of Navalar's

---

94 John H. Piet, *A Logical Presentation of Śaiva Siddhānta Philosophy* (Madras: The Christian Literature Society for India, 1952), pp. 163–4.

Caivatusanaparikaram (Remedy for Invective on Saivism), which was available in southern India at that time and attracted his attention, especially the hermeneutical potential of the Hebrew scriptures, strengthened him for his impending battles against missionaries.[95] Before we look at that, let me give some background details which influenced and prompted Suttampillai's hermeneutical activity. Conversion to Christianity paved the way for those who were denigrated by the Hindu caste system to climb the social ladder and challenge some of the caste-based restrictions. One of the controversial victories notched up by the depressed classes was the right of their women to wear upper-cloth. The dispute was known as the upper-cloth controversy. The depressed classes challenged the custom which permitted higher-caste women to wear the *tolcilai*,[96] but forbade the lower-caste women either to wear it or to cover the upper part of their body. Ironically, the depressed-class converts who were able to free themselves from some of the caste prejudices in society, with the help of a compliant colonial administration, found themselves rendered powerless in their own church. They were seen by the missionaries as needing careful nurturing and paternalistic protection. Some of the missionaries were suspicious of the newly converted depressed-class Christians and were reluctant to show them any respect. They saw Indian Christians as 'weak, especially more ignorant' and still clinging on to some of the 'old habits, old superstitions and old heathen rules'.[97] One of those who found that the old marginalization in society was replaced by a new marginalization was Suttampillai. He was trained at a seminary run by the Society for the Propagation of the Gospel (SPG). A man of considerable intellect, he had studied Hebrew and Greek and won several prizes as a seminarian. A Shanar[98] himself, Suttampillai found

---

95 See Dennis D. Hudson, 'The Responses of Tamils to Their Study by Westerners 1600–1908', in *Comparative Civilizations Review* 13&14 (1986), 189. I have not myself seen Suttampillai, who cites the works of many western scholars, acknowledging Navalar, a forceful voice which missionaries would have recognized.

96 A Tamil word which means shoulder cloth; *tol* means shoulder and *cilai* means cloth. The literature on the background to the upper-cloth controversy is voluminous. For a succinct narrative of the issues and how the controversy was looked upon by the various players – the upper caste, lower caste, missionaries and the colonial administration – see Koji Kawashima, *Missionaries and a Hindu State: Travancore 1858–1936* (Delhi, Oxford University Press, 1998), pp. 60–70.

97 Joseph Mullens, *Missions in South India* (London, W. H. Dalton, 1854), p. 113.

98 Shanars are hereditarily devoted to cultivating and climbing palmyra palms, and they adopted the name Nadars (lords of the soil). In the fourfold division of the caste system they are placed outside the fourfold division of priests, warriors, merchants and labourers.

the paternalistic attitude of the missionaries unacceptable. He particularly disliked two of the SPG missionaries, A. F. Caemmerer and Robert Caldwell. Suttampillai worked under Caemmerer as a catechist. Even by the intolerant colonial standards, Caemmerer was thought to be an obnoxious missionary with a very low opinion of the converts from the depressed classes. Suttampillai's irritation with Caemmerer was both theological and personal. Suttampillai objected to the placing of the cross on the altar, which he interpreted as a sign of idolatry and against the biblical injunction, but it was a personal matter which finally cracked Suttampillai. Caemmerer refused to accept the girl to whom Suttampillai was engaged and wanted him to marry the girl he himself had selected for him, which Suttampillai rejected outright. This led to his dismissal.

Suttampillai's anti-missionary feeling was further fuelled by Robert Caldwell's *The Tinnevelly Shanars*,[99] a quasi-ethnographical study of this community, which unfortunately included passages disparaging the ethical behaviour and communitarian arrangements of the Shanars. In Caldwell's view, they were the 'least intellectual people found in India',[100] and only a few among them possessed any ability. The majority were marked by apathy, indifference, ignorance and vice, and were unable to engage in rational thinking. He found the newly emancipated Negroes to be 'superior to the Shanars in intellect, energy, and vivacity',[101] and castes inferior to the Shanars to have a sharper intellect – 'even their expressions and pronunciation are more accurate'.[102] The distinctive feature of their religion was seen as 'systematic worship of demons' which was characterized by devil dances and bloody sacrifices. As a consequence of such worship, Shanars had 'sunk in moral depravity',[103] and were 'incapable of exercising moral restraint'.[104] The religion of the Shanars, in Caldwell's view, was a 'school of immorality'.[105] Under such depraved conditions, Caldwell asked, 'How could they be gentlemen?'[106] The Shanars, who were now in social ascendency, as Caldwell himself recognized, and as vouchsafed by another missionary, 'year by year rising in

---

99 R. Caldwell, *The Tinnevelly Shanars: A Sketch of Their Religion, and Their Moral Condition and Characteristics, as a Caste; with Special Reference to the Facilities and Hindrances to the Progress of Christianity amongst Them* (Madras, Christian Knowledge Society's Press, 1849).
100 Ibid., p. 61.   101 Ibid., p. 62.   102 Ibid., p. 63.
103 Ibid., p. 38.   104 Ibid., p. 36.
105 Ibid., p. 37.   106 Ibid., p. 65.

intelligence, wealth and influence',[107] found such remarks undermining their newly emerging status.

It was against this missionary dominance and condescension that Suttampillai tried to re-cast Christianity into a nativistic and nationalist framework and started his Hindu Christian Church of Lord Jesus Christ in 1857.[108] The year is significant. While an uprising was raging in northern India against British political dominance, a much smaller but highly significant uprising was rattling the power of western Christendom in Tinnevelly in the south. Suttampillai was engaged in a twofold hermeneutical battle to settle his old scores with the missionaries. Negatively, he tried to discredit the Christianity which came with the missionaries, thus undermining their authority and presence. Positively, he latched onto Judaism, and massively over-projected it as an antidote to what the missionaries were trying to impart. He showed his antagonism towards missionary Christianity by exposing the decadence, sexual immorality and materialism rampant among westerners, both in India and in Europe. He validated his accusations by referring to the writings of westerners who were trying to offer an internal critique of their own society, their government's imperial involvement and evangelistic endeavours in the empire. He cited the works of both secular and Christian writers such as John Parker, William Howitt, Robert Southey and the Abbé Dubois. These writers spoke of the savage nature of Saxons, their drunken behaviour, the rampant prostitution in western capitals and polygamous marriage practices. Suttampillai selected those elements which could be profitably used against the missionaries. His intention was to expose and castigate the lifestyle of Europeans. He was particularly severe on divorce and remarriage, and the offspring of such unions. In his view, the Holy Church and the country were 'greatly polluted (Jer. 3.1; Lev. 18.24–8) by unscrupulously admitting to the Church-communion, such despicable families procreating culpable offspring'.[109] He exposed

---

107 Frederic Baylis's note in *The Evangelical Magazine and Missionary Chronicle* 37 (1859), 442.
108 In dealing with Suttampillai and his Hindu Christian Church of Lord Jesus Christ, I have greatly benefited from the works of Vincent Kumaradoss, 'Negotiating Colonial Christianity: The Hindu Christian Church of Late Nineteenth Century Tirunelveli', *South Indian Studies* 1 (1996), 35–53 and 'Creation of Alternative Public Spheres and Church Indigenisation in Nineteenth Century Colonial Tamil Nadu: The Hindu-Christian Church of Lord Jesus and the National Church of India', in *Christianity is Indian: The Emergence of an Indigenous Community*, ed. Roger E. Hedlund (Mylapore, MIIS, 2000), pp. 3–23; and M. Thomas Thangaraj, 'The History and Teachings of the Hindu Christian Community Commonly Called Nattu Sabai in Tirunelveli', *Indian Church History Review* 5:1 (1971), 43–68.
109 A. N. Suttampillai, *A Brief Sketch of the Hindu Christian Dogmas* (Palamcottah, Shanmuga Vilasam Press, 1890), p. 6.

the missionaries for their syncretistic tendencies. He was astute enough to see that the western form of Christianity was a mixture of gospel, politics, power and European customs. He accused them of incorporating their national customs into their Christianity, thus polluting '"the sincere milk of the word of God" by mingling with it the poison of your own impure national traditions'.[110] In contrast to the familiar pattern of missionaries blaming the natives for polluting the gospel by fusing indigenous elements, here was the colonized accusing the colonizer of commingling gospel and culture. He denounced the missionaries for leading a life which was full of 'unscriptural manners', an indication of 'the progress of the immoral European Christianity'.[111] What was more, they subscribed to and encouraged idols, which was against biblical teaching. This 'New idolatry' included replicating the popish practice of 'succession of priesthood and baptism', and European Christians paying obeisance to pictures of God's image. In his view, European Christians had rendered 'ineffectual the other laws concerning the sacred times and other duties of public worship, which are neither to be discarded nor changed, but are to be binding upon all nations at all times as a direct guide to heaven (Isa. 66.22, 23; Zech 14.16–21; Col. 2.16, 17)'.[112] European Christians were guilty of several 'cardinal sins' since they incurred the wrath of the Almighty by their 'perversion of the sincere word of God'.[113] Such a devastating critique of the western form of Christianity served a double purpose. First, it exposed the failure of western Christians to match their manner of living to the message they were trying to transmit. Secondly, it was a telling riposte to Caldwell's negative portrayal of the Shanars. By raking up these examples of the spiritual and material degeneration of the West, Suttampillai was able to demonstrate that when it came to depravity and licentiousness, Europeans were as good as, or even better than Shanars.

Positively, Suttampillai saw the Hebrew scriptures as resonating with his own hermeneutical agenda. Unlike most reformers who aspired to rectify the distortion of the Christian message by resorting to the core gospel of Jesus, Suttampillai sought to recover the essence of Christianity in the law and liturgical practices of the Hebrew Bible. He appropriated elements from the Hebrew scriptures and affirmed them as an authentic and unadulterated form of Christianity. Suttampillai believed that his new church was the fulfilment of the prophecy of Isaiah:

110 Ibid., p. 30. 111 Ibid. 112 Ibid., p. 4. 113 Ibid., p. 25.

And the foreigners who join themselves to the Lord, to minister to him, and to love the name of the Lord, and to be his servants, everyone who keeps the Sabbath, and does not profane it, and holds fast my covenant – these I will bring to my holy mountain, and make them joyful in my house of prayer; their burnt offerings and their sacrifices will be accepted on my altar; for my house shall be called a house of prayer for all peoples (Isa. 56.6, 7).[114]

Suttampillai drew heavily on Jewish ritual practices and modelled his nativized church on the Jewish pattern, refashioning, embellishing and assimilating.[115] His claim was that 'the disciples of God Incarnate instituted Holy Churches, among all Gentile nations throughout the Roman Empire called "the world" (Lk. 2.1) but only in conformity with the congregational worship of the Jewish synagogues (Acts 13.42, 15.21)'.[116] In keeping with Jewish practices, his church observed Saturday as the Sabbath, which he tirelessly pointed out had scriptural endorsement in the aforementioned Isaiah verse and in other passages. He introduced the blowing of a horn to invite the faithful to the assembly, citing the verse, 'Make two silver trumpets' and 'you shall use them for summoning the congregation (Num. 10.1, 2)', thus replacing the European habit of ringing bells to summon the congregation to worship. His church followed such customs as the purificatory act of washing one's feet before entering the sanctuary, having a clean body and clean clothes. He found in Genesis 35.2 scriptural support for this: 'Put away the foreign Gods that are among you, and purify yourselves and change your garment'. In keeping with Numbers 19.16, anyone who touched a corpse or a grave was treated as unclean for seven days. His church followed the Jewish calendar and celebrated festivals 'ordained in the Hebrew Scriptures',[117] such as the New Moon festival (Isa. 66.23), the Festival of the Trumpets, the Day of Atonement, the Feast of the Tabernacles (Zech. 14.16–21), the Passover Feast and the Days of Unleavened Bread, the Day of Pentecost and the New Year Festival. In keeping with the Jewish tradition, he placed the Bible on the altar wrapped in a cloth.

It was his understanding of Jesus and the early church which provided Suttampillai with biblical legitimacy for such practices. For him, Jesus

---

114 Thangaraj, 'The History and Teachings of the Hindu Christian Community Commonly Called Nattu Sabai in Tirunelveli', 56–7.

115 Except circumcision and animal sacrifices. But later Suttampillai introduced animal sacrifices, which led to a substantial exodus. It is this breakaway group which is in existence today. See, Thangaraj, 'The History and Teachings of the Hindu Christian Community Commonly Called Nattu Sabai in Tirunelveli', 51.

116 Suttampillai, *A Brief Sketch of the Hindu Christian Dogmas*, p. 4.

117 Ibid., p. 10.

never thought of abolishing the Law. Suttampillai's pamphlet *A Brief Sketch of the Hindu Christian Dogmas* began with the statement: 'It is enjoined by God Incarnate that even the least commandment contained in the Hebrew Scriptures, called the "Law" and the "Prophets" ought not to be overlooked, but to be strictly observed by His Holy Church. Matt. 5.17–18; Lk. 24.44–8'. Jesus' observance of Jewish festivals, his interest in and endorsement of the temple in such acts as its cleansing, his telling the healed leper to show himself to the priest as Moses had commanded, and, more significantly, his saying 'Think not that I have come to abolish the law and the prophets. I have not come to abolish them but to fulfil them' (Matt. 5.17) were seen as subscribing to Jewish customs and practices. It was claimed that the early church held on to Jewish purificatory customs. The Apostolic decree read: 'But we should write to them to abstain from the pollutions of idols and from unchastity and from what is strangled and from blood. For from early generations Moses has had in every city those who preach him, for he is read every Sabbath in the Synagogues' (Acts 15.20). Paul, too, was seen as confirming the practices of Suttampillai's 'National Church': 'Therefore let no one pass judgement on you in questions of food and drink or with regard to a festival or a new moon or a sabbath' (Col. 2.16).

More significantly, Arumainayagam replaced the western hymn-book with a book of Psalms rendered by him into Tamil and set to Indian classical tunes. His use of classical Indian music for Christian purposes was probably an early attempt at indigenization. This was his way of redefining a Christianity which had come with western cultural paraphernalia and placing it within a Jewish and Indian milieu. He felt that his Tamil Psalms would be a suitable hymn-book for his church. Thomas Thangaraj who comes from Tinnevelly, explains Suttampillai's preference for the Psalms as an alternative to western hymns: 'Though the choice of the Psalms came from the Anglican tradition he grew up in, the choice of South Indian classical music was deliberate with a keen desire to inculcate the gospel idiom'.[118] An innovative missiological achievement of Arumainayagam was to make the Hebrew Psalms attractive to a wider audience. He achieved this by employing different phrases and words which broadened their appeal, as indicated, for instance, by his choice of words for God:

---

118 M. Thomas Thangaraj, 'Hymnody as Biblical Hermeneutics: Tehillim by Sattampillai of Hindu-Christian Community', Paper Presented at the Annual Meeting of the Society of Biblical Literature, (Orlando, November 1998), p. 4.

The wide range of terms he uses signals his interest to speak to different sections of the society. He uses both *theivam* and *thevan*. *Thevan* has the masculine ending whereas *theivam* is neuter, meaning godhead. *Thevan* is the word most Christians are familiar with since that is the term that is used to translate YHWH in the Hebrew Bible and *Theos* in the New Testament. Most frequently he employs the name Jehovah (*ekova*) and *karthar* (Lord) as well. He reaches a much broader section of Tamil society when he uses terms such as *paran* (often used for Shiva), *rasa* and *arase* (terms for king) and *sami* (popular and colloquial term for God). The use of multiple terms for God indicates Sattampillai's commitment to a broader horizon of understanding of his hearers.[119]

Another interpretative tactic employed by Suttampillai to gain acceptance for his community was to see both the biblical Jews and the Shanars of Tinnevelly as parts of the wider family of the people of God. Suttampillai affirmed a common pedigree, the idea of a single act of creation and the dispersion of people to different destinations. His attribution of a common Jewish origin resonated with the monogenetic theory prevalent at that time.[120] He alleged that Jews and Hindus were the survivors of the 'Great Deluge', and that the Jews proceeded to settle in the north and the Hindus in the south. He even identified Aryavarta in the Himalayas as the place where Noah's ark landed after the 'Great Flood'. He also claimed that the Jews were entrusted with the commandments of God, but that these were meant for all. He never advocated mere transposition of Jewish customs. He clearly distinguished between universal practices which Christians should follow, and indigenous customs which were in keeping with God's laws, and which could be adopted. He argued against adhering to all Jewish customs, especially against the circumcision of Gentile converts, asserting that it was 'prescribed solely for the use of the Jewish nationality'.[121] Just as he introduced Jewish practices in his worship services, he also accommodated a number of indigenous practices to ensure that the Shanars were not denied their 'own agency' and to make clear that their native customs were noble enough to be accepted in the assembly of God. He found scriptural warrant for following one's own national customs. The 'respective national customs'[122] he advocated in his church included the Indian habit of prostrating before the deity, the use of frankincense, sitting on the floor, and worshipping God with folded hands.[123] While missionaries

119 Ibid., pp. 6–7.
120 Marshall (ed.), *The British Discovery of Hinduism in the Eighteenth Century*, p. 23.
121 Suttampillai, *A Brief Sketch of the Hindu Christian Dogmas*, p. 4.
122 Ibid., p. 1.
123 Kumaradoss, 'Creation of Alternative Public Spheres and Church Indigenisation', p. 10.

discouraged the Hindu custom of offering food to deities, Suttampillai encouraged his church members to observe such acts. He promoted the offering of 'food, drink and perfume' to Christ. Suttampillai reckoned that it was perfectly acceptable to offer these 'spiritual nourishments'. His justification was that Jesus still had a 'human frame' although he was in perfect union with God, and that he 'personally enjoyed all the sacrificial things (in the course of 34 years)'.[124]

Suttampillai's replication of Jewish religious practices suggests that he was able to see a connection between the biblical Jews and the Shanars of Tinnevelly. He saw the Shanars of his new community as like the Israelites called by God to be God's own people. For him, the Hindu Christian community chosen by God was small in numbers like the 'little family of Noah', and 'a lonely distressed Israel'.[125] He claimed that it was

foretold in the Hebrew Scriptures that the temporal power of the Jewish nation, which was in a manner supporting the Church of God until the time of the Holy Incarnation (Gal. 4.1–5), would cease to exist at the prescribed time (Gen. 49.10) and the Gentile converts would be incorporated with the Jewish Holy Church with full liberty to practise such of their own respective national customs (1 Cor. 7.17–20).[126]

By associating the Shanars with the biblical Jews, Suttampillai was thus able to elevate his community from the degraded state in which they were placed. Suttampillai's aim in this respect was to impress on the missionaries that Shanars had not altogether fallen into total darkness, because they followed the customs and precepts of the Mosaic religion. He was trying to conform and reconcile the Shanars' customs and practices with those of the Jews. He conceded the superiority of biblical faith: 'On the whole, my diligent search of nearly half a century for the necessity of my own salvation, has brought me to the conclusion that the Holy Scripture cannot be surpassed by the books of any other religion, either anciently existing in or recently introduced into India'.[127] At the same time, as we have seen, Suttampillai never failed to acknowledge the potential of national customs.

Despite his iconoclastic streak, Suttampillai remained a conservative as far as the role of women in his church was concerned. He uncritically accepted the low status accorded to women in the Hebrew scriptures. Women were expected to follow the defilement regulations and purificatory rites listed in the priestly code (Lev. 12 and 15) and still evident in

124 Suttampillai, *A Brief Sketch of the Hindu Christian Dogmas*, pp. 11–12.
125 Ibid., p. 29.   126 Ibid., p. 1.   127 Ibid., p. 28.

Anglican practice, as he would have observed in the Tinnevely church. This included the declaration of women as unclean during menstruation, and their observation of a readmission process after childbirth, before being allowed to participate in normal community and ritual life. Suttampillai unwittingly replicated the codes which were devised to perpetuate androcentric expectations and definitions of holiness and purity. He supported levirate marriage because it was sanctioned by the Hebrew scriptures. He found support for this in the Book of Ruth and rewrote it in Tamil *ammanai* form, a ballad-like narrative style.[128] He juxtaposed Jewish and Sanskrit texts to establish his case. He placed Hebrew texts such as Deuteronomy 25.5–10, Genesis 38.8–10, and Ruth 3.12, 13 and 4.1–13 alongside elitist Hindu texts such as the Laws of Manu 9.56–63, 145–7 in order to reinforce his case. He never tried to destabilize Tamil values regarding male–female relationships. He assigned women to the domestic sphere and denied them a public space and a public role. He was very unsupportive of women's preaching. They were 'only gifted with the spirit of dreams and visions'.[129] He likened the women preachers of the Salvation Army to performers in concert halls and theatres. In his view, women acting in the public sphere went against 'the permanent divine law perpetually binding the whole human race from the creation of Adam to the end of the world'.[130] The powerful women portrayed in the Bible were dismissed as isolated characters who were 'not to be imitated by womenkind in general'.[131] He even ridiculed some biblical women for their liberative attitude. Regarding the Magnificat of Mary, which spoke of a reversal of fortunes whereby the mighty would be brought down and the lowly lifted up, Suttampillai sarcastically wondered whether, 'if this doctrine be a true one', there would be a 'universal change of human body, by which the act of child-bearing is to be transferred to the male sex, or its pangs are to be relieved from the female sex'. He pointed out that these prophetesses were permitted to perform their ministry within the privacy of their homes and make 'known their revelations at critical movements from their residences' (Acts 21.8, 9; 2 Kings 22.14–20).[132] His essentially conservative stance could be traced to his misogynistic reading of the Hebrew scriptures, and his subscription to the behavioural patterns of the Tamils, who distinguished between *akam* (inside, house, private) and *puram* (outer, exterior, public). Translated into gender roles, women

---

128 A. N. Suttampillai, *Ruthamavai* (Palamcottah: Church Mission Press, 1884). He claims in this booklet that he had rewritten Lamentations (1854) and Proverbs (1864) using Tamil poetic tradition. So far my attempts to locate them have proved fruitless.
129 Ibid., p. 23.   130 Ibid.   131 Ibid.   132 Ibid.

were confined to the home and were expected find their salvation through service and sacrifice. His contention was that 'the pious and social manners of the females' handed down to us by the ancient church had to be upheld. What was paramount was the establishment of a national church distinct from 'the corrupt form of Christianity professed by Europeans'[133] in order to regain national pride against the aspersions cast by missionaries. In that overarching aspiration, women's causes were subsumed and sacrificed.

Suttampillai's hermeneutical enterprise knocked wind out of the sails of Caldwell's claim that there was no single Shanar 'who really appears able to think for himself on any point of Christian doctrine or scriptural interpretation, or on any social question'.[134] His grasp of biblical data, his clever use of western writings to turn the tables on Europeans, and his articulation of the strengths of his own community challenged Caldwell's claim that Shanars were prone to 'dullness of apprehension and confusion of ideas'.[135] He was intrinsically nationalistic even before such a concept entered the discourse. He warned the British that if they did not reform their ways, they would be ousted, as had once happened to the nations in Palestine: 'Reform at once (Eph. 5.1–12). "That the land spue not you out also, as it spued out the nations that were" once in Palestine (Lev. 18.28)'.[136] Rammohun Roy viewed the British occupation as a divine boon to bolster India, and Navalar perceived the missionary presence not as the work of the white-man's God, but as that of Siva to galvanize the Saivas, but Suttampillai entertained no such notions. For him, Europeans and their brand of Christianity led to the destruction of 'the social, moral and economic usages traditionally peculiar to their nationality'.[137] He even went on to claim that 'the European Christians and their colonies are hereditarily overwhelmed for ages with various gross sins'.[138]

Missionaries who were adept at handling native protestations and even their pagan practices found themselves in the awkward position of being confronted by natives projecting the very biblical tenets which they regarded as irrelevant to their hermeneutical cause. Unlike these missionaries, who made hermeneutical judgements from a Christian apologetic point of view, treated the cultic practices mentioned in the Hebrew

133 Ibid., p. 8.
134 Caldwell, *The Tinnevelly Shanars*, p. 63.
135 Ibid., p. 2.
136 Suttampillai, *A Brief Sketch of the Hindu Christian Dogmas*, p. 30.
137 Ibid., p. 8.   138 Ibid., p. 19.

scriptures as a mark of the decadence of Judaic religion and elevated the teachings of the prophets as ethically superior, Navalar and Suttumpillai saw temple practices in a positive light. While Rammohun Roy and Thomas Jefferson were extolling the superior moral fabric of the gospels and eschewed ritual in religion, Navalar and Suttampillai did the reverse.

What looms large in Arumuka Pillai's and Suttampillai's hermeneutical enterprise is the significance of the Hebrew Bible. For them, the Hebrew scriptures were not to be treated as inferior or irrelevant, or attached tenuously to the most glorious of narratives – the New Testament. Ironically, both found the cultic practices of the Hebrew scriptures to be recognizable and useful, and the theology of Protestant missionaries deriving from Paul to be foreign and unhelpful. They did not often follow the customary Christian habit of calling the Testaments Old and New. Navalar, in his relentless rebuttal, often used phrases like 'your religious book', 'your sacred books', 'your scriptures' and 'viviliam' (literal translation of *ta biblia*). In his *Brief Sketch of Hindu Christian Dogmas* Suttampillai referred to the Old Testament as the 'Hebrew Scriptures' and the New Testament as the 'Greek Scriptures', and when he meant both, he used 'Holy Scriptures'. This was perhaps his way of providing scriptural warrant for his enterprise by underlining the two Testaments as a continuum of one revelation. The New Testament was important because it resonated with the customs and religious practices in the Hebrew scriptures. His privileging of the Hebrew scriptures was based on the authority of Jesus and the early church: 'It is enjoined by God Incarnate that even the least commandment contained in the Hebrew Scriptures called "the Law" and "the Prophets" ought not to be over-looked, but to be strictly observed by His Holy Church (Matt. 5.17–19; Lk. 24.44–8)'.[139] Jesus 'distinctly announced' to the disciples 'the excellent authority of the Hebrew Scripture' and they were to 'think nothing above what is written' in the said books.[140] For him, there were no other 'books of Divine authority besides the said Hebrew Scriptures'.[141] He saw the Bible brought by the Europeans as a two-edged sword by which they themselves were be condemned.

The choice of texts by Navalar and Suttampillai from the Hebrew scriptures was, as we have seen, limited to those which promote liturgical and cultic practices. It was not the maniacal and punitive passages which galvanized the Victorian preachers, as we saw in the previous chapter, which were central to Suttampillai and Navalar but the narratives which

139 Ibid., p. 1.   140 Ibid., p. 5.   141 Ibid.

dealt with ceremonies, rituals and liturgy. The texts dealing with the poor, widows, orphans and sojourners, which became pivotal for Third World interpreters a century later, did not excite their attention. For them, the contested space was not economics but culture. They did not challenge social inequalities but aimed to create positive forms of communal identity which would rectify the misrepresentation of them by the missionaries. Navalar made the Hebrews into honorary Saivites. He reckoned that the Hebrews of old, in their liturgical ideas and thought acted like Saivites. Suttampillai brought legitimacy to his debased community by indigenizing it with elements from Hebrew and Aryan customs.

The use of biblical texts by Arumuka Pillai and Suttampillai, in the light of today's highly professionalized biblical scholarship, would be seen as pre-critical. They were engaged in their heremeneutical task before modern criticism hit the biblical world. They interpreted the biblical narratives on the basis of their own understanding of the situations described in the texts. Theirs was an imaginative but orthodox employment of texts marked by a mixture of liberalism and conservatism. Suttampillai relied on Thomas Scott's *The Holy Bible with Original Notes*, which was first published in 1788 and went through several editions, being revised by Scott in 1828. The overarching theological presupposition of the commentary was that the Bible was God's oracle and God's law. Scott's explanatory notes were based on the Authorized Version and his book was renowned for three things. It was addressed to ordinary people, it reflected the evangelical mood of the time and it offered practical guidance. Scott's intention was: 'first to explain in the notes the primary meaning . . . and then, in practical observations, to shew what we may learn from each passage, allowing for all difference in circumstance'.[142] Scott's commentaries made clear that biblical texts gained significance through performance and practice. Suttampillai must have been enthused by Scott's call for practical enactment of biblical teachings, which resonated with his own hermeneutical intent. Navalar's penchant for texts was not necessarily influenced by the Protestant approach, but the relentless use of the text by the missionaries no doubt had an impact on him. The revealed scriptures as accepted orthodoxy were part of Saiva tradition.

Suttampillai and Navalar were in a way precursors to the current reader-response readings. Their hermeneutical work was undertaken

142 John Eadie, 'Preface by Dr Eadie', in *The National Comprehensive Family Bible: The Holy Bible with the Commentaries of Scott and Henry, and Containing Also Many Thousand Critical and Explanatory Notes, Selected from the Great Standard Authors of Europe and America*, ed. John Eadie (Glasgow, W. R. M'Phun, 1860), p. xiii.

before biblical narratives were subjected to historical scrutiny. Their prime aim was to find out the function of the texts in the lives of the people. What was crucial to them was the practical meaning of worship for ordinary biblical Jews and how it coincided with their own hemeneutical agendas. If Navalar tried to Saivize Judaism, Suttampillai endeavoured to Judaize Christianity. It is apparent that their attitude to the Hebrew scriptures was in total contrast to that of another Hindu revivalist of the time, Dayananda Saraswati (1824–83). His fulminations were many,[143] and he was particularly critical of the references to animal sacrifice in the Old Testament, which Navalar and Suttampillai conveniently avoided. Commenting on the Exodus, Dayananda Saraswati said: 'What a fine thing did this God of the Christians do! How like a burglar, at midnight He mercilessly killed children, and not had least pity on them . . . When the God of the Christian is a flesh-eater, what can He have to do with *pity* and compassion?' His conclusion was, 'may such a God and such a book remain far from us. In this alone lies our good'.[144] Unlike Arumuka Pillai and Suttampillai, Dayananda Saraswati did not search for similarities or correspondences between Vedic and biblical teaching. True, Dayananda Saraswati did search the Bible, but his intention was to demolish its teaching and to prove that the Vedas alone contained truth which was universally valid.

From a postcolonial perspective, the Navalar and Suttampillai readings fall in the category of identity hermeneutics. The emphasis on caste is manifest in their writings. The Vellala and Shanar elements are very much in evidence. Those who are inclined to think that identity-politics is narrow and does not take into account the aspect of class will find the work of these men unsatisfactory. Identity-politics has its virtues. It affirms the right to self-definition and a sense of agency in order to fight discrimination, and, in the case of these men, it helped them to deal with the calumnies heaped upon them by the colonizers. Far from navel-gazing, Navalar and Suttampillai challenged and constructed a hermeneutical argument against their opponents with the very issue, namely caste, which the missionaries found abominable and were set on eradicating. In Navalar's case, his comparative hermeneutics provided him with a heightened sense of Saiva social superiority, moral excellence

143 He found both Testaments, in contrast to Vedic or Aryan Hinduism, consisted of silly and savage stories. See Chiranjiva Bharadwaja (tr.), *Light of Truth* or *An English Translation of the Satyarth Prakash, the well-known work of Swami Dayananda Saraswati* (Allahabad, K. C. Bhalla, n.d.), pp. 583–644.
144 Ibid., pp. 605–6.

and, more specifically, of the exemplary characteristics of Saiva worship. In the case of Suttampillai, it was a matter of turning the once degraded community into respectable citizens. This he was able to achieve by selectively appropriating two priestly codes – Hindu and Hebrew. It was the commonsensical or idiosyncratic hermeneutical mannerisms of Suttampillai and Navalar, depending on one's view, which enabled them to advance their communities.

CONCLUDING REMARKS

At a time when new empires are being talked about, the Hebrew scriptures become an important source for studying the role of empires. Let me end the chapter with what the Old Testament has to say about empires. Political circumstances of the Old and New Testaments were totally different. Imperial impulses and ambitions are recurrent themes in the Hebrew scriptures. In the Old Testament we see how a group of loosely knit tribes evolved into a people with a communal identity and eventually culminated in a nation possessing territory, even becoming an empire for a short time. Under King David, Israel was transformed into an imperial power. David was able to make Israel a dominant power, and 2 Samuel 8 lists the names of the nations he conquered. In a short span of time he was able to annex Syria, Moab, Ammon, Amalek and Edom. More importantly, the capture of Edom, which commanded the ports on the Red Sea, and the treaty with Tyre enabled Israel to control the trade route which set her on the path of commercial prosperity. The territorial and commercial success had theological implications. At that point, Israel is seen as specially mandated by God to subjugate other peoples and occupy their lands: 'The impact of all this on Israelite religion must have been profound. David's conquests were also Yahweh's, so Yahweh too ruled an empire; its religious centre was the pavilion erected by David on Jerusalem's acropolis to enshrine the Ark, an object symbolic of divine presence during the earlier period of the league (2 Sam. 6; cf. Ps. 132)'.[145]

Thus a new era began in which Yahweh became the patron deity of an imperial nation-state which had a royal shrine located in the capital of Jerusalem with the protection of the king. We see the emergence of the theology of empire based on God's special relationship with the people he has chosen. In addition, there is a promise for the monarch of an enduring

---

145 S. Dean McBride, 'Biblical Literature in Its Historical Context: The Old Testament', in *Harper's Bible Commentary*, ed. James L. Mays (San Francisco, Harper and Row, 1988), p. 16.

dynasty and an assurance by the deity of his lasting presence in the royal shrine:

The Lord swore to David a sure oath from which he will not withdraw: 'Your own offspring I will set upon the throne; one of the sons of your body I will set on your throne. If your sons keep my covenant and my testimonies which I shall teach them, their sons also for ever shall sit upon your throne. For the Lord has chosen Zion; he has desired it for his habitation: This is my resting place for ever; here I will dwell, for I have desired it'.

(Ps. 132.11–14)

From now on, the God of Israel is seen to be at work not only in the internal affairs of the Israelites, but also in international affairs on their behalf. The New Testament, on the other hand, hardly recognizes the concept of a nation at all. We do not encounter newly formed Christian communities engaging in political struggles or vying to establish a nation for themselves. The paramount and the sole political duty of a believer is to reverence the powers that be. The prophets were patriots and citizens who were striving to establish a just society within their national boundary and national identity. The apostles and disciples, on the other hand, were sojourners and pilgrims looking towards the kingdom of heaven. Although most of the New Testament writing emerged in the context of Roman colonialism, there are no explicit references to the empire or its oppressive presence. The exception is the Book of Revelation, though even here the account of the situation is couched in allegory and imagery.

At a time when right-wing political commentators like Robert Cooper and Niall Ferguson[146] are arguing for strong nations such as the United States of America to intervene and topple 'rogue' nations which threaten western values, the Old Testament has a telling message: misuse power and you will be punished. Empires are seen as condemned both for their predatory nature and for their arrogance. Empires are double-edged swords. Sometimes they are seen as having a providential role as liberating agents, but, more often than not, they themselves are subjected to stern punishment. Empires are raised as a scourge to punish wicked nations and in turn they themselves are punished for the oppressive measures which affect the subjugated nations. Syrians are condemned for violently abusing the vanquished people of Gilgad; the Philistines for the inhuman act of slave-trading; the Phoenicians for breaking a treaty and enslaving; the Edomites for their violence; the Ammonities for the massacre of innocent women; and the Moabites for dishonouring the dead bodies of their

146 See Afterword, pp. 223–4 for details of their writings.

enemies. The first two chapters of Amos are a warning to nations and empires. The injustices identified include the evils of plunder, aggression, and cruel treatment of the subject people (Isa. 10.13–14; Amos 1.3, 6, 9, 11, 13). Assyria, seen as God's weapon against godless nations, including Israel, is castigated not only for the terror tactics it unleashes among the subjects it has conquered, but also for the failure to acknowledge that its achievements are the result of God's power. Assyria uses divine dispensation to plunder and conquer other nations. Assyria has wiped out national borders and looted their treasures (Isa. 10.13). Similarly, Babylonians (Chaldeans) are ordained to chastise the wicked Habbakuk (1.5–11) – though who is wicked is ambiguous here. But the point is that the Babylonians themselves will be judged for their destructive militarism and the way they have mercilessly overstepped the limits set for them (Hab. 1.17). The Hebrew scriptures seem to suggest that empires, because of their military strength and the power that comes with it, are more than likely to behave arrogantly. Discrimination, oppression, inhumanity, cruelty and all forms of barbarity are no less barbarous because they are carried out by nations chosen as God's instrument. Presidents and prime ministers who seek biblical support for the messianic role of empires do well to realize that the same Bible has another harrowing message. Empires are an unreliable way of solving the world's problems, and those who take the sword will inevitably die by it.

CHAPTER 5

Imperial fictions and biblical narratives: entertainment and exegesis in colonial novels

> But the one rule to remember is: the sacred text is actually enemy of every other.
>
> William H. Gass

This chapter focusses on the employment of the Bible in two colonial novels: Sydney Owenson's *The Missionary: An Indian Tale* (1811) and Akiki K. Nyabongo's *Africa Answers Back* (1936).[1] Sydney Owenson (1783–1859), who later became Lady Morgan through marriage to a knighted English physician, Charles Morgan, was an Irish literary figure. Her literary production extended over six decades; it included novels, poems and travel and political writings. She was a complex personality. She championed the cause of Irish nationalism but was reluctant to support women's participation in politics.[2] Nyabongo, an African chief from Uganda, was educated at Yale and Oxford and played a critical role in Uganda before and after independence. Besides his political involvement, he was visible in international literary guilds and acted as the editor of *African Magazine*.[3]

Both novels, *The Missionary* and *Africa Answers Back*, were shaped by a confused mixture of religious enthusiasm, colonial attitudes to people, and the forces of modernity which came in the wake of colonialism. The *Missionary* takes a Eurocentric view of India and of colonial practices, in which identities of both the colonizer and the colonized are questioned and reframed. *Africa Answers Back*, on the other hand, takes a nativist

---

1 The novel also appeared under the name *The Story of an African Chief* (Charles Scribner's Sons, New York, 1935).

2 For a helpful introduction to the historical and literary context of her life and work, see Julia M. Wright, 'Introduction', in *The Missionary: An Indian Tale*, ed. Julia M. Wright (Peterborough, Ontario, Broadview Press, 2002), pp. 9–63.

3 Details about Nyabongo are scarce. For a brief entry on his life and work, see *Who's Who in African Literature: Biographies, Works, Commentaries*, ed. J. Jahn et al. (Tubingen, Horst Erdmann Verlag, 1972), pp. 277–8.

view of colonialism and seeks to invoke through the main character the uneasiness and uncertainty of the colonized 'other'. Both novels expose intra-Christian differences which have implications far beyond Europe. In Owenson's novel it is internecine doctrinal disputes between Spanish Jesuits and Portuguese Franciscans, whereas in Nyabongo's narrative it is between the Protestants and the Catholics. When the missionaries make a case for their denominations, asserting their superiority and in the process castigating each other before the Bugandan King, Mutesa, the confused King comments: 'We see that every White man seems to have his own religion, and thinks it is the only true one'. What he is further prompted to say casts doubt on the future of the mission enterprise: 'We must assert our strength. We shall have nothing more to do with … the religion of the Whites. We shall return to the religion of our forefathers. Each of the missionaries called the others liars, and our prophet has found that none of them is correct'.[4] Nevertheless, these Christian denominations might have had their internal differences but, as the novels make clear, in their aim to convert the natives they acted with one accord.

The Missionary first appeared in 1811, a narrative interspersed with a number of pieces of documentary evidence. In one of her footnotes Owenson refers to the Vellore Mutiny of 1806.[5] The implication is that the novel explores the same basic tension as had provoked the Vellore Mutiny: the violent and forceful nature of European colonial rule. She reissued the novel in 1859, soon after the Indian uprising of 1857. The revised version had a new title – *Luxima, the Prophetess: A Tale of India*. The supplanting of the European hero, Hilarion, the missionary, with the Indian Brahmin woman, Luxima, could be interpreted as an indication of the pointlessness of missionary labours in the aftermath of the 1857 Indian uprising. The novel, set in a seventeenth-century colonial context, has further colonial complications. Goa was a Portuguese territory, but Portugal itself had recently come under Spanish rule. The novel thus addresses two kinds of colonialism: one that existed within Europe and

---

4 Akiki K. Nyabongo, *Africa Answers Back* (London, George Routledge & Sons Ltd, 1936), p. 19.
5 The sepoy rebellion of Vellore, South India, was a result of a number of factors. There was resentment among the sepoys over the new changes introduced by the East India Company; these had to do with caste marks, new uniforms and the amount of facial hair one could have. These new changes were interpreted by the sepoys as an indirect means of converting everyone to Christianity. Their conditions of service and low-scale pay were the other sore points. There was also an alleged collusion between the sepoys and the family of the deposed Tipu Sultan, who was interned in the Fort of Vellore, with a view to restoring him to power. For a succinct introduction to the causes, see S. K. Mitra, 'The Vellore Mutiny of 1806 and the Question of Christian Mission to India', in *Indian Church History Review* 8:1 (1974), 75–82.

the other between Europe and India. Owenson's text can be read at many levels and functions simultaneously as travelogue, romance and missionary history. It is essentially about a mission undertaken by the Portuguese monk Hilarion, who fashions himself as a latter-day St Paul, 'consumed with an insatiable thirst for the conversion of souls'.[6] Initially, Hilarion goes to Portuguese Goa as the apostolic nuncio, and then to a 'remote and little known province' of Kashmir in order to carry out his evangelistic activities. In Kashmir, Hilarion is encouraged by a Brahmin pundit, who tells him that once the conversion of Luxima, 'the priestess of Cashmire', is effected, it will lead to the 'redemption of her whole nation'.[7] Her example would cast a spell on her compatriots and the follower of Brahma will 'fly from the altar of his ancient gods, to worship in that temple in which she would become a votarist'.[8] Spurred on by the Indian pundit, Hilarion invests all his evangelistic zeal and energy in the single purpose of converting Luxima. His earnest design and his passionate dream is that one day he will 'shade the brow of the Heathen Priestess with the sacred veil of the Christian Nun'.[9] With this in mind, Hilarion pursues his prey. A fair amount of the narrative is devoted to the unconsummated and, in Hilarion's case, unstated romance that exists between the two protagonists of the novel. This association with a woman leads to Hilarion's Inquisition. The officers of the Inquisition charge Hilarion with two crimes – 'heresy' and 'seduction'.[10] His heresy is that he loses his zeal for proselytization and neglects his mission. His seduction has to do with his entering into a tie with his 'lovely associate' and her being 'companion in his wanderings', thus breaching his monastic vows. For these crimes, Hilarion is condemned to be burnt at the stake. The novel ends in tragedy. Luxima is killed by an arrow which is meant for Hilarion, and Hilarion himself languishes in the Kashmir valley, a lost soul. More will follow on the doomed mission of Hilarion as the chapter progresses.

The importance of Nyabongo's novel, *Africa Answer Back*, lies in the fact that it contains a heady mixture of colonialism and the Bible. The author, a descendant of the Toro kings, was born in Uganda. The novel is autobiographical and mixes both fact and fiction, imagination and memory. The story is set in Buganda at the turn of the nineteenth century and spans fifty years. As the title indicates, it is a subversive African tale

---

6 Sydney Owenson, *The Missionary*, ed. Julia M. Wright (Peterborough, Ontario, Broadview Press, [1811] 2002), p. 77.

7 Ibid., p. 96.   8 Ibid., p. 98.   9 Ibid., p. 100.   10 Ibid., p. 238.

which answers colonial discourse by rupturing and remoulding it. The novel reverses a seemingly successful missionary story, turning it into a narrative of the empowerment and emancipation of the missionized. The novel is about the hero, Abala Stanley Mujungu, and his journey of self-discovery as he tries to straddle both the ancient culture that his parents want to maintain and the modern western culture introduced by the missionary Hubert, and about how Mujungu is finally transformed from exemplary mission-school student into African reformer.

THE BIBLE — ALLUSIONS AND RESISTANCE

For our purposes, the significance of these two novels lies in the use of biblical texts and images throughout the narrative, sometimes obliquely and at other times explicitly. My intention is not to engage with the biblical texts as such, but to elucidate how they are appropriated by the two authors in order to challenge and comment on the colonial presence.

In *The Missionary* biblical references are alluded to and are incidental rather than overt in the text. What we find is a clever blending of biblical allusions and phrases in the narrative. Analogous biblical figures, too, crop up. In the early part of the novel, a Bible is exchanged between the two protagonists, an exchange which does not produce the desired results. The hero, Hilarion, who is besotted with Luxima, a 'soul so bewildered, so deep in error', gives her a 'scriptural volume, translated into the dialect of the country', with the express intention of convincing her of the superiority of his religion. Presenting her with the book, he tells her of the sacrifices he has made so that many might follow the precepts contained in it. With a view to convincing Luxima, Hilarion provides a list of the things he has had to give up – youth, rank, status, his own country – and tells how he has had to cross dangerous seas and encounter pain and hardship so that others might 'follow the divine precepts which this sacred volume contains'. He gives her the book with these words: 'Judge, then, of its purity and influence, by the sacrifices it enables man to make. Take it; and may Heaven pour into thy heart its celestial grace, that, as thou readest, thou mayst edify and believe'.[11] His hope in presenting the Bible is that, just as he himself has been moved by its contents, Luxima too will be attracted by it. The Bible is envisaged as a totemic power, at least in the mind of Hilarion, a power to move and captivate people.

---

11 Ibid., p. 127.

Luxima graciously accepts the book. But, on the very next occasion
when she sees Hilarion, she gives it back to him with the words:
'Christian, take back thy Shaster, for it should belong to thee alone.
'Tis a wondrous book! and full of holy love; worthy to be ranked with
the sacred *Veidam*, which the great Spirit presented to Brahma to
promote the happiness and wisdom of his creatures'.[12] It is Luxima who
ratifies the Bible, saying that it is as good as her own Vedas and to be
placed alongside the sacred books of the East. The imported book is put
on a par with indigenous texts. The Bible, which later came to be seen as
the mediator of morality and an instrument of colonial power and
authority, is here deemed to echo the seminal tenets of the sacred books
of the East. Confounded by such a confident tone, the Franciscan monk
tries to tell the Brahmin priestess that her observations about the book are
accurate and that the 'inspired book' he tried to put in her hands is 'full of
holy love; for the Christian doctrine is the doctrine of the heart', and 'is
full of that tender-loving mercy, which blends and unites the various
selfish interests of mankind, one great sentiment of brotherly affection
and religious love!' Such eulogizing of the Book is too much for Luxima.
She cuts down to size the missionary's sacred book by saying that the
claims Hilarion has made for it are already encapsulated in her own
religious texts: 'Such is that doctrine of mystic love, by which our true
religion unites its followers to each other, and to the Source of all good;
for we cannot cling to the hope of infinite felicity, without rejoicing in the
first daughter of love to God, which is charity towards man'.[13] The
Christian Bible, which was to become the focal point of vigorous debate
in the nineteenth – century colonial expansion, in this instance does not
encourage dialogue, nor is it in a position to effect an impact. It is not
seen as the authority to which all other texts should be submitted. In this
encounter it is the colonial text which emerges as ambivalent and insecure
when placed alongside indigenous texts. It also suggests the hazard of
adding another sacred text in a land which is already brimming with
religious writings.

Later in the novel, the missionary gives the scripture back to Luxima
again. The book and its contents appear not to have created any great
effect on Luxima's sense of spiritual well-being. On their final and fateful
journey to Goa, Luxima reveals her true intention in following
Hilarion:'it was *thou* I followed, and not thy doctrines; for, pure and

12 Ibid., p. 139.   13 Ibid., p. 140.

sublime as they may be, they yet came darkly and confusedly to my soul'.[14] She subsequently makes it clear where she stands in relation to the new faith. Immediately before her death, she tells Hilarion, 'now *I die* as Brahmin women *die*, a *Hindu* in my feelings and my faith – dying for him I loved, and believing as my fathers have believed'.[15] It was not the foreign book but the Franciscan monk who had attracted Luxima's attention and inspired her love.

The Missionary is peppered with biblical allusions which easily fit into the narrative. None of these allusions has specific attribution to a biblical writer. Nor are they provided with many hints that single them out as scriptural citations. The only concession the author allows for their sacred status is in sometimes italicizing them. On the other hand, the Victorian readers, for whom the novel was written and who would have been fairly conversant with the King James Version, might not have needed such chapter and verse identifications. These allusions function on two levels. On the first level, the characters in the novel are compared to biblical figures such as Paul, Jesus and Mary Magdalene. The stories related to these biblical personalities are not recounted in the novel. The allusions are sufficient to make the points Owenson was trying to make. The two leading protagonists of the novel are given characteristics and placed in situations which signify biblical linkage. The character of Hilarion, the hero, provides multiple allusions. Sometimes he is seen as Paul and at other times as Jesus. In the opening section of the novel Hilarion is presented as a reflection of Paul, replicating the twin tasks for which Paul was distinctly renowned, namely evangelization and debating with theological opponents. Hilarion himself chooses the subject of Paul as the topic of his discourse which he delivers on the eve of the festival of St Hilarion, a third-century Palestinian convert who lived as an ascetic in Egypt. The monks who are listening to his talk are inspired to say: 'It is not of St Paul alone he speaks, but of himself; he is consumed with an insatiable thirst for the conversion of souls; for the dilatation and honour of the kingdom of Christ. It is through him that the heretical tenets of the Jesuits will be confounded and exposed'.[16] This was the time when the Portuguese in Goa were groaning 'under the tyranny of the Spanish Jesuits'. As anticipated by his Franciscan monks, Hilarion fulfils his role as a skilful debater like Paul when he argues with his fellow missionaries, the Jesuits, about their unscrupulous mission practices. Like Paul, who

14 Ibid., p. 231.   15 Ibid., p. 257.   16 Ibid., p. 77.

questioned the motives and methods of his theological opponents, Hilarion too is trying to correct the abuses in the Jesuit practices which hindered the progress of the gospel.[17] Later, when Hilarion sees Luxima indulging in the Hindu practice of offering her worship to heaven and earth, his reaction is Paul-like. Hilarion's words of admonition are a paraphrase of Paul's letter to the Romans, where the apostle charges the Gentiles with substituting the 'truth about God' with a 'lie' and with worshipping and serving the creature rather than the creator: 'Mistaken being! know you what you do? That profanely you offer to the created, that which belongs to the creator only!' (Rom. 1.25).

At other times Hilarion is seen as a Jesus-figure. For instance, when describing Hilarion's first entry to Kashmir, where he was supposed to undertake the great mission of preaching the gospel, the author activates a biblical passage from Zechariah which is quoted by Matthew as well: 'he came riding on an ass' (Zech. 9.9; Matt. 21.5). This biblical reference has a twofold message, both parts of which fit in with the narrative flow of the novel. One is ominous: the original passage from Zechariah is placed within a chapter which has oracles of God against foreign nations saying that these nations will be defeated and come under Yahweh, which is probably a veiled reference to the future annihilation of heathen nations such as India by the white-man's God. Jesus' entry into Jerusalem was a final invitation to the people and the religious authorities to make a public choice between God and Satan, a choice which India too would soon have to make. The other message is a premonitory one. Like Jesus, Hilarion is going to be a righteous servant who will pass through the crucible of suffering. The difference between Jesus and Hilarion is that Jesus was finally vindicated, but Hilarion is totally abandoned by his God and his own church.

Luxima's character too is portrayed using biblical allusions. At one point in the novel, she is described as a 'Christian Magdalene'. From the narrative it is clear that the reference is not to the Mary Magdalene of popular imagination, a repentant prostitute, which Luxima was definitely not. The reference is to Mary Magdalene, the faithful follower of Jesus, who was present at his crucifixion and a testifier to his resurrection. Just like the biblical Mary, Luxima is a steadfast admirer and a devotee of Hilarion; she remains with him until the end, witnesses his sufferings and makes a brave attempt to rescue him.

17 Ibid., p. 81.

The second level of allusion happens on the level of communication between the author and the reader. Such citations create a feeling of intimacy and immediacy between the reader and the author, the reader and the text, and facilitate an easy link between the activated biblical text and the novel.

The second category of biblical allusions is used in a number of ways. Firstly, the allusions have a symbolic significance. When Luxima is excommunicated by the Guru of Kashmir at a public ceremony and forfeits her brahminical status, she is emotionally overwhelmed. She gazes at her country, parents and friends, and weeps; at this point in the narrative Owenson inserts words from Jeremiah, 'and would not be comforted' (Jer. 31.15). This verse was part of the poem announcing the return and comforting of Rachel, the mother of Israel, who is weeping painfully for her lost children. Like any mother who loses her children, she refuses to be comforted, because they are no more. God's message to the bereaved mother is that they will come back from the land of the enemy. Perhaps this is an indication that, in the end, Luxima too will go back to her faith, which she indeed does at the end of the novel. The poem also ends with a puzzling line: 'A woman shall encompass a man'. Literally translated, it means a female surrounds the warrior. A possible meaning could be that in a reconstituted society there could be a reversal of roles for women, by which they become guardians of warriors.[18] As the reader will come to know, towards the end of the novel, amidst the pandemonium and fighting, it is Luxima who protects Hilarion and in a sense redeems him. There is another instance of a symbolic use of allusion when Hilarion is arrested by the papal emissaries. When he is told that charges will be brought against him, Hilarion is shocked and cannot believe that this is happening to him. He who has made resisting oppression and avenging insult his vocation does not resist, but rather recollects the words of Jesus on the Sermon on the Mount: when one cheek is smitten, turn the other. Unlike Luke, who had personal adversaries in mind, Matthew had enemies of the church persecuting Christians for their faith. The subtext is that now the church, in the form of the papal inquisitors, is persecuting faithful Christians such as Hilarion.

Secondly, there are misapplications of allusions, which distort the original biblical text, thus misrepresenting it. When Portugal regained its independence, the occasion was celebrated by paraphrasing the

---

18 I owe this point to Kathleen M. O'Connor, 'Jeremiah', in *The Women's Bible Commentary*, ed. Carl A. Newsom and Sharon H. Ringe (London, SPCK, 1992), p. 176.

Magnificat: 'the mighty had fallen, and the lowly were elevated; the lash of oppression had passed alternately from the grasp of the persecutor to the hand of the persecuted; the slave had seized the sceptre, and the tyrant had submitted to the chain'.[19] The irony of the allusion is that a one-time oppressor is now recast as victim, and this victim status is further emphasized by quoting a text which celebrates the reversal of fortune of the *anawim*, God's little people. This is a textual travesty, where an aggressor is seen as an amiable victim.

Thirdly, allusions are also used in a sarcastic way, to mock and expose pomposity and bigotry. When one of the two European travellers, who later turns out be the inquisitor, questions and finds fault with Hilarion for not zealously propagating the Christian faith, Hilarion replies that his enthusiasm has not diminished, but that he is conscious that what he has to say to Indians should not sound like tinkling brass. In the original Corinthians context, the comparison with sounding brass and clanging cymbal suggests pretentious and spiritually insincere utterance. Translated into the seventeenth-century Goan context, Hilarion's comment refers to the vacuous and vain preaching of the Jesuits of the time.

These biblical allusions act as a decoder and help the reader to see symbolic significances and discern biblical echoes. Though biblical texts are not quoted overtly, the use of them demonstrates that for the author the Bible is an important resource. Biblical allusions in Owenson's novel are neither a form of argument nor a form of narration; rather, they supply the narrative with a kind of language which accords status, seriousness and sanctity to it.

Split reading – aural and textual

In *The Missionary* the Bible is incidental, indirect, or hinted at, but in *Africa Answers Back* it becomes central to the narrative. Biblical texts are quoted here in full though, as in the case of Owenson, they appear without chapter and verse references, and are not even italicized to signal their scriptural status.

Curiously, at the beginning of the novel, the Bible, the Englishman's book, not only is seen as an opaque and awkward text to understand but also loses its pre-eminence as a record of God's deeds. True to colonial cliché, the Bible arrives in Buganda with the gun. It is the legendary explorer Stanley who, making an appearance in the novel in search of

19 Owenson, *The Missionary*, p. 259.

David Livingstone, introduces both the Bible and the gun to the King of Buganda. According to the narrative, he is the first European to visit Buganda; he presents the King with a gun which 'could kill quicker than a spear' and also introduces the Bible as a book 'from my country'. Horrified by the way the King tests the potency of the gun by killing one of his slaves, Stanley, by way of recompense, offers to read from the other gift of the empire, the Bible. His introduction of the Bible does not go well. He reads the first three verses from St John's prologue: 'In the beginning was the Word, and the Word was with God, and the Word was God. The same was in the beginning with God. All things were made by Him; and without Him was not any thing made that was made. In Him was life; and the life was the light of men'. But as Stanley is not well-versed in his religion, according to the narrative, he is not able to explain the meaning of these words. The Bible, a product of translation and the most translated of books, is at risk of being untranslated and not understood. Ironically, the Johannine prologue itself was an attempt to translate the gospel to a Greek context. The opacity of this passage prompts Stanley then to go on to read passages which are transparent. This time he reads to the King the story of the Israelites crossing the Red Sea. The King's response is: 'Hm, that's just like our story, because when the Gods came from the north they reached the River Kira and the waters stopped flowing, so that they could get across. Isn't it strange that his story and ours should be the same?'[20] For the King, all stories have in them the nucleus of all other stories, pouring out from some mysterious universal source. Instead of confronting and dislodging the heathen story, the 'White man's mythology' as the King calls it, now has a rival, a parallel 'heathen' version to vie with it for attention and authority. The Bible is not totally rejected but is seen as overlapping with indigenous stories. It is seen as part of a continuum of various stories of the people.

The Bible's standing and status are undermined on another occasion when the wives of a certain Chief Ati come to regard it as just one more form of literature rather than the deposit of God's oracles. When the Chief's son, Mujungu, comes home for his vacation and wants to display his new skill in reading, the wives of the Chief wants to know whether the book contains any stories – stories about fighting, strong handsome men, and girls falling in love with kings, and such like. The guiding book of the white-man's religion is now turned into another form of entertaining and interesting literature.

20 Nyabongo, *Africa Answers Back*, p. 10.

The Bible first becomes a complicated book in *Africa Answers Back* when the art of reading is introduced in the mission school run by Hubert, the missionary. Hubert introduces western literature and biblical stories to the class with a condescending attitude, saying that his students would not 'grasp the full significance of the White Man's Bible'.[21] Learning to read does not provide an immediate release from the control of missionary interpretation but it does offer access to one of the most powerful instruments of their oppressors, the Bible. Mujungu, who has learnt to read, is no longer at the mercy of Hubert and is free to interact with the text for himself. Like the real William Ngidi before him, whose questioning of the historical accuracy and moral validity of biblical narratives had set John Colenso thinking, Mujungu's relentless intervention in the class has an impact on the missionary, in this case making Hubert ineffective and diminishing his authority. Whatever the story, Jonah, Adam and Eve, or the virgin birth, Mujungu finds them impossible to accept rationally. He disputes the Jonah story by asking 'how could a whale swallow a man whole?' and wonders 'how could a man go through so small a throat unharmed?'[22] He questions the story of the creation in Genesis by pointing out that 'no woman came from a man's rib'. His deepest suspicion is reserved for the story of the virgin birth. He wants an unequivocal answer whether 'Jesus was the son of Joseph or Jesus was a bastard'.[23] For him it is a fairy-tale, since it was recorded by only two of the evangelists and, in any case, is biologically impossible: 'Sir, how could the seed of a man get into the womb of a woman without intercourse? And if Joseph didn't do it, I expect one of the servants acted for the Holy Spirit'.[24] When Hubert tries to get out of the difficulty by saying that Mary had two husbands, God and Joseph, Mujungu's immediate riposte is: 'You won't baptize the children of men with two wives, yet John baptized Jesus',[25] an obvious dig at the missionary's refusal to baptize him because his father is engaged in polygamous relationships.

Arguing from what he regards as a commonsensical and rational point of view, Mujungu undermines, if only temporarily, God's word, the English book. He not only renders the sacred book irrelevant but also disarms its interpreter, Hubert. The missionary, instead of engaging in dialogue with Mujungu, dismisses him as jeopardizing evangelization and retreats into the safety of authoritative dogma and the missionary homiletical practice of simultaneous denunciation and pastoral care: 'There is

21 Ibid., p. 233.   22 Ibid., p. 224.   23 Ibid., p. 227.
24 Ibid., p. 226.   25 Ibid.

no hope for you. You are dangerous to the faith of the rest of the class. I shall pray for you'.[26] Unlike Colenso, who, faced with a similar attack on the literal accuracy of the Bible, tried to resolve it by rational means and by reframing the biblical religion as the 'Fatherhood of God and the brotherhood of man', Hubert turns to the immaculate authority of the written word, and blames the weakness of the human mind in grasping God's mysterious ways. His way of addressing the issue is to reinforce the inerrancy of biblical texts and impose his authority as an interpreter. Unable to control his temper, Hubert sternly answers Mujungu's probing: 'We know, my boy, that the Holy Scriptures are the word of God. If we do not understand how things happened, that is due to our own ignorance. Only those who are impudent dare to ask *if* it could have happened. *It did happen!* The particular whale which swallowed Jonah was big enough to do so'. Mujungu still persists and rubs it in further with the knowledge he acquired from science class: 'Then how did Jonah live in the stomach? Why, we were learning the other day that there are juices in the stomach which digest food. Yet here your Bible says Jonah came out unharmed'. This is too much for Hubert. The only way Hubert knows how to handle this is to yell at the boy: 'You say *my* Bible. It is not my Bible, or your Bible. It is God's Bible, therefore our Bible. It is yours whether you accept it or not. But if you reject it, you will surely go to hell!'[27] In Hubert's view, Mujungu has eaten the forbidden apple of reading and thus has sinned. He concludes that Mujungu has read 'too much' and the only way to stop him from further 'misreadings' or sinning is to banish him from class, as Adam was cast away. He cannot forbid Mujungu from reading. He is well aware that once the art of reading has been acquired, it cannot be untaught, and, more ominously, there is no limit to what one reads. He suspects that Mujungu has learnt these arguments from some book he picked up from a trader. The best recourse under these circumstance is to isolate and ignore him and refuse to dialogue with him. In this way Hubert manages to maintain his own authority and pre-empts any further questions: 'I will not tolerate your talking back to me, as you have just done. I am the master of the school'.[28] The superiority of the Christian text is established through Hubert's assertion of his power as headmaster of the school rather than by cogently presenting its case. Not only the Bible, in Hubert's view, but his interpretation too has come under severe attack and is seen as fallible. For

---

26 Ibid., p. 228.   27 Ibid., p. 224.   28 Ibid., pp. 218–19.

Hubert, his way of reading biblical narratives is beyond contestation and doubt. He has become as authoritative as God in reminding Mujungu that he is the head of the school. The implication is that to challenge Hubert is to stage a rebellion against God. Reading and education, the very instruments which Hubert has introduced, have been turned against him. The problem has been caused by Mujungu, who does not confine his reading to the prescribed text, nor does he read the way Hubert expects him to read. He reads whatever satisfies his private and intellectual needs.

Mujungu has the last word. Deprived of his holidays as a punishment for raising impertinent questions, he is asked to accompany the missionary as his interpreter on his visits to different churches. Mujungu uses his experience in mission school and his knowledge of the Bible to warn his listeners that Hubert's intentions to teach people 'the new ways' will result in disrespect for their elders and their culture. Handicapped by not being able to speak the native language, the missionary accepts defeat and announces that further evangelizing mission activities are over.[29] Hubert's desire to produce spiritually Christian Africans out of heathen Africa ends with his decision to make no further converts.

The sacredness and authority of the Bible have not been totally dislodged It is projected as on a par with African oral tradition. When Hubert pays a visit to Mujungu to offer his condolences on the death of his father, a conversation fraught with frosty exchanges between the two, Mujungu's dialogue is suffused with biblical quotations and African proverbs. When Hubert expresses his sympathy, Mujungu philosophically paraphrases the words of Job: 'God has given and has taken away'. At the same meeting, Mujungu reminds Hubert of his failure to turn up when his people were ravaged by the smallpox epidemic. This time, to show his displeasure, Mujungu uses the local proverb: 'He who forgets you when you are in trouble is no friend. He who remembers you when you are in trouble is your true friend'.[30]

While the modern practice of reading emphasized the authority of the printed text, the Bible gained a new lease of life through the oral transmission of biblical narratives in a missionary context. When the Bible was read aloud in public, it was recognized as the record of the spoken word. The oral reading of biblical texts enabled Ati and his wives to hear its stories. Being read to not only freed them from any of the constraints of formal, institutionally based reading, but also allowed them to comment, challenge and interrupt freely. The Chief and his wives had

29 Ibid., p. 234.   30 Ibid., p. 263.

not mastered the technique of reading but listened intently to what was read to them by their literate son. The portions of the Bible which referred to Solomon and his seven hundred wives, when read aloud, immediately spoke to them. They were able to recognize that the very practice abhorred by the missionary was documented and practised in the foreign book which was introduced by the Englishman as the 'guiding book of our religion'.[31] On hearing the biblical story, the many wives of the Chief were able to assess for themselves how they had been deceived by the missionary. They were able to establish a written validity for one of their pivotal practices – polygamy. The written word had been put to the service of the oral culture. Hearing what was being read aloud made Ati's wives realize that what was scripted spoke to their cultural situation. The book, which had first attracted the attention of the wives as a collection of entertainment literature, had now become a work of practical information which had direct relevance to their lives.

Reading aloud in public permits non-literate cultures, as in the case of the illiterate Ati and his wives, to participate and challenge the claims of written documents. By confronting Hubert with the contents of the printed Bible, they were able to engage with the literary culture. Their scepticism about the claims of the missionary was an indication that one need not be a modern literate in order to master the significance of texts. The lack of literacy on the part of Ati and his wife did not mean that they were incapable of coping with the issue at hand, namely polygamy. They grasped the issue as well as Hubert did, and as well as the task required.

Unlike the modern and the Protestant habit of reading the text in silence and isolation, the Bible was read aloud and heard publicly. *Africa Answers Back* harks back to days when scripture reading was primarily oral. The Chief and his wives were not passive listeners. Far from it. The vocalization of biblical narratives generated a dynamic relationship between the written word and the audience. The text was no longer mute or static. They heard it intimately and this allowed them to interact with it.

For Ati and his wives reading was 'auditing' in the medieval sense of the term. Clanchy has clarified auditing as the the 'habit of listening to rather than seeing an account'. Though accounts in the medieval period were available on parchment rolls and wooden tallies, they were often conveyed

---

31 Ibid., p. 9.

by reading aloud. In other words, 'inspecting a document meant hearing it read aloud'.[32] As far as Chief Ati and his wives were concerned, polygamy was an ideal form of social arrangement. They were not hearing the book for its narrative power and much less for accessing its divine truth, but to measure the veracity it claimed to possess, and that Hubert claimed for it.

Writing shifted the mode of assessing the truth from speech to documents. Intently listening to the stories about Solomon's many wives, the Chief had reappropriated the stories without the benefit of literacy. Both the missionary and the Chief were insisting on the absolute literal accuracy of scriptural texts, and where Hubert differed was in the authority he accorded to the Old Testament. When Ati went on harassing the missionary about Solomon and his many wives, the answer Hubert came up with was the classic Christian one: Solomon was not a Christian and was not baptized; such practices were allowed under the old dispensation but, with the arrival of the new covenant, the old had been replaced and the practices were prohibited in the Christian church. Hubert chose to overlook the fact that both monogamous and polygamous marriages occur in the Hebrew scriptures. He was not dismissive of the practice because it would have been too risky to challenge what is recorded in Holy Writ. His conservative theological position would not permit him to question the record of polygamous practices, but he saw a polygamous social system as a temporary state which befitted the lower stages of life and which one had to leave behind. He used with confidence a single biblical verse, 'that a man may have one wife', to proscribe the practice of polygamy and decreed that monogamous marriages were universally prescribed. The tension was caused between Hubert and Ati because of the two different ways in which they appropriated the Bible. Hubert saw Ati's interpretation as unruly, unbalanced and unrefined, whereas Ati felt the missionary's interpretation was rigid, anti-egalitarian and unpastoral. The missionary and his great instrument of truth were called into question. Hubert was seen as a liar, untrustworthy and antisocial. As one of Chief Ati's wives put it, 'this man was not telling us the truth'.[33] The white-man's book, representing power and correctness, failed to satisfy Ati and his wives, and the interpreter's authority and the potency of his book were diminished in their view.

32 M. T. Clanchy, *From Memory to Written Record: England 1066–1307* (Oxford, Blackwell, 1993), p.267.
33 Nyabongo, *Africa Answers Back*, p. 207.

MISSIONARY METHODS, MULTIPLE MARRIAGES

Both novels, *The Missionary* and *Africa Answers Back*, addressed crucial concerns which came in the wake of Christianization, that is, the potential pitfalls of proselytization, and the place and function of cultural practices such as polygamous marriage. *The Missionary* offered a critique of prose-lytization and illustrated more specifically the agonies of converts who try to relate to both the old faith they have left behind and the new faith they are embracing. Hilarion's evangelistic project did not leave any space for holding on to aspects of more than one religious affiliation. Whereas Brahmin converts such as Upadhyay and Tilak, two hundred years later, were trying to negotiate religious identities which embraced both Hindu and Christian elements, Hilarion wanted Luxima to abandon her former life and with it the memories of her traditions. Professing that she belonged to a 'religion which unites the most boundless toleration to the most obstinate faith; the most perfect indifference to proselytism, to the most unvanquishable conviction of its own supreme excellence', Luxima could not comprehend Hilarion's obsession that she should altogether renounce her faith.[34] She accepted baptism but this was for her merely an outward ritual which did not affect her beliefs and her attachment to her earlier religious practices. More significantly, she was immediately recognizable as a '*Hindu*'.[35] Even when she was baptized, and when Hilarion was uttering the words of the baptismal rite, Luxima's attention was not on the ceremony. Her gaze was somewhere else. Her eyes were fixed upon the 'Pagoda, the temple of her devotion'. When Hilarion saw the Brahminical rosary with the image of Kamadev, the god of love, tied around her wrist and told her that these were not the 'ornament[s] of a Christian vestal', Luxima's reply captured the distress of countless converts who were tormented by attachment to the religion they had left behind:

Oh! thou wilt not deprive me of these also? I have nothing left now *but these!* nothing to remind me, in the land of strangers, of my country and my people, save only these: it makes a part of the religion I have abandoned, to respect the sacred ties of nature; does my new faith command me to break them? This rosary was fastened on my arm by a parent's tender hand, and bathed in Nature's holiest dew – a parent's tender tears; hold not the Christians relics, such as these, precious and sacred? Thou hast called thy religion the religion of the heart; will it not respect the heart's best feelings?[36]

34 Owenson, *The Missionary*, p. 125.   35 Ibid., p. 222.   36 Ibid., pp. 193–4.

Conversion to Christianity in the modern West is seen as a subjective, and a self-determinative act, whereas Luxima's words indicated that for her it could not be divorced from family ties and parental affection.

As Hilarion himself observed, at a time of distress it was to her former gods that Luxima turned for 'support and comfort'.[37] She 'involuntarily bowed before the objects of her habitual devotion',[38] and continued to invoke the deities 'whom she still believed to have been as the tutelar guardians of the days of innocence and her felicity'.[39] As she herself put it, 'Alas! I have but changed the object, the *devotion* is still the same'.[40]

Luxima clung to relics of her earlier life in the community from which she had been cast out. With the image of Kamadev adorning her wrist, and a cross dangling from her neck, Luxima alternately resembled a 'Christian Magdalene or a penitent Priestess of Brahma'.[41] The radical break from Indian cultural and religious ties which missionary practice demanded and expected did not materialize in the case of Luxima. Instead, she remained tied to Indian culture and opted to observe the religious tradition with which she was familiar. Although she was supposed to have abandoned her previous religion – 'less from conviction than for love'[42]– her former religious practices continued to have their place in her life. As Sydney Owenson put it, 'it was the heart of the woman he had seduced and not the mind of the heathen he had converted'.[43] It was not the religion of Hilarion she chose but Hilarion himself. When he put it bluntly to Luxima that 'either thou art a Pagan or a Christian', her reply was, 'Then I will believe and follow thee'.[44] The implication was clear.

It was through kindly acts that Hilarion was able to win his way with Luxima. He rescued her fawn and saved Luxima from a venomous snake. This method of attracting potential converts by humanitarian actions resonated with the sixteenth-century Portuguese missionary practice. Studying the methods and motives of Portuguese conversion during that period, Rowena Robinson has identified three strategies employed by them to woo new converts: humanitarian acts (namely taking care of unwanted children), a system of patronage whereby privileges were bestowed on promising candidates, and a system of mixed marriages whereby Portuguese soldiers were encouraged to marry widows and

37 Ibid., p. 175.   38 Ibid., p. 208.   39 Ibid., p. 219.
40 Ibid., p. 231.   41 Ibid., p. 184.   42 Ibid., p. 218.
43 Ibid., p. 220.   44 Ibid., p. 151.

children of Muslim men who had been killed in battle.[45] It was by the first method, caring for others, that Hilarion appeared to be insinuating himself into Luxima's life.

The putative conversion of Luxima to Christianity stands in contrast to the large-scale conversion of lower-caste Indians which happened in nineteenth-century India. These were not individual conversions but groups of people moving from one faith to another. Motivations for this mass exodus were mixed, and included gaining material advantage and escaping from the collective caste abuse and hurt caused by Brahminical Hinduism. Luxima's conversion, on the other hand, was clearly an individual act, not prompted by the injuries caused by Hindu caste practices. It was not forced but neither was it prompted by a deep spiritual thirst. It did not result in the intense psychological disturbance which normally attends such conversions. Her apparent conversion was not a true commitment to the Christian faith but a manifestation of her love for a Christian, Hilarion. In Luxima's own words, 'it was *thou* I followed and not thy doctrines'.[46]

The novel draws attention to the ineffectiveness and unethical nature of Christian proselytization. Luxima's message to Hilarion was that Christian preaching should be directed not only to Hindus but also to Christians. Her advice was that future missionary exhortations should reflect a different kind of homiletical tone and thrust. In a long speech delivered towards end of the novel, she spoke her mind:

[T]hou shalt preach, not to the Brahmins only, but to the Christians, that the sword of destruction, which has this day been raised between the followers of thy faith and mine, may be for ever sheathed! Thou wilt appear among them as a spirit of peace, teaching mercy, and inspiring love; thou wilt soothe away, by acts of tenderness, and words of kindness, the stubborn prejudice which separates the mild and patient Hindu from his species; and thou wilt check the Christian's zeal, and bid him to follow the sacred lesson of the God he serves, who, for years beyond the Christian era, has extended his merciful indulgence to the errors of the Hindu's mind, and bounteously lavished on his native soil those wondrous blessings which first tempted the Christians to seek our happier regions. But, should thy eloquence and thy example fail, tell them my story! tell them how I have suffered, and how even thou hast failed: – thou, for whom I forfeited my caste, my country, and my life; for 'tis too true, that still *more loving* than

45 Rowena Robinson, 'Sixteenth Century Conversions to Christianity in Goa', in *Religious Conversion in India: Modes, Motivation, and Meanings*, ed. Sathianathan Clarke and Rowena Robinson (New Delhi, Oxford University Press, 2003), p. 302 and also p. 321.

46 Owenson, *The Missionary*, p. 231.

enlightened, my ancient habits of belief clung to my mind, thou to my *heart*: still I lived thy seeming proselyte, that I might *still live thine*; and now I *die* as Brahmin women *die*, a *Hindu* in my feelings and my faith – dying for him I loved, and believing as my fathers have believed'.[47]

In the revised version *Luxima* makes clear the futility of flaunting power and wealth in order to convert. In a narrative which appears in both versions, where the Pundit tells Hilarion that 'you may seize on an opportunity of advancing your doctrines, as, by throwing off your European habit, and undergoing purification in the consecrated tanks of the temple, you become qualified to enter the temple', Owenson adds a sentence which serves as a warning: 'you must go alone, an ostentatious mission would destroy all hope of success and perhaps risk your life'.[48]

If baptism is a contentious issue in *The Missionary*, it is the indigenous practice of polygamy which comes under severe scrutiny in *Africa Answers Back*. The missionary's attempt to wean the African away from the practice is vigorously contested, and, most tellingly, the very book which the missionary claimed as denouncing the practice was exposed and found dubious. When Chief Ati requested that his son, Mujungo, be baptized by Hubert, the missionary refused the request on the grounds that the Chief had many wives, which went against biblical teaching. He told Chief Ati: 'It is written in the Holy Scripture that a man may have one wife',[49] and then went on to blame the African for living in sin. For Hubert, polygamy was nothing more than adultery and Ati was a sinner. For Ati and the Africans it was a beneficial social system, which took care of widows and war-widows and was a way of sharing wealth. Ati retorted and reversed the accusation. In Ati's view, it was Hubert and Christians like him who were sinners because they were basically selfish and did not want to share their wealth, a pratice which promoted the welfare of the people: 'You think you are *not* a sinner, but I can call you one too if you marry one wife, and don't marry or enslave those whom you capture in war, and keep your wealth selfishly to yourself. If your work is not benefiting society, then *you* are a sinner'.[50] It was during this frosty conversation that Chief Ati confidently predicted that his son, whom Hubert refused to baptize, would one day learn the new ways and find out the truth about Hubert's teaching: 'He will learn whether you have told me the truth concerning the way your religion works in your own country. He will read your Bible,

---

47 Ibid., p. 257.
48 Sydney Owenson, *Luxima, the Prophetess: A Tale of India* (London, Charles Westerton, 1859), p. 34.
49 Nyabongo, *Africa Answers Back*, p. 66.   50 Ibid., p. 69.

your books, and translate to me the truth. I hope it coincides with what
you have given to me. Then only will I believe what you say'.[51] As we saw
above, Hubert's claim that the Bible endorsed monogamous marriages
was shown to be untrue in the middle of the novel when Mujungu
returned home on holiday and read aloud from the Hebrew scriptures
about King Solomon and his seven hundred wives and three hundred
concubines. Ati, his father, and his wives were astonished to find that the
practice of polygamy, the very practice condemned elsewhere in the
Englishman's book, was approved here. Solomon's many wives and
concubines became a talking, even a laughing, matter among the villagers.
The book and the missionary were, as they saw it, now exposed for their
double standards. After hearing the story read, one of the wives of Ati
exclaimed: 'Ha, ha, your son will find him out. He can read his books,
too! The Reverend Mr. Hubert can't tell us lies any more'.[52]

Hubert's being the sole interpreter and making the Africans rely on
him as a pastoral guide to their practices such as polygamy had come
under severe strain. It was the introduction of literacy, the imported evil
of teaching the natives to read, write and think, which eventually made
the Book and its interpreter lose their potency and control. In a culture
where oral witness holds primacy over the written word, the oral claim of
the missionary that one should have only one wife was tested against the
written word and found wanting.

Unlike Luxima, who was apathetic towards the seemingly harsh Indian
social system, Mujungu was troubled by the native practice of acquiring
many wives. Centred and immersed as he was in his own culture, he
nevertheless questioned the nature of such practice. When he assumed the
leadership of his community, he tried to abolish the practice and himself
sent away many wives, retaining only one. But such a reform was given
short shrift. The retained wife persuaded him to reverse his decision and
take more wives. She said that his people saw him as a 'radical with a lot of
theories and no experience'.[53] Among the arguments advanced by his wife
were the very ones his father deployed against the missionary, Hubert: the
newly acquired western ways had made Mujungu selfish and uncaring for
the poor. She used another trump-card, the ultimate shame to a son:
'Your father would have disowned you if he had known you were going to
act like this'.[54] The novel ends with Mujungu listening to the arguments
put forward by his wife and finally agreeing to take further wives. Like

---

51 Ibid., p. 70.   52 Ibid., p. 207.   53 Ibid., p. 278.   54 Ibid., p. 276.

Luxima, Mujungu went back to his roots. The solution he arrived at was an inter-subjective, existential, one which tried to transcend the native values in which he was steeped and the western values which he had acquired more recently. He solved this tension by taking a few more wives, not hundreds as his father had, but a total of four. This way he thought that his people would leave him alone to carry on with his reforms, or, as the narrative put it, 'Then he might have some peace to carry out his plans'.[55] His desire to incorporate modernist views had to accommodate his people's deeply entrenched belief in their cultural practices and social etiquette. His social status and standing among his clan prevented him from making any radical departure. He resorted to a second-best recourse – compromise.

Mujungu, like Luxima, was baptized, in his case twice – one baptism being in the traditional manner and the other Christian. His education, too, was both indigenous and western. Western methods did not replace or rescind the local ways of learning but the two co-existed. He learnt the modernist literary pursuit of reading and writing at the white-man's school, and during the holidays he was sent to his grandmother in order to absorb and broaden his indigenous wisdom in the form of oral 'proverbs, histories, riddles, stories, all sorts of games, and the customs of his clan'. Five of his old teachers, along with his grandmother, tested him on various subjects ranging from the African way of naming the stars[56] to solving riddles. They were elated at the way he answered their questions, and their unanimous verdict was: 'He hasn't forgotten a thing'.[57] The fact that the African elders acknowledged that Mujungu remembered the African ways of learning was an indication that the formal education he received at the missionary school had not entirely displaced indigenous knowledge.

Both novels predict doom for Christian work and enterprise in Africa and in India unless there is radical rethinking. The failure of mission practice in Africa was attributed in *Africa Answer Back* to the narrow views held by people like Hubert. In their last meeting, Mujungu told Hubert that he was 'too fixed' in his views. The novel portrays religious enthusiasts, such as Hubert, and Stanley before him, as suspicious about local customs and manners, whereas the western medical personnel who came to work during an outbreak of smallpox were willing to learn from indigenous medical practices. In stark contrast to the attitude of the

---

55 Ibid., p. 278.   56 Ibid., p. 171.   57 Ibid., p. 173.

missionaries, the doctors were impressed by the techniques of the native doctors. One of the things that fascinated them was the African way of treating broken bones. One of them said: 'We could probably learn many things from these people if we weren't obsessed with the idea that we are better than they in everything'.[58] True to their word, the foreign doctors proved willing to learn from African practices.

Unlike *The Missionary*, which initially states a belief in the need to eradicate Indian indigenous practices through reason and the Christian message, *Africa Answers Back* advocates an amalgamation of western and African methods which could be of benefit to both. The narrative ratifies the profitability and the potency of creatively mixing the traditional ways and western methods. One classic example is how, at the height of a smallpox epidemic, the urgently needed doctors and vaccines were called for from nearby countries like Zanzibar and Kenya by means of a drum message. Nyabongo said the message would have normally taken nearly two months but to the astonishment of the foreign doctors, Mujungu sent it through the drums within a day. A German doctor compared the ancient system of communication to the modern-day wireless; time-honoured methods were appropriated to the situation. Ancient communication methods were aligned with modern medicine in order to solve the problem. The German doctor summed up: 'We have all of us something to learn'.[59]

Mission work failed to make any positive impression where its practitioners were unable and unwilling to adapt and accommodate their message to the situation. When Hubert was adamant that science and religion could not mix, Mujungu told him forthrightly: 'Your religion can't'. This was because, unlike the scientists, he had 'exalted thoughts'.[60] What that narrative signals is that Africa prized not so much the white-man's religion as his technology and the benefits that came with it. Unlike the propagators of religion, the scientists and medical people were open and were willing to incorporate indigenous methods. As one of the doctors put it: 'We are here to learn and to co-operate with you. If some of your old traditional methods are better than ours, then we should like to see them. We must exchange our ideas'.[61] The problem with Hubert was that he saw the Christian faith as an unchanging and un-changeable deposit. When we last hear of Hubert, he 'looked old, thin and discouraged'. The authorial voice sums up his work thus: 'His work

58 Ibid., p. 254.   59 Ibid., p. 246.   60 Ibid., p. 264.   61 Ibid., p. 257.

has been a failure. His influence among Mujungu's people was at an end'.[62]

What *The Missionary* argues for eventually, after its initial negative approach, is a missionary undertaking that is warmer, gentler and kinder and which would help to remove the misconceptions of Hindus that Christianity is an arrogant and aggressive faith. More significantly, the narrative proposes that missionary work should recognize and build on the moral and religious heritage of India. The revised perception of mission comes through clearly at the Inquisition when, in his defence, Hilarion produces a textbook-like mission statement which would simultaneously please missiologists of a liberal disposition and annoy those who take a hard line on matters relating to mission:

> The zeal of Christianity should never forsake the mild spirit of its fundamental principles; in the excess of its warmest enthusiasm, it should be tempered by charity, guided by reason, and regulated by possibility; forsaken by these, it ceases to be the zeal of religion, and becomes the spirit of fanaticism, tending only to sever man from man, and to multiply the artificial sources of aversion by which human society is divided, and human happiness destroyed.[63]

For the interrogators of Hilarion, it was the aggressive policy of the Christian Church which made the Christian faith successful. Had the Church persisted with tolerance, moderation and freedom of opinion – marks of the 'heathen philosophy' – and had the disciples of Christian faith showed such a leniency, 'never would the cross have been raised upon the remotest shores of the Eastern and Western oceans'.[64] Hilarion's reply was that any aggressive policy would have been counter-productive. It would have fatally affected the moral strength of a religion which was supposed to preach peace, love and salvation. Conversion methods also came under scrutiny. When asked whether he disapproved of the methods of conversion practised by the Jesuits, Hilarion's answer was that what he opposed was their manner, the way in which the Jesuits went about achieving their goals. He advocated building on the positive elements already embedded in the religious tradition of India, showing kindness, courtesy and love to Indians and slowly enticing them into the Christian fold rather than employing highhanded tactics as the Jesuits did. His answer to his Inquisitors on the question of conversion was a model for all interfaith dialogue, and one of which Vatican II would have been proud:

---

62 Ibid., p. 265.   63 Owenson, *The Missionary*, p. 225.   64 Ibid.

It is by a previous cultivation of their moral powers, we may hope to influence their religious belief; it is by teaching them to love us, that we can lead them to listen to us; it is by inspiring them with respect for our virtues, that we can give them a confidence in our doctrine: but this has not always been the system adopted by European reformers, and the religion we proffer them is seldom illustrated by its influence on our lives. We bring them a spiritual creed which commands them to forget the world, and we take from them temporal possessions, which prove how much *we live for it.*[65]

The conversion that Hilarion was looking for was not through coercion but through conviction. In his view, force could not induce conviction of faith but it was an 'act of private judgement, or of freewill, which no human artifice, no human authority can alter or controul [*sic*]'.[66] The commitment to the Christian cause remained but the method is radically revised.

Hilarion's story is the classic case of the evangelizer being evangelized. Whereas Hubert remained rigid in his attitude, Hilarion slowly opened up and the Indian experience became a journey of self-discovery for him. He distanced himself from the conversion of the natives, the very project which initially prompted him to go to India. As Owenson put it, 'Yet he dared no longer seek the "highways and public places" to promulgate his doctrines and to evince his zeal'.[67] This change of attitude provided the Inquisition with the perfect excuse to arrest him. Hilarion himself has moved from his earlier position in which he firmly believed that Hinduism could be 'perfectly eradicated by the slow operation of expanding reason'[68] and 'universally subverted by a train of moral and political events, which should equally emancipate [Hindu] minds from the antiquated error'.[69] As the novel progresses, Hilarion realizes, after seeing Luxima's silent tears and uncomplaining suffering, that her faith was uncertain, and that she 'purchased the sacred truths of Christianity at the dearest price'.[70] Hilarion, who had modelled himself on Paul, progressively veered from his earlier fanatical stance to a fairly tolerant one. More significantly, his faith underwent a discernible change – from an unambiguous commitment to one faith to an indeterminate position which tried to combine and incorporate elements from many faith traditions. From an earlier monocentric Christian stance, Hilarion gradually aligned himself with a pluralistic position which put God at the centre. In one of his last attempts to convince Luxima of the new faith, he

---

65 Ibid., p. 226.   66 Ibid.   67 Ibid., p. 196. See Matt. 22.9–10; Lk. 14.23.
68 Owenson, *The Missionary*, p. 194.   69 Ibid., p. 196.   70 Ibid., p. 219.

quoted one of the rare Pauline passages which puts God at the centre, 'God in all and all in God' in the novelist's version (1 Cor. 15.28),[71] thus according a secondary role to Jesus and subordinating him to God. As the Corinthian passage indicates, the son gives up the sovereignity and the power to God who will be all in all. Hilarion, too, conceded that eventually all belongs to God. As the narrative makes clear, he himself realized at the end the amount of hardship and pain he had caused and the untold psychological misery he had brought upon his only half-hearted convert, Luxima:

He almost looked upon the mission, in which he had engaged, as hopeless; and he felt that the miracle of that conversion, by which he expected to evince the sacred truth of the cause in which he had embarked, could produce no other effect than a general abhorrence of him who laboured to effect it, and of her who had already paid the forfeit of all most precious to the human breast, for that partial proselytism, to which her affections, rather than her reason, had induced her.[72]

As a result of such a discovery, Hilarion now 'lived in a world of newly connected and newly modified ideas'.

If we see Hubert as a sorry figure, confused and entrenched in his own ways, we see Hilarion struggling to find his religious identity. The earlier arrogance and confidence now has gone. As we saw earlier, at the beginning of his missionary odyssey, an Indian pundit gave him advice as to how to Indianize and modify his Christianity in order for it to thrive and be successful in an alien context. His suggestion was that Hilarion should try to lose his European manners and immerse himself in Indian culture. What the pundit implied was that Christianity must assume a Hindu appearance in order to be attractive. Ironically, the pundit's advice is actualized at the end of the novel when the reader is shown Hilarion as 'a wild and melancholy man, whose religion was unknown, but who prayed at the confluence of rivers, at the rising and setting of the sun'.[73] The verdict of the narrative was that Hilarion and Luxima were '*victims of mistaken zeal*'.[74]

EMPIRE AND RELIGIONS

Religious differences are blurred and any claim to Christian uniqueness collapses on a number of occasions in *The Missionary*. When Hilarion twice attributed his spectacular acts of rescue to his religion, both times he

71 The other being 1 Cor. 11.3: 'the head of Christ is God'.
72 Owenson, *The Missionary*, p. 196.   73 Ibid., p. 260.   74 Ibid., p. 239.

was rebutted and corrected by Luxima. On the first occasion when he saved one of Luxima's fawns, which he used as a ruse to attract her attention, Luxima expressed her appreciation by saying that he was a kind but polluted infidel, and that he acted as a 'Hindu would have acted'.[75] As she spoke these words, she noticed that Hilarion himself had been hurt in rescuing the animal. Seeing his wounds, Luxima commented that, unlike the other infidels, Hilarion was tender towards suffering animals. Hilarion attributed his kindly act to his Christian faith: 'My religion teaches me to assist and to relieve all who suffer'.[76] For Luxima, such an act was not an extraordinary one as Hilarion implied but a normal practice for a Hindu. In her perception, he had done what a Hindu would have done in a similar situation, and she went on to praise Vishnu who 'protects those who are pure in heart, even though their hands be polluted'.[77] On the second occasion when Luxima offered her gratitude to Hilarion for saving her from a venomous snake, his response, again, was to attribute his exemplary behaviour to his religion. The act he performed to save Luxima, he would have done for others as well, because he was inspired by his religion: 'That which I have done *for thee*, I would have done for another, for it is the spirit of the religion I profess, to sacrifice the selfish instinct of our nature to the preservation of a fellow-creature whose danger claims our interference, or whose happiness needs our protection'.[78] Luxima's immediate retort not only corrected Hilarion's self-righteous notion that it was the duty of a Christian to help those who were in need but also reinforced the Hindu notion of the inherent divinity in each one which prompts good actions:

Refer not to thy faith alone, a sentiment inherent in thyself; let us be more just *to him* who made us, and believe that there is in nature a feeling of benevolence which betrays the original intention of the Deity, to promote the happiness of his creatures. If thou art prone to pity the wretched, and aid the weak, it is because thou wast thy self created of those particles which, at an infinite distance, constitute the Divine essence.[79]

Luxima's answer not only nullified any privileged status claimed by Hilarion for Christianity, but also reiterated the Advaita philosophy of the divine presence in human beings. What the narrative proposes is that with regard to humanitarian acts, the differences between religions break down. All compassionate activities are human responses to God's

---

75 Ibid., p. 118.　　76 Ibid., p. 117.　　77 Ibid.
78 Ibid., p. 215.　　79 Ibid., p. 214.

presence. It is denied that public-spirited acts are the privilege of a Christian, and similar benevolent acts seen as part of Hindu tradition are thus also universalized.

There was another indication of the irrelevance of religious doctrines when Hilarion participated in theological debate with various sects of Hinduism and Buddhism. While members of these religious sects were 'contented to detail their own doctrines, rather than anxious to controvert doctrines of others', Hilarion boldly proclaimed the object of his mission and, in the process, exposed the weaknesses of the various attributes of the Hindu divinities, especially of Vishnu and his various incarnations. Although Hilarion denounced Hinduism, he did not, contrary to the standard missionary approach, deem it useless and vain. He saw some value in it, however erroneous, and these useful elements could be employed as a hermeneutical base for mounting the Christian truth. He told the religious dignitaries assembled that, though Hinduism was a 'pure system of natural religion', it was 'not unworthy to receive upon its gloom the light of a divine revelation'.[80] But the Guru of Kashmir, the presider, who listened to the discourses of the various disputants, went on to affirm the superiority of Hindu faith, and, what is more, praised the very God whom Hilarion belittled:

I set my heart on the foot of Brahma, gaining knowledge only of him: it is by devotion alone that we are enabled to see the three worlds, celestial, terrestrial, and ethereal; let us, then, meditate eternally within our minds, and remember that the natural duties of the children of Brahma are peace, self-restraint, patience, rectitude, and wisdom. Praise be unto Vishnu.[81]

Read again the last sentence of the Guru. He reinforced the notion that godly acts were performed by all the devotees of God, and that they were not special to Christians. What Owenson's novel reiterates is that metaphysical speculations and doctrinal formulations are largely irrelevant. Religious adherence is not merely about subscribing to certain credal postulations, it is about right conduct and behaviour, or, as liberation theologians were to put it later, orthopraxis.

There are times when the narrative advances the equality of all religions. One occasion was when Prince Solyman, a character who makes a fleeting appearance in the novel and who tries and fails to win the affection of Luxima, demanded to know whether she was a Christian and an apostate from her religion. Luxima's answer was: 'I am not a

80 Ibid., p. 94.   81 Ibid., p. 95.

Christian! not *all* a Christian! His God is indeed mine; but Brahma still receives my homage: I am still his Priestess, and bound by holy vows to serve him'. She affirmed the openness of her faith, saying that only in 'innocence and truth' had she listened to the 'precepts of the holy man'.[82] Luxima's answer was a typical Vedic position which celebrates the fact, that irrespective of what one worships, one's devotion is ultimately directed to the one power which has many manifestations: 'It is called Indira, Mitra, Varuna, and Agni, and also Garutman. The real is one, though by different names' (*Rigveda* 1, 164.46). The other occasion when the equality of religions was affirmed was when Hilarion's appearance caused curiosity among the Indians. They perceived him as 'a sanaisse, or pilgrim, of some distant nation, performing tupseya in a strange land'. Hilarion availed himself of this opportunity again to explain the purpose and object of his coming from a distant country. The Indian onlookers were not interested in his religion. After listening to him, they came up with the standard Indian answer to the multiplicity of religions – one infinite religion manifesting itself in manifold ways. They told Hilarion plainly: 'God has appointed to each tribe its own faith and to each sect its own religion: let each obey the appointment of God, and live in peace with his neighbour'.[83] Owenson's narrative was a subtle attack on the imperialist dream of evangelizing the benighted natives, and also a plea to think again about the superiority of their doctrines and practices.

CONCLUDING REMARKS

The Bible is introduced in bits and pieces in these two novels. The biblical passages are plucked out of their natural habitat, fragmented and broken into recognisable, pithy texts to underscore various points. The fact that the biblical phrases appear in the novels without any identifiable markers is an indication that it was an era when 'the gossip of the street and tramcar is continually given a sort of distinction by the instructive use of Bible phrases'.[84] The novels, especially *Africa Answers Back*, reinstate the historical and literal accuracy of the Bible. Both Mujungu's modernistic private scrutiny and Chief Ati's and his wives' vocalized reading are examples of this.

---

82 Ibid., p. 167.   83 Ibid., p. 106.
84 Dark, Sidney, 'Christianity and Culture', *The New Green Quarterly* 2:2 (1936), 85.

It is not entirely clear from these novels whether the presence of the Bible in India and Africa is welcome. It has been invalidated as a governing discourse and its eminence and exclusivity are constantly called into question. Biblical teachings do not act as the absolute standard in matters related to morality and humanitarian acts. It is no more the sole source of saving knowledge. It has to compete with and take its place beside sacred books of the East and African folk traditions. The universal presence of God is found not only in the Bible but in the multitude and variety of sacred texts.

Both novels offer a critique of empire and provide a site for a debate on the implications of postcolonialism for the colonized as well the colonizer. In one, the criticism is internal, undertaken from within, and put forward as a European perspective. In the other, the critique is from the outside and undertaken from the native's point of view. Owenson's novel represents the best facet of liberalism, a capacity for self-criticism and disinterestedness. Nyabongo, on the other hand, not only offers resistance but also advocates a critical synthesis of Africa and the West, indigenous practices and Christian values. As Mujungu puts it: 'By gradually changing their old culture, but not by throwing it away entirely, I hope to amalgamate what is good in the old and the new'.[85] When caught up in the double bind – indigene customs and imported values, ancient practices and modern methods – the viable option advanced by Nyabongo is to negotiate between the contradictory demands of the old and the new. The idea is not to produce a neat synthesis of the two but to reconfigure the identity and culture so as to allow one to remain within the native space and at the same time imbibe the benefits of modernization. The novel both celebrates and compromises indigenous and imported values.

Let me end with a couple of undercurrent messages from the two novels which have relevance for our time: any change imposed from outside has only limited value; local rejuvenation is possible only when the indigenous resources are strengthened in conjunction with outside resources. Both novels propose the advantages of a local transformation with assistance from outside which animates the indigenous traditions rather than annihilating them. Both narratives establish that the reform or solution should emanate from and be engineered by those who are part of the indigenous system. This is particularly highlighted in Nyabongo's novel by the German doctor, who, after seeing how deftly Mujungu

---

85 Nyabongo, *Africa Answers Back*, p. 246.

adapted both indigenous and imported methods, says: 'If you initiate a change, your people will probably accept it more readily than if someone else does'.[86] In essence, both novels check the missionary success story and try to establish the importance of native agency and the wealth of native cultures. At a time when, in the name of globalization, western agricultural, medical and educational practices are imposed on the developing nations, the novels urge the interveners to be less self-important and less uncompromising, appealing to them not to presume that western methods and ways of life are the proper norm for all. The words of two thinkers, one an academic, Tzvetan Todrov, and the other a film maker, Satyajit Ray, resonate with the novels. Granted that their articulations emanate from different disciplinary landscapes, these thinkers, in my view, enunciate the overwhelming idea shared by Owenson and Nyabongo. I will leave you with their quotations, the first by Todrov, and the second by Satyajit Ray:

In the past, we have mistaken for universal values what was merely the reflection of our traditions and desires. A little modesty or circumspection is in order.[87]

All artists imbibe, consciously or unconsciously, the lessons of past masters. But when a film maker's roots are strong, and when tradition is a living reality, outside influences are bound to dwindle and disappear and a true indigenous style evolve.[88]

86 Ibid.
87 Tzvetan Todrov, 'Right to Intervene or Duty to Assist?', *in Human Rights, Human Wrongs*, ed. Nicholas Owen (Oxford: Oxford University Press, 2002), p. 32.
88 Satyajit Ray, *Our Films Their Films* (Hyderabad, Orient Longman, 1976), p. 157.

Afterword

We don't do empire.

Donald Rumsfeld

One man's Bible is another man's fish wrapper.

Albert Scardino

As a way of bringing this volume to a close I offer, a few thoughts on the present status of empire and the Bible. Both the Bible and the empire are trying to stage comebacks and are undergoing vigorous makeovers to meet their changing contexts. Both are being refurbished and reinvented. The old territorial empire has now given way to an informal one which is as menacing as the one which it is trying to replace. The earlier empire's biggest export – the English Bible, on which it was said at the time, 'the sun never sets'[1] – is assuming new forms in the new situation. It is no coincidence that the current boom in books on empire and the Bible is taking place at a time when America is trying to assume the role of a new imperialist.

The old empire was engaged in a civilizing project of bringing light to dark places. The new imperium is about righting wrongs. The old empire spoke in terms of eradicating ignorance and enlightening the benighted natives with Christian values. The new empire is also on a mission, but sees its task as removing erring rulers who undermine corporate authority (read American authority), violate human rights and threaten American financial interests. Tony Blair spoke of the new empire in missiological terms. In his speech, the British Prime Minister told the US Congress: 'I feel a most urgent sense of mission

---

1 John Eadie, 'Preface by Dr. Eadie', in *The National Comprehensive Family Bible: The Holy Bible with the Commentaries of Scott and Henry, and Containing Also Many Thousand Critical and Explanatory Notes, Selected from the Great Standard Authors of Europe and America,* ed. John Eadie (Glasgow, W. R. M'Phun, 1860), p. vi.

today'.[2] The new missionary command is to preach the gospel of freedom, democracy, human rights and market economy, distinctly as defined by its western interests. The new missionaries who effect these changes are the coalition soldiers; they are seen not as military personnel but as evangelizing emancipators who bring liberty and luxury to those who are under 'shadow and darkness'.[3] Unlike the traditional missionaries who targeted erring individuals, the new missionaries target erring nation-states. Their weapons, according to Blair, are not 'guns but our beliefs'. Like the disciples of old, they, too, cast out demons in forms such as that of Saddam Hussein. Those who question this project are seen as anti-Christ, those who are not with us. The old evangelizers assured those who accepted the Christian gospel that they were on the side of the saved. The new evangelizers tell those who accept the western gospel that they are on the side of civilization. In an earlier era, those who did not practise the Christian way of life were called 'savages'. Now those liberation movements which question the imposition of western ways of living are demonized as terrorists. The new conquest is presented as liberation and the new economic enslavement is interpreted as setting free those benighted natives. These military missionaries who die in their mission efforts are the new martyrs. Echoing the vocabulary of the Victorian church and of the Authorized Version, Blair reassured his listeners in the US Congress that these soldiers 'did not strive or die in vain, but through their sacrifice future generations can live in greater peace, prosperity and hope'.[4]

This new imperium is marked by a series of books, articles, documentaries and films on empire. The books are produced by historians, bureaucrats and cultural critics from different social and ideological backgrounds. Chief among them are Niall Ferguson,[5] David Cannadine,[6] Robert Cooper[7] and Michael Ignatieff.[8] The first two deal with the old

---

2 British Prime Minister Tony Blair's phrase. For the full text of his speech to the US Congress, see *Sydney Morning Herald*, 18 July 2003.

3 Ibid., p. 2.

4 Ibid.

5 Niall Ferguson, *Empire: How Britain Made the Modern World* (London, Allen Lane, 2003).

6 David Cannadine, *Ornamentalism: How the British Saw the Empire* (London, Allen Lane, 2001).

7 Robert Cooper, 'The Post-Modern State', in *Re-Ordering the World: The Long-Term Implications of 11 September*, ed. Mark Leonard (London, The Foreign Policy Centre, 2002), pp. 11–20; and Robert Cooper, *The Breaking of Nations* (New York, Atlantic Monthly Press, 2003).

8 Michael Ignatieff, *Empire Lite: Nation-Building in Bosnia, Kosovo and Afghanistan* (London, Vintage, 2003).

empire, the other two with the new. This may not be the right place to evaluate their work, nor I am the right person to do it, but let me venture a few comments.

There are certain common characteristics that run through the writings of this group. They speak about how Asia and Africa were impoverished and chaotic before the advent of colonialism. The initial European empires were seen as buccaneering and predatory outfits but later turned into immensely benevolent instruments of moral and economic uplift-ment. For these writers, colonialism was a noble undertaking which provided practical projects such as schools, hospitals, railways and irriga-tion schemes. It opened up markets and helped to spread western science and literature. The writers routinely recall the empire's role in the aboli-tion of slavery, sati and polygamy. For them, these public achievements and visible markers of moral and material improvement outweigh lurid tales of imperial savagery – the genocide of Aborigines, the atrocity of General Dyer or even the reintroduction of slavery in the form of inden-tured labour. For these commentators, the empire was not about race and colour but about class, ceremony, chivalry and status. They also bemoan the end of the empire and put the blame squarely on the legacy bequeathed by empire – the nation-state – which has failed in Africa and the Middle East, both of which have become breeding grounds for terrorists and dictators, and more importantly, threaten the security of western powers and western ways of life. These writers conveniently overlook the role played by western politicians who, in concert with native lackeys, foster this mess. Their prescription for this sorry state of affairs is to re-invent the empire as 'voluntary', or to re-invade and rearrange the world to suit western interests. This re-invasion is called variously 'liberal', 'humanitarian', 'altruistic' and 'moral' intervention. These writers are astute enough to know that older forms of empire are not easy to introduce and that it is far more difficult now to reverse the nationalistic fervour which is running through these countries. A possible alternative is to assist these 'messy' nation-states with a Machiavellian prescription of 'good laws' and 'good armies'. The aim of the new empire is to create 'order in border zones essential to the security of great powers'. Ignatieff captures the strategy of the new empire: 'It is imperial, finally, because while nominal power may return to the local capital – Kabul, Sarajevo, and Pristina – real power will continue to be exercised from London, Washington and Paris'.[9]

9 Ibid., p. 109.

These books are postmodern restatements of a traditional, conservative and highly romantic history of empire. They may bolster the thirst for knowledge of the empire, but they tell only a highly selective story. They lament the opportunities on which 'natives' failed to capitalize. They talk chiefly about the interests of the conquerors and minimize the feelings of the conquered, and especially what it means to be at the receiving end of imperialism. True, the orientalists unearthed enormous textual treasures from India's past, as the new historians affirm, but the their motives were not always pure. M. Monier-Williams, the Boden Professor of Sanskrit at Oxford, disclosed one of their less pure intentions: 'But it seems to me that our missionaries are already sufficiently convinced of the necessity of studying these works, and of making themselves conversant with the false creeds they have to fight against'.[10] What these recent books on the empire often forget is that empires always act in their own interests, they are often insensitive to indigenous cultures and their best intentions are likely to end up being unhelpful. Their message is that the West has the power to recast the rest of the world in its own image. Asians, Africans and Arabs are depicted as incapable of effecting changes that would lead to peace and prosperity. In short, what these books on empire try to convey is that it is time for westerners to don khaki shorts and topees, to remove the burden from the natives and to place it on the shoulders of the white man.

A SURFEIT OF SACRED TEXTS

Like the new crop of empire books, there is also a crop of books on the English Bible. Like the empire books, these emerge from different stables and are written by a disparate group of theologians and historians.[11] At the risk of oversimplifying the arguments, let me summarize their salient points. All of the books tell us how the English thirsted for scripture, how the medieval church deprived them of it and how they were

10 M. Monier-Williams, *The Holy Bible and the Sacred Books of the East: Four Addresses; to which Is Added a Fifth Address on Zenana Missions* (London, Seeley & Co., 1887), p. 10.
11 Benson Bobrick, *The Making of the English Bible* (London, Weidenfeld & Nicolson, 2001); Christopher De Hamel, *The Book: A History of the Bible* (London, Phaidon Press Ltd, 2001); Alister McGrath, *In the Beginning: The Story of the King James Version and How It Changed a Nation, a Language and a Culture* (London, Hodder and Stoughton, 2001); David Daniell, *The Bible in English: Its History and Influence* (New Haven, Yale University Press, 2003); Adam Nicolson, *Power and Glory: Jacobean England and the Making of the King James Bible* (London, Harper Collins Publishers, 2003); David S. Katz, *God's Last Words: Reading the English Bible from the Reformation to Fundamentalism* (New Haven, Yale University Press, 2004).

forbidden to read without a special licence. The English Bible joined many other vernacular Bibles in Europe. The writers describe in great detail how the physical shape of the Bible changed over the years, from being the monumental volumes of the Middle Ages to portable single-volume copies, small enough to be carried in a satchel. They remind the readers that, unlike the continental vernacular versions, the English Bible was not an exclusive product of a single hand, but the result of the united labours of a group of dynamic scholars who put together what has become the greatest book in the English language in spite of bad printing and many errors. The impression given is that the English Bible, like English laws and the constitution, grew through a slow process of absorption and conservation and did not erupt suddenly onto the scene. Out of this gradual process emerged a monument which was nobler than the original, and which has earned the affection of countless admirers and has become the 'paradigm of how mankind should deploy words'.[12] – God's last word. Some of the writers, not necessarily Christians, deviate from such beliefs, seeing the Bible as a cultural artefact and as a result of human inventiveness, erudite scholarship and manipulation of the market. But all of these writers use a similar rhapsodic vocabulary when narrating the impact of the English Bible on the lives of the English, their literature, music, art and painting. These writers recycle one another's ideas, indicating the extent of their common enthusiasm.

So far this is fine. But the intriguing part is not what these wide-eyed enthusiasts say about the finer qualities of the English Bible but what they conceal. There are three notable omissions from these books: the English Bible's contribution to English nationalism; the Bible's role as a superintendent in adjudicating the moral and theological worth of other sacred texts in the colonies; and the promotion of the English Bible as an instrument which inculcates obedience and respect for those in authority. The language of the English Bible, especially the Old Testament, provided the English with a vocabulary, unavailable until then, to capture the new realization of a chosen people with a divine destiny.[13] George Smith put the new self-designated role thus:

But the teaching of India is pre-eminently the first and the greatest duty of the English speaking Aryans, who have been chosen as the servants of Jehovah for this end as truly as the great Cyrus was in the Old Testament, that the Jews

---

12 Katz, *God's Last Words*, p. 214.
13 Krishan Kumar, *The Making of English National Identity* (Cambridge, Cambridge University Press, 2003), pp. 103–4.

might fulfil their preparatory mission to the world, and might in their turn bring in the fullness of the nations.[14]

The content of the 'Englishman's blessing' – the Bible – became a benchmark by which to evaluate the ethical qualities of other religious texts. In comparison to the Bible, Monier-Williams declared confidently that other religious texts were 'corruptions and lamentable impurities'.[15] The English Bible, which had been seen as a 'symbol of opposition to authority'[16] by the Lollards, was presented in the colonies as promoting order, obedience and respect for those in power and authority. A perfect example of this was the way the Tribute Money incident in the Synoptic gospels was exegeted during the colonial period. 'Render therefore to Caesar the things that are Caesar's' was interpreted as denouncing the revolutionary leanings of zealots, and advocating the payment of tax as a sign of obedience and respect to the Roman ruler whose reign had produced security and a stable government. The implication of such a reading not only legitimized British colonial rule, but also encouraged the 'natives' to show loyalty and deference to authority.[17] The only mention of the Bible's entanglement with the empire comes in the form of reference to the translation activity that went on in the colonies. Even here, the report of such activities centred around single heroic missionary figures like William Carey, and the role of native translators was either minimized or written out. The proliferation of books on the Bible in a way reverses the current trend in biblical scholarship. Whereas the present focus has moved from the text to the reader, these new tomes redirect the attention of the reader back to the book. The focus is on the book and its materiality and raises questions about the social, class and economic functions of its production.

Along with a spate of books on the Bible there is a proliferation of Bibles as well. The King James Version, once an undisputed universal script, has given way to a number of Bibles designed to lure specific audiences. Now there is a *Green Bible*, a *Gay and Lesbian Bible*, an *African Bible*, *The Amplified Bible*, *New American Bible*, *Youth Bible*, *The Bible in Cockney* and a *People's Bible*. A book that was in every sense, an

14 George Smith, *The Conversion of India: From Pantaenus to the Present Time* (London, John Murray, 1893), p. 5.
15 Monier-Williams, *The Holy Bible and the Sacred Books of the East*, p. 35.
16 Gillian Brennan, 'Patriotism, Language and Power: English Translations of the Bible, 1520–1580', *History Workshop: A Journal of Scientist and Feminist Historians* 27 (Spring 1989), 27.
17 R. S. Sugirtharajah, *The Bible and the Third World: Precolonial, Colonial and Postcolonial Encounters* (Cambridge, Cambridge University Press, 2001), pp. 255–7.

'establishment Bible', with 'impeccable social and intellectual creden-
tials'[18] is now fragmented into several splinter Bibles, and, far worse, it
has become part of the entertainment industry. Endless endeavours to
bring the Bible to target-specific audiences have resulted in what David
Clines calls 'marketization of the Bible'. Holy Writ is now seen as a
commodity to be packaged as 'infotainment'.[19] Supreme examples of
niche Bibles are: the Canongate Bible, *The Scroll: The Tabloid Bible*,
The Street Bible, and *Revolve*, the teenage Bible. While the first three aim
at a secularized post-Christian British clientele, the last one targets a
narrowly defined Christian readership in America.[20]

The Canongate Bible was the idea of the Edinburgh publisher who
brought out individual books of the King James Version with an
introduction by a leading cultural or literary luminary. For instance,
the pop star Bono wrote an introduction to the book of Psalms and
the novelist P. D. James provided the preamble to the Acts of the
Apostles.[21] Nick Page's *The Scroll: The Tabloid Bible* recasts the biblical
material in a racy, sensational and easy-to-read sound-bite style. This
introduces the peccadilloes of David with the words: 'David – The
Adultery, Rape, and Incest Years will be published next week, with a
10-page pull out supplement on Ten Great Slappers of Israel. As ever –
dignity is our key word'.[22]

The Street Bible is the work of Rob Lacey, a media personality, and is
aimed at urban audiences.[23] It is structured as a website format and the
epistles are in the form of emails. For instance, Paul's First Letter to the
Corinthians begins:

(Email No. 2. – No. 1 got wiped)

From: paul.benson@teammail.org

---

18 Harry S. Stout, 'Word and Order in Colonial New England', in *The Bible in America: Essays in Cultural History*, ed. Nathan O. Hatch and Mark A. Noll (New York, Oxford University Press, 1982), p. 25.

19 David Clines, 'Biblical Studies at the Millennium', *Religious Studies News* 14:4 (1999), p. 9.

20 For the Bibles produced and marketed mainly for Christian audiences in America, see Mark Fackler, 'The Second Coming of Holy Writ: Niche Bibles and the Manufacture of Market Segments', in *New Paradigms for Bible Study: The Bible in the Third Millennium*, ed. Robert Fowler, Edith Blumhofer and Fernando F. Segovia (New York, T. & T. Clark International, 2004), pp. 71–88.

21 For a detailed analysis of the Canongate Bible, see R. S. Sugirtharajah, *Postcolonial Reconfigurations: An Alternative Way of Reading the Bible and Doing Theology* (London, SCM Press, 2003), pp. 51–73; American edition: Chalice Press.

22 Nick Page, *The Scroll: The Tabloid Bible* (London, Harper Collins Publishers, 1998), p. 76.

23 Rob Lacey, *The Street Bible* (Grand Rapids, Zondervan, 2003).

To: jim@corinth.org.gr

Date: A D 54-ish

Subject: your letter re hassles and questions, and some . . .[24]

The language is a combination of modern-day media- and management-speak. The disciples are now called the 'team', the crowd that follow Jesus are the 'troupe of groupies', and the proclamation of good news is now 'breaking the news'. Here is an example of 'pure' management-speak which will make Tyndale turn in his grave. Jesus' words to Nicodemus: 'No one in this world gets to see God's world unless he is reconceived, redeveloped, redelivered, and then reborn'.[25]

Revolve is a Bible for teenage girls, in which the entire New Testament writings are presented in a fashion-magazine format. The volume is full of colour spreads of smiling smart young women and has all the ingredients of a teenage glamour magazine: question and answer, boxed items which provide succinct biographical details of leading personalities – not pop stars, but biblical figures. One thing missing from the regular teenage magazine format is the horoscope. *Revolve* offers beauty tips with biblical texts. Here is an example of how to keep the skin fresh and glowing: 'Do you want to look happy, healthy and glowing? Remember that because Christ lives in you, his light is to shine through you for the entire world to see (read Matthew 5.14–16). Your face should have a glow that comes from the joy of the Lord, a glow that is beyond compare!'[26] A delicious sample of question and answer:

Q. Is it wrong to wear a bra that fills out your shirt a little more?

A. 1. How old are you? 2. Why do you want to do it? If you are still young, just be patient. Your body is still in the process of filling out. In fact, it will continue to do this all through college. So don't give up hope and think that you will be forever flat-chested. If you're trying to get guys to like you more, it may work. But do you really want to date a guy who wouldn't go out with you if you were one cup-size smaller? I mean, seriously, what are his priorities? And check your priorities. Read Proverbs 31 to see what God says an attractive woman looks like.[27]

The publishers of these versions have their own rationale. They cite biblical precedents for their ventures. If Jesus spoke in the everyday

---

24 Ibid., p. 402.   25 Ibid., p. 290.
26 *Revolve: The Complete New Testament* (Thomas Nelson Bibles, 2003), p. 248.
27 Ibid., p. 361.

language of Aramaic, why not make the Bible available in the language of the ordinary people of today. They see their versions as modern day Targums – 'an effort to make text accessible to everyone'.[28] They draw attention to examples from mission fields where undecipherable Middle Eastern images are replaced by local images: 'African translations have changed "snake" to "scorpion" in cultures where snakes are a luxury'.[29]

A detailed study of these Bibles has to wait for a later date. Two things are immediately noticeable. One is that these versions have given a new lease of life to the Bible, which is otherwise in danger of being dismissed as an antiquated book written in difficult English. The other is, more worryingly, the hijacking of the language of liberation hermeneutics. *Revolve* presents Jesus as the 'truest revolutionary of all time', and *The Street Bible* portrays him as the 'liberator'. This Jesus is more recognizable to the class which frequents shopping malls and is familiar with investment trusts than to the urban or rural poor. The Parable of the Talents is retold in the language of the stock market – shares, profits and inflation.[30] The radical message of the Nazareth Manifesto is sanitized and presented as offering consolation to the emotional needs of the poor. 'Top news for the poor' is that Jesus was sent 'to mend broken hearts' and 'to announce the news – that this is the era of God going gentle on his people'.[31] The liberation agenda is recast in an apolitical terminology which eviscerates the biblical texts and soothes the sentiments of the urban middle class. The Bible's true liberative potential has a very different significance, and for a very different subaltern readership.

Protestants once abolished indulgences and made the Bible a bestseller. Now the bestseller is turned into a form of indulgence and sold in attractive formats to select audiences. Not for the first time, the Bible has been accommodated to imperial interests and becomes part of the new empire – the corporate world. Once 'a people nurtured on the Bible' were seen as 'essentially a cultured people'.[32] Now the Bible is introduced into various subcultures where a niche is carved out for it. The Bible which was hailed as a universal word, transferable to all cultures irrespective of time and space without contaminating the purity of its message, is now being marketed tarnished with traces of the very cultures it once abhorred. Now it is treated as an easily consumable commercial object. This market-ization of the Bible is fraught with ambivalence. On the one hand, these

28 Lacey, *The Street Bible*, p. 1.   29 Ibid.
30 Ibid., pp. 301–2.   31 Ibid., p. 295.
32 Sidney Dark, 'Christianity and Culture', *The New Green Quarterly* 2:2 (1936), 85.

attempts, imbued with theological conservatism and suffused with gim-
mickery, make the Bible readable and accessible to an audience which has
little incentive to read more formal versions of the Bible – a postmodern
fate for an artefact which emerged as a shining example of modernity. On
the other hand, such commercial razzmatazz raises the question of how to
maintain the Bible's status as a sacred text. There is no easy resolution of
this in sight.

What of the future? Empires do not last. They emerge, dominate and
then, due to their own hubris and vanity and to national resistance, they
disintegrate, though often paving the way for other empires. As for the
Bible, there are two ways of perceiving its future survival. These two ways
are exemplified in Salman Rushdie's *Haroun and the Sea of Stories*, a novel
about the fate of stories. One understanding of the Bible could be equated
with Kattum Shud, the character in the novel, the monstrous hater and
arch-enemy of all stories, who would like to control all stories; or the
Bible could be likened to the Ocean of the Stream of Stories, the biggest
library of stories, which the Water Genie introduced to the eponymous
Haroun. In this library, stories are held in 'fluid form' and they retain 'the
ability to change, become new versions of themselves, to join up with
other stories and so become yet other stories'.[33] One way of perceiving is
about control, single interpretation, sticking to the letter and denial of any
imagination, and the other is about the ability to move, mingle and mix
and morph into other stories and become new ones so that 'even the
oldest ones, would taste as good as new'.[34] Stories flourish on innovative
revitalization. They lose their appeal and die when they are tethered to
their ancient origins, declare too much veneration for the past and insist
on their own purity. The Bible can either become a mono-text or become
part of a mosaic of texts. The choice is either to become a fish wrapper, as
the epigraph put it, a roll-up paper for a cartridge as we saw in the
Introduction, or to become part of the Ocean of the Stream of Stories,
which is 'made up of a thousand thousand thousand and one different
currents, each one a different colour, weaving in and out of one another
like a liquid tapestry of breathtaking complexity'.[35] The Bible's future,
I incline to think, lies in the second option. This is not too much to ask
of a book which has all along proved its adaptability. As a character
in Rushdie's novel puts it. 'Any story worth its salt can handle a little
shaking up!'[36]

33 Salman Rushdie, *Haroun and the Sea of Stories* (London, Granta Books, 1990), p. 72.
34 Ibid., p. 175.   35 Ibid., p. 72.   36 Ibid., p. 79.

Select bibliography

BIBLICAL HERMENEUTICS: COLONIAL AND POSTCOLONIAL

A Brief Narrative of the Operation of Jaffna Auxiliary in the Preparation of a Version of the Tamil Scriptures (Jaffna, Strong and Asbury Printers, 1868).

Adams, Dickinson W. (ed.), *Jefferson's Extracts from the Gospels: 'The Philosophy of Jesus' and 'The Life and Morals of Jesus'* (Princeton, Princeton University Press, 1983).

Arnold, Thomas, *Sermons, with An Essay on the Right Interpretation and Understanding of the Scriptures*, vol. 11 (London, B. Fellowes, 1854).

Arumuka Pillai, *Caivatusanaparikaram* (Madras Jubilee Press, 1890).

Bates, Ernest Sutherland, *The Bible Designed to Be Read as Literature* (London, William Heinemann Ltd, 1937).

Clines, David, 'Biblical Studies at the Millennium', *Religious Studies News* 14:4 (1999), 9.

Colenso, John William, *The Pentateuch and Book of Joshua Critically Examined* (London, Longman, Green, Longman, Roberts, & Green, 1862).

The Pentateuch and Book of Joshua Critically Examined, Part 111 (London, Longman, Green, Longman, Roberts, & Green, 1863).

The Pentateuch and Book of Joshua Critically Examined, Part 1v (London, Longman, Green, Longman, Roberts, & Green, 1864).

The Pentateuch and the Book of Joshua Critically Examined, Part v (London, Longmans, Green & Co., 1865).

'On the Efforts of Missionaries among Savages', *Journal of the Anthropological Society* 3 (1865), 248–89.

Natal Sermons: A Series of Discourses Preached in the Cathedral Church of St Peter's, Maritzburg (London, N. Trübner & Co., 1866).

Natal Sermons: Second Series of Discourses Preached in the Cathedral Church of St Peter's, Maritzburg (London, N. Trübner & Co., 1868).

Natal Sermons, Series 111 (n.p., n.d.).

Natal Sermons, Series 1v (n.p., n.d.).

The Pentateuch and Book of Joshua Critically Examined, Part 1v (London, Longmans, Green & Co., 1871).

Lectures on the Pentateuch and the Moabite Stone (London, Longmans, Green & Co., 1873).

The Pentateuch and Book of Joshua Critically Examined, Part vii (London, Longmans, Green and Co., 1879).

'What Doth the Lord Require of Us?: A Sermon Preached in the Cathedral Church of St Peter's Maritzburg on Wednesday, March 12, 1879', reprinted in *Natalia* 6 (1879), 15–23.

Three Sermons Preached in the Cathedral Church of St Peter's, Maritzburg (Pietermaritzburg, P. Davis & Sons, 1883).

Eadie, John, 'Preface by Dr Eadie', in *The National Comprehensive Family Bible: The Holy Bible with the Commentaries of Scott and Henry, and Containing Also Many Thousand Critical and Explanatory Notes, Selected from the Great Standard Authors of Europe and America*, ed. John Eadie (Glasgow, W. R. M'Phun, 1860).

Frazer, James George, *Passages of the Bible: Chosen for Their Literary Beauty and Interest* (London, A. & C. Black, 1927).

Glover, Willis B., *Evangelical Nonconformists and Higher Criticism in the Nineteenth Century* (London, Independent Press Ltd, 1954).

Goodspeed, Edgar J., 'Thomas Jefferson and the Bible', *Harvard Theological Review* 40:1 (1947), 71–6.

Hipsley H., *The Bible in the School: A Question for India* (London, Alfred W. Bennett, n.d.).

Horton, Robert F., *The Bible: A Missionary Book* (Edinburgh, Oliphant, Anderson and Ferrier, 1904).

Jefferson, Thomas, *The Jefferson Bible: The Life and Morals of Jesus of Nazareth* (Boston, Beacon Press, 1989).

Jowett, Benjamin, 'On the Interpretation of Scripture', in *Essays and Reviews. The Sixth Edition* (Longman, Green, Longman, & Roberts, 1861), pp. 330–433.

Kelley, Shawn, *Racializing Jesus: Race, Ideology and the Formation of Modern Biblical Scholarship* (London, Routledge, 2002).

Kulandran, S., 'The Tentative Version of the Bible or "The Navalar Version"', *Tamil Culture* 7 (1958), 229–50.

Lapham, Henry A., *The Bible as Missionary Handbook* (Cambridge, W. Heffer and Sons, 1925).

Long, James, 'Peasant Degradation an Obstacle to Gospel Propagation', Church Missionary Meeting, Calcutta (8 April 1856).

'Address by the Rev. James Long at the Anniversary Meeting of the Family Literary Club', in *The Second Anniversary Report of the Family Literary Club* (Calcutta, Sundaburson Press, 1859).

'Address by the Rev. James Long at the Anniversary Meeting of the Family Literary Club', in *The Third Anniversary Report of the Family Literary Club* (Calcutta, C. H. Manuel & Sons, 1860).

'Bengali Proverbs', in *Calcutta Christian Observer*, 28 April 1860, pp. 179–85.

'Address of the Reverend James Long to the Court', in *Trial of the Rev. James Long, for the Publication of the 'Nil Durpan'; with Documents Connected with Its Official Circulation, Including Minutes by the Hon. J. P. Grant, Statements by W. S. Seton-Karr, and Resolution by the Governor-General of India in Council* (London, James Ridgeway, 1861), pp. 19–21.

'The "Nil Darpan" Controversy-Statement', in *The Friend of India*, 27 June 1861, pp. 712–13.

Russia, Central Asia, and British India (London, Trübner and Co., 1865).

Scripture Truth in Oriental Dress, or Emblems Explanatory of Biblical Doctrines and Morals, with Parallel or Illustrative References to Proverbs and Proverbial Sayings in the Arabic, Bengali, Canarese, Persian, Russian, Sanskrit, Tamul, Telegu and Urdu Languages (Calcutta, Thacker, Spink and Co., 1871).

Bible Teaching and Preaching for the Million by Emblems and Proverbs (n.p., 1874).

How I Taught the Bible to Bengal Peasant Boys (London, Christian Vernacular Education Society for India, 1875).

'Oriental Proverbs in Their Relations to Folklore, History, Sociology with Suggestions for Their Collection, Interpretation, Publication' (15 February 1875).

'On Eastern Proverbs, Their Importance and the Best Mode of Making a Complete Collection, Classified with the Native Interpretations', Oriental Congress, Berlin, September 1881.

'On the Importance and Best Mode of Making a Collection of Oriental Proverbs', Oriental Congress, Leiden, September 1883.

Marshman, Joshua, *A Defence of the Deity and Atonement of Jesus Christ, in Reply to Ram-Mohun Roy of Calcutta* (London, Kingsbury, Parbury, and Allen, 1822).

Maurice, Frederick Denison, *The Indian Crisis* (Cambridge, Macmillan and Co., 1857).

McBride, S. Dean, 'Biblical Literature in Its Historical Context: The Old Testament', in *Harper's Bible Commentary*, ed. James L. Mays (San Francisco, Harper and Row, 1988), pp. 14–26.

Monier-Williams, M., *The Holy Bible and the Sacred Books of the East: Four Addresses; to which Is Added a Fifth Address on Zenana Missions* (London, Seeley & Co., 1887).

Moulton, Richard G., *A Short Introduction to the Literature of the Bible* (London, D. C. Heath, 1900).

Moxnes, Halvor, 'The Construction of Galilee as a Place for the Historical Jesus – Part I', *Biblical Theology Bulletin* 31:1 (2001), 26–37.

'The Construction of Galilee as a Place for the Historical Jesus – Part II', *Biblical Theology Bulletin* 31:2 (2001), 64–77.

Niditch, Susan, *War in the Hebrew Bible: A Study in the Ethics of Violence* (New York, Oxford University Press, 1995).

Norton, David, *A History of the Bible as Literature*, vol. II: *From 1700 to the Present Day* (Cambridge, Cambridge University Press, 1993).

O'Connor, Kathleen M., 'Jeremiah', in *The Women's Bible Commentary*, ed. Carl A. Newsom and Sharon H. Ringe (London, SPCK, 1992), pp. 169–77.

Phillips, Godfrey E., *The Old Testament in the World Church: With Special Reference to the Younger Churches* (London, Lutterworth Press, 1942).

Quiller-Couch, Arthur, 'On Reading the Bible (11)', in *The English Bible: Essays by Various Authors*, ed. Vernon F. Storr (London, Methuen & Co. Ltd, 1938).

Reventlow, Henning Graf, *The Authority of the Bible and the Rise of the Modern World*, tr. John Bowden (London, SCM Press, 1984).

Richardson, Alan, *The Bible in the Age of Science* (London, SCM Press, 1961).

Roy, Rammohun, *The Precepts of Jesus. The Guide to Peace and Happiness; Extracted from the Books of the New Testament, Ascribed to the Four Evangelists* (Calcutta, The Baptist Press, 1820).

Sheridan, Eugene R., *Jefferson and Religion* (Thomas Jefferson Memorial Foundation, 1998).

Smith, George Adam, *Modern Criticism and the Preaching of the Old Testament: Eight Lectures on the Lyman Beecher Foundation, Yale University, USA* (London, Hodder and Stoughton, 1901).

Stanley, Brian, *The Bible and the Flag: Protestant Missions and British Imperialism in the Nineteenth and Twentieth Centuries* (Leicester, Apollos, 1990).

Sugirtharajah, R. S., 'Wisdom, Q, and a Proposal for a Christology', *The Expository Times* 102:2 (1990), 42–6.

Asian Biblical Hermeneutics and Postcolonialism: Contesting the Interpretations (Sheffield, Sheffield Academic Press, 1999).

The Bible and the Third World: Precolonial, Colonial and Postcolonial Encounters (Cambridge, Cambridge University Press, 2001).

Postcolonial Criticism and Biblical Interpretation (Oxford, Oxford University Press, 2002).

Postcolonial Reconfigurations: An Alternative Way of Reading the Bible and Doing Theology (London, SCM Press, 2003) (American edition: Chalice Press).

Suttampillai, A. N., *Ruthamavai* (Palamcottah: Church Mission Press, 1884).

A Brief Sketch of the Hindu Christian Dogmas (Palamcottah, Shanmuga Vilasam Press, 1890).

Wilson, Daniel, *Humiliation in National Troubles: A Sermon Delivered at St Paul's Cathedral on Friday, July 24th, 1857* (Calcutta, Bishop's College Press, 1857).

Prayer the Refuge of a Distressed Church: A Sermon Delivered at St Paul's Cathedral, Calcutta on Sunday, June 28th, 1857 (Calcutta, Bishop's College Press, 1857).

Wright, G. Ernest, 'The Old Testament: A Bulwark of the Church Against Paganism', *Occasional Bulletin from the Missionary Research Library* 14:4 (1963), 1–10.

Wright, Julia M., 'Introduction', in *The Missionary: An Indian Tale*, ed. Julia M. Wright (Peterborough, Ontario, Broadview Press, 2002), pp. 9–63.

Wrigley, Francis, *The Old Testament in the Light of Modern Scholarship: Abbreviated and Arranged for Use in Home, School and Church* (London, Independent Press, 1932).

Young, Robert J. C., *Postcolonialism: A Very Short Introduction* (Oxford, Oxford University Press, 2003).

EMPIRE: RELIGIONS AND THEOLOGY

Anderson, Olive, 'The Reactions of Church and Dissent towards the Crimean War', *The Journal of Ecclesiastical History* 16 (1965), 209–20.

'The Growth of Christian Militarism in Mid-Victorian Britain', *The English Historical Review* 86:338 (1971), 46–72.

Banerjee, Sumanta, *The Parlour and the Streets: Elite and Popular Culture in Nineteenth Century Calcutta* (Calcutta: Seagull Books, 1989).

Bharadwaja, Chiranjiva (tr.), *Light of Truth* or *An English Translation of the Satyarth Prakash, the Well-known Work of Swami Dayananda Saraswati* (Allahabad, K. C. Bhalla, n.d.), pp. 583–644.

Caldwell, R., *The Tinnevelly Shanars: A Sketch of Their Religion, and Their Moral Condition and Characteristics, as a Caste; with Special Reference to the Facilities and Hindrances to the Progress of Christianity amongst Them* (Madras, Christian Knowledge Society's Press, 1849).

Chatterjee, Shyamal K., 'Rammohun Roy and the Baptists of Serampore: Moralism vs. Faith', *Religious Studies* 20:4 (1984),669–80.

Chinard, Gilbert (ed.), *The Literary Bible of Thomas Jefferson: His Commonplace Book of Philosophers and Poets* (Baltimore, The Johns Hopkins Press, 1928).

Gandhi, M. K., *Christian Missions: Their Place in India* (Ahmedabad, Navajivan Press, 1941).

Ganeri, Jonardon (ed.), *Indian Logic: A Reader* (London, Curzon Press, 2001).

Hilton, Boyd, *The Age of Atonement: The Influence of Evangelicalism on Social and Economic Thought 1785–1865* (Oxford, Clarendon Press, 1991).

Hudson, Dennis D., 'The Responses of Tamils to Their Study by Westerners 1600–1908', *Comparative Civilizations Review* 13&14 (1986), 180–200.

'Violent and Fanatical Devotion among Nāyanārs: A Study in the *Periya Purāṇam* of *Cēkkilār*', in *Criminal Gods and Demon Devotees: Essays on the Guardians of Popular Hinduism*, ed. Alf Hiltebeitel (New Delhi, Manohar Publications, 1990), pp. 373–404.

'Arumuga Navalar and the Hindu Renaissance among the Tamils', in *Religious Controversy in British India: Dialogues in South Asian Languages*, ed. Kenneth W. Jones (Albany, State University of New York Press, 1992), pp. 27–51.

'Winning Souls for Siva: Arumuga Navalar's Transmission of the Saiva Religion', in *A Sacred Thread: Modern Transmissions of Hindu Tradition in India and Abroad*, ed. Raymond Brady Williams (Chambersburg, Anima Publications, 1992), pp. 23–51.

'A Hindu Response to the Written Torah', in *Between Jerusalem and Benares: Comparative Studies in Judaism and Hinduism*, ed. Hananya Goodman (Albany, State University of New York Press, 1994), pp. 55–84.

'Tamil Hindu Responses to Protestants: Nineteenth-Century Literati in Jaffna and Tinnevelly', in *Indigenous Responses to Western Christianity*, ed. Steven Kaplan (New York, New York University Press, 1995), pp. 95–123.

Kenyatta, Jomo, *Facing Mount Kenya: The Tribal Life of the Gikuyu* (London, Secker and Warburg, [1938] 1968).

Kumaradoss, Vincent, 'Negotiating Colonial Christianity: The Hindu Christian Church of Late Nineteenth Century Tirunelveli', *South Indian Studies* 1 (1996), 35–53.

'Creation of Alternative Public Spheres and Church Indigenisation in Nineteenth Century Colonial Tamil Nadu: The Hindu-Christian Church of Lord Jesus and the National Church of India', in *Christianity is Indian: The Emergence of an Indigenous Community*, ed. Roger E. Hedlund (Mylapore, MIIS, 2000), 3–23.

Maurice, Frederick Denison, *The Religions of the World and Their Relations to Christianity* (London, Macmillan and Co., 1886).

Piet, John H., *A Logical Presentation of the Śaiva Siddhānta Philosophy* (Madras: The Christian Literature Society for India, 1952).

Rajaiah Paul D., *Triumphs of His Grace* (Madras, The Christian Literature Society, 1967).

Rangachari, R. (tr.), *Saint Sekkizhar's Periya Puraanam* (Tiruvannamalai, Sri Ramanasramam, 1992).

Robinson, Rowena, 'Sixteenth Century Conversions to Christianity in Goa', in *Religious Conversion in India: Modes, Motivations, and Meanings*, ed. Sathianathan Clarke and Rowena Robinson (New Delhi, Oxford University Press, 2003), pp. 291–322.

Thangaraj, M. Thomas, 'The History and Teachings of the Hindu Christian Community Commonly Called Nattu Sabai in Tirunelveli', *Indian Church History Review* 5:1 (1971), 43–68.

'Hymnody as Biblical Hermeneutics: Tehillim by Sattampillai of Hindu-Christian Community', Paper Presented at the Annual Meeting of the Society of Biblical Literature (Orlando, November 1998). Unpublished paper.

Thangasamy, D. A. (ed.), *The Theology of Chenchiah with Selections from His Writings*, Confessing the Faith in India Series No. 1 (Bangalore, The Christian Institute for the Study of Religion and Society, 1966).

Young, R. F. and Jebanesan, S., *The Bible Trembled: The Hindu–Christian Controversies of Nineteenth-Century Ceylon* (Vienna, Institüt fur Indologie der Universität Wien, 1995).

COLONIAL HISTORY AND LITERATURE

Ahmed Khan, Syed, *The Causes of the Indian Revolt*, Oxford in Asia. Historical Reprints (Karachi, Oxford University Press, [1873] 2000).

Bhabha, Homi K., *The Location of Culture* (London, Routledge, 1994).

Bhadra, Gautam, 'Four Rebels of Eighteen-Fifty-Seven', in *Selected Subaltern Studies*, ed. Ranajit Guha and Gayatri Chakravorty Spivak (New York, Oxford University Press, 1988), pp. 129–75.

Bhattacharya, Pradyumna, 'Rammohun Roy and Bengali Prose', in *Rammohun Roy and the Process of Modernization in India*, ed. V. C. Joshi (Delhi, Vikas Publishing House, 1975), pp. 195–228.

Boyd, Julian P. (ed.), *The Papers of Thomas Jefferson* vol. I : *1760–1776* (Princeton, Princeton University Press, 1950).

    (ed.), *The Papers of Thomas Jefferson*, vol. XII : *7 August 1787 to 31 March 1788* (Princeton, Princeton University Press, 1955).

Cannadine, David, *Ornamentalism: How the British Saw the Empire* (London, Allen Lane, 2001).

Clanchy, M. T., *From Memory to Written Record: England 1066–1307* (Oxford, Blackwell, 1993).

Collet, Sophia Dobson, *The Life and Letters of Raja Rammohun Roy*, ed. Dilip Kumar Biswas and Prabhat Chandra Ganguli (Calcutta, Sadharan Brahmo Samaj, 1900).

Cox, George W., *The Life of John William Colenso, D.D. Bishop of Natal*, vol. I (London, W. Ridgway, 1888).

    The Life of John William Colenso, D.D. Bishop of Natal, vol. II (London, W. Ridgway, 1888).

Dark, Sidney, 'Christianity and Culture', *The New Green Quarterly* 2:2 (1936), 83–9.

Das, Sisir Kumar, 'Rammohun and Bengali Prose', in *Rammohun Roy: A Bi-Centenary Tribute*, ed. Niharranjan Ray (New Delhi, National Book Trust, 1974), pp. 133–41.

David, Saul, *The Indian Mutiny 1857* (London, Viking, 2002).

Davies, Alan, *Infected Christianity: A Study of Modern Racism* (Kingston, McGill-Queen's University Press, 1988).

Duff, Alexander, *The Indian Rebellion: Its Causes and Results in a Series of Letters* (London, James Nisbet, 1858).

Edgecombe, Ruth (ed.), *John William Colenso: Bringing Forth Light. Five Tracts on the Bishop Colenso's Zulu Mission* (Pietermaritzburg, University Press, 1982).

Edwardes, Michael, *Red Year: The Indian Rebellion of 1857* (London, Cardinal, 1975).

Hibbert Christopher, *The Great Mutiny: India 1857* (London, Penguin Books, 1980).

Horton, Robert F., *An Autobiography* (London, George Allen and Unwin Ltd, 1917).

Jefferson, Thomas, *Notes on the State of Virginia*, edited with an introduction and notes by William Peden (Chapel Hill, The University of North Carolina Press, 1955).

Writings, ed. Merril D. Peterson (New York, Library Classics of the United States, 1984).

Jones, William, *The Works of Sir William Jones in Six Volumes* (London, G. G. and J. Robinson, 1799).

Kawashima, Koji, *Missionaries and a Hindu State: Travancore 1858–1936* (Delhi, Oxford University Press, 1998).

Kulandran, S., *The Word, Men and Matters (1940–1983): Being a Rescript in Five Volumes of the Writings of the Rt Rev. Dr S. Kulandran, Bishop of Jaffna Diocese C.S.I. 1947–1970)*, vol. 1, ed. D. J. Ambalavanar (Chunnakam, Institute for the Study of Religion and Society, 1985).

Kumar, Krishan, *The Making of English National Identity* (Cambridge, Cambridge University Press, 2003).

Kumar, Krishna, *Prejudice and Pride: School Histories of the Freedom Struggle in India and Pakistan* (New Delhi, Penguin Books, 2002).

Long, James, 'Introduction' to *Nil Durpan: The Indigo Planters' Mirror, A Drama Translated from the Bengali by a Native* (Edinburgh, Myles Macphail, 1862), pp. 2–3.

Macaulay, T. B., 'Minute of the 2nd of February 1835', in *Speeches by Lord Macaulay with His Minute on Indian Education*, ed. G. M. Young (London, Oxford University Press, 1935), pp. 345–61.

Majumdar, Jatindra Kumar (ed.), *Raja Rammohun Roy and Progressive Movements in India: A Selection from Records (1775–1845)* (Calcutta: Art Press, 1941).

Marshall, P. J. (ed.), *The British Discovery of Hinduism in the Eighteenth Century* (Cambridge, Cambridge University Press, 1970).

Marshall, P. J and Williams, Glyndwr, *The Great Map of Mankind: British Perceptions of the World in the Age of Enlightenment* (London, J. M. Dent and Sons Ltd, 1982).

Marx, Karl, 'The Indian Revolt', in *The Portable Karl Marx*, ed. Eugene Kamenka (New York, Penguin Books, 1983).

Maurice, Frederick (ed.), *The Life of Frederick Denison Maurice Chiefly Told in His Own Letters*, vol. 11 (London, Macmillan and Co., 1884).

McKenzie, D. F., *Bibliography and the Sociology of Texts* (Cambridge, Cambridge University Press, 1999).

Mitra S. K., 'The Vellore Mutiny of 1806 and the Question of Christian Mission to India', *Indian Church History Review* 8:1 (1974), 75–82.

Mullens, Joseph, *Missions in South India* (London, W. H. Dalton, 1854).

Nandy, Ashis, *Time Warps: The Insistent Politics of Silent and Evasive Pasts* (Delhi, Permanent Black, 2001).

Nyabongo, Akiki K., *Africa Answers Back* (London, George Routledge & Sons Ltd, 1936).

Oddie, Geoffrey, *Missionaries, Rebellion and Proto-Nationalism: James Long of Bengal 1814–87* (Richmond, Curzon Press, 1999).

Owenson, Sydney, *Luxima, the Prophetess: A Tale of India* (London, Charles Westerton, 1859).

The Missionary: An Indian Tale, ed. Julia M. Wright (Peterborough, Ontario, Broadview Press, [1811] 2002).

Perusek, Darshan, 'Subaltern Consciousness and Historiography of Indian Rebellion of 1857', in *Economic and Political Weekly*, 11 September 1993, pp. 1931–6.

Ray, Satyajit, *Our Films Their Films* (Hyderabad, Orient Longman, 1976).

Richter, Julius, *A History of Missions in India*, tr. Sydney H. Moore (Edinburgh, Oliphant Anderson and Ferrier, 1908).

Roy, Rammohun, *The English Works of Raja Rammohun Roy*, vols. I–IV, ed. Jogendra Chunder Ghose (New Delhi, Cosmo Publications, 1906).

Rushdie, Salman, *Haroun and the Sea of Stories* (London, Granta Books, 1990).

Said, Edward W., *Culture and Imperialism* (London, Chatto & Windus, 1993).

Humanism and Democratic Criticism (New York, Columbia University Press, 2004).

Sarkar, Sumit, 'Rammohun Roy and the Break with the Past', in *Rammohun Roy and the Process of Modernization in India*, ed. V. C. Joshi (Delhi, Vikas Publishing House, 1975), pp. 46–68.

Savarkar, V. D., *The Indian War of Independence: National Rising of 1857* (London, 1907).

Sherring, M. A., *The History of Protestant Missions in India from Their Commencement in 1706 to 1881* (London, The Religious Tract Society, 1884).

Smith, George, *The Conversion of India: From Pantaenus to the Present Time* (London, John Murray, 1893).

Smith, Vincent A., *The Oxford History of India: From the Earliest Times to the End of 1911*, second edition (Oxford, Clarendon Press, 1923).

Stout, Harry S., 'Word and Order in Colonial New England', in *The Bible in America: Essays in Cultural History*, ed. Nathan O. Hatch and Mark A. Noll (New York, Oxford University Press, 1982), pp. 19–37.

Tagore, Saumyendranath, *Raja Rammohun Roy* (New Delhi, Sahitya Akademi, 1966).

Young, Robert J. C., *Postcolonialism: A Very Short Introduction* (Oxford, Oxford University Press, 2003).

THE ENGLISH BIBLE

Bobrick, Benson, *The Making of the English Bible* (London, Weidenfeld & Nicolson, 2001).

Brennan, Gillian, 'Patriotism, Language and Power: English Translations of the Bible, 1520–1580', *History Workshop: A Journal of Scientist and Feminist Historians* 27 (Spring 1989), 18–36.

Calvocoressi, Peter, *Who's Who in the Bible* (London, Penguin Books, 1990).

Daniell, David, *The Bible in English: Its History and Influence* (New Haven, Yale University Press, 2003).

De Hamel, Christopher, *The Book: A History of the Bible* (London, Phaidon Press Ltd, 2001).

Fackler, Mark, 'The Second Coming of Holy Writ: Niche Bibles and the Manufacture of Market Segments', in *New Paradigms for Bible Study: The Bible in the Third Millennium,* ed. Robert Fowler, Edith Blumhofer and Fernando F. Segovia (New York, T. & T. Clark International, 2004), pp. 71–88.

Katz, David S., *God's Last Words: Reading the English Bible from the Reformation to Fundamentalism* (New Haven, Yale University Press, 2004).

Lacey, Rob, *The Street Bible* (Grand Rapids, Zondervan, 2003).

McGrath, Alister, *In the Beginning: The Story of the King James Version and How It Changed a Nation, a Language and a Culture* (London, Hodder and Stoughton, 2001).

Nicolson, Adam, *Power and Glory: Jacobean England and the Making of the King James Bible* (London, Harper Collins Publishers, 2003).

Page, Nick, *The Scroll: The Tabloid Bible* (London, Harper Collins Publishers, 1998).

Revolve: The Complete New Testament (Thomas Nelson Bibles, 2003).

NEW EMPIRE

Cooper, Robert, 'The Post-Modern State', in, *Re-Ordering the World: The Long Term Implications of 11 September,* ed. Mark Leonard (London: The Foreign Policy Centre, 2002), pp. 11–20.

The Breaking of Nations (New York, Atlantic Monthly Press, 2003).

Ferguson, Niall, *Empire: How Britain Made the Modern World* (London, Allen Lane, 2003).

Ignatieff, Michael, *Empire Lite: Nation Building in Bosnia, Kosovo and Afghanistan* (London, Vintage, 2003).

Todrov, Tzvetan, 'Right to Intervene or Duty to Assist?', in *Human Rights, Human Wrongs,* ed. Nicholas Owen (Oxford: Oxford University Press, 2002), pp. 28–48.

Index of biblical references

Index of names and subjects